Son of Karbala

Shaykh Fadhlalla Haeri

BOOKS

Winchester, UK
Washington, USA

First published 2006 by O Books
O Books is an imprint of John Hunt Publishing Ltd., The Bothy,
Deershot Lodge, Park Lane, Ropley, Hants, SO24 0BE, UK
office@johnhunt-publishing.com
www.O-books.net

Distribution in:

UK
Orca Book Services
orders@orcabookservices.co.uk
Tel: 01202 665432
Fax: 01202 666219 Int. code (44)

New Zealand
Peaceful Living
books@peaceful-living.co.nz
Tel: 64 7 57 18105
Fax: 64 7 57 18513

USA and Canada
NBN
custserv@nbnbooks.com
Tel: 1 800 462 6420
Fax: 1 800 338 4550

Singapore
STP
davidbuckland@tlp.com.sg
Tel: 65 6276
Fax: 65 6276 7119

Australia
Brumby Books
sales@brumbybooks.com
Tel: 61 3 9761 5535
Fax: 61 3 9761 7095

South Africa
Alternative Books
altbook@global.co.za
Tel: 27 011 792 7730
Fax: 27 011 972 7787

Text: © 2006 Zahra Trust
Design: Jim Weaver Design
Cover design: BookDesign™, London
ISBN 13: 978 1905047 51 2
ISBN 10: 1 905047 51 7

A CIP catalogue record for this book is
available from the British Library.
Printed in the USA by Maple-Vail Press

Contents

Acknowledgements

In writing this book, all members of my immediate family have participated in varying degrees. Several relatives confirmed and reminded me of past events, others helped in transcribing and editing the manuscript. In addition, a number of my students and friends have helped at various stages of the writing. My special gratitude goes to those who spent much time and effort in shaping this book.

I am deeply indebted to my family, friends, associates and students, who have enriched my life in form and meaning. My heartfelt love and acknowledgement goes to all those who have touched my life (in any way) and my sincere apologies to those whom I have hurt or upset, knowingly or otherwise.

Foreword I

The name "Karbala" is etched in the consciousness of present day Westerners through presentation in the mass media of bloody scenes, fearsome battles and tragic destruction of the past few years following the invasion of Iraq by America and other coalition forces. But for Muslims, and especially Shi 'ites, it is associated with another and very different kind of bloody event, one that took place nearly fourteen centuries ago and involved the spilling of the blood of "the prince of martyrs", Imam Husayn ibn 'Ali, the grandson of the Prophet of Islam. It was here that Husayn met his death while seeking to present the authenticity of the Islamic message and the administration of justice on the basis of the truth that Islam teaches. His body was buried in the desert where he and other members of his family were killed. And from this event there came into being the city of Karbala, built over the centuries around the mausoleum of the supreme martyr of Islam. The dome and minarets of the tomb of the Imam still dominate the city's landscape.

Subsequently, Karbala became a major center of pilgrimage and religion activity, visited by countless pilgrims from all over Iraq, Persia, the Indian subcontinent and many other lands. Over the centuries the faithful have also tried to be buried near Imam Husayn and many bodies of pious Muslims have been brought from near and far to Karbala, for that purpose. Moreover, the city became a major center of Islamic learning where many migrated to sit at the feet of masters in its schools and also in Najaf nearby. Even the earth of Karbala is considered to contain special blessings and to this day devout Shi 'ites put a piece of that earth before them on the ground during the daily prayers and place their forehead on it during the act of prostration so as to be able to touch the earth near where the body of Imam Husayn is buried.

Being a major religious center and site of pilgrimage, Karbala retained its traditional character longer than Baghdad and was still to a large extent dominated by traditional Islamic culture until the mid – 20th century. It was in this still Islamic ambience that Shaykh Fadlallah Haeri was born and brought up. Like many distinguished families of Karbala, his family was both Persian and Arab having some members who lived in Iraq and others who lived in Persia, where the family is said to have originated. The riveting autobiography that follows describes in moving prose and with a strong sense of narrative the life of an exceptionally gifted member of the religious and social aristocracy of that city.

We read about this early years set in a completely traditional family and social context followed by the gradual penetration of modernism and Westernization into his life. We read about his attraction to the West, going to England to study , his spiritual and intellectual crisis, his return to Iraq as a Westernized Muslim and his return to the West. Of greatest interest is how he re-discovered Islam while he was in the West and especially the fact that this transformation took place through the agency of a Hindu and with the help of Sufism. This process has become prototypic for many a Muslim and depicts an early example of what can be observed among many Muslim students coming to the West these days. But it was less common when Shaykh Fadlallah experienced it.

As someone who is somewhat older than Shaykh Fadlallah, and who underwent a very similar transformation a decade earlier than him. I can vouchsafe the authenticity of such a life transforming process. Reading this biography reminds me very much of my own life. I too was born in a distinguished Shi 'ite family in Persia and my father in fact knew Shaykh 'Abd Allah Ha'iri, a famous Sufi master, who was a great uncle of our author. I still recall that as a child I was taken by my father to meet this master. He put me on his lap, smiled and recited prayers for me. His son, Hadi Ha'iri, the greatest authority on Rumi in his day, was like my uncle and one of my important teachers in Sufi literature. I too was to go at a young age to the West, become immersed in Western culture, in my case American rather than British, become attracted to Hinduism through which the metaphysical and mystical dimensions of Islam were to open to me and I subsequently re-discovered the integral Islamic tradition. It is even more remarkable that in Shaykh Fadlallah's case as in mine there came into being a meeting at the highest level between Shadhili spirituality and Shi'ism, something that has been rare in Islamic history. I can therefore speak from personal experience about the authenticity of the salient features of Shaykh Fadlallah's life and works and can bear witness to the importance of his variegated and diversified life for a better understanding of the dynamics of the encounter between Islam and the West in the mind and soul of many Muslims today.

Shaykh Fadlallah has adorned his autobiography with many Quranic citations and the events of his life has been described in such a way that they have become imbued with moral and spiritual character and serve as ethical and religious lessons. His autobiography is therefore not only engaging in itself and revealing as far as the life of an important contemporary Muslim personality is concerned, but it is also emblematic of the life of a deeply rooted present day Muslim thrown into the chaos of the modern world but able finally to find his moorings and return with even greater certitude than before to the world of faith. His work can in fact be a guide for many a Muslim confronted with a similar situation.

Shaykh Fadlallah Haeri has already written a member of valuable books and especially penetrating works on the Noble Quran. He has also guided numerous young spiritual aspirants, both Muslim born and of Western origin, in America, Europe, Africa and Asia. Moreover, he has carried out very valuable acts of philanthropy and continues to do so. I pray for him to have a long and continuously fruitful life in service to God and His creatures. His life demonstrates the fact that to "God belong the East and the West" and that wheresoever we turn "there is the Face of God".

Seyyed Hossein Nasr, Bethesda, Maryland, U. S. A.
Dhu'l-qa'dah 1426 AH
December 2005

Seyyed Nossein Nasr is Professor of Islamic Studies at George Washington University, Washington DC.

Foreword II

"Son of Karbala", the memoirs of Shaykh Fadhlalla Haeri, are an extraordinary testament to the man, place and time. At one level it is a fitting tribute to one of the most significant shrine cities of Islam, and also, and more importantly, a record of the passing away of an entire way of life. At another level, it is the fascinating story of a true seeker after wisdom and enlightenment, and the paths that he had to tread, and the incredible people that he met, before he emerged as one of the recognised modern masters of authentic spirituality.

Karbala, after the Second World War, mirrored the decline of traditional society that was occurring elsewhere in Iraq and indeed throughout the Muslim World. The fragility of its age-old structures were all too evident as the emergent generation abandoned nearly all of its legacy and replaced it with a crude modernism devoid of any civilising virtue. A close-knit, organically connected and mutually supportive culture was unable to cope with the allure of materialism, an ever-expanding state, and the siren calls of false ideologies. The author describes in lyrical terms the warmth and common decency that pervaded human relations in the Karbala of his childhood; the sense of responsibility that governed people's every actions; and the sinews of mutual obligations that provided the safety net for the poor and the weak, and that combined power and privilege with a profound consciousness of service to society's disadvantaged. His family occupied the commanding heights of Karbala's society, combining an elevated status in the religious hierarchy of the city, with a wide recognition of their authority as hakims, or masters of the inner dimensions of Islam. Shaykh Ahmad Haeri, the author's father, was an accomplished practitioner of alchemy. He was sought out for his spiritual advice and guidance from as far a field as India. Through his intense spiritual practices and devotions, he was able to reach very high levels of inner awareness and consciousness, one of whose by-products being an ability to discern patterns in events which were beyond the normal capacities of humans. Shaykh Fadhlalla Haeri must have inherited these qualities from the long line of his illustrious predecessors.

As the tides of change began to overwhelm his native town, the young Fadhlalla adapted, though not uncritically, to the ways of the new order. He continued his higher education in Britain and then joined the fast-expanding oil industry of Iraq, where he rapidly rose in the organisation of the major foreign-owned oil company, the Iraq Petroleum Co. But correctly sensing that the politics of the country were about to become more tyrannical and violent, he left Iraq, and established himself as a successful oil consultant and entrepreneur. It was while on one of his numerous business trips in the Middle East that he came across the figure who would challenge his way of life directly and rekindle in him the passionate yearning for the truth that would set the pattern for his future. Swami Chinmaya, an Indian spiritual master, confronted Fadhlalla with the great questions of life and the significance of all authentic traditions in mapping the path that can lead to self-realisation and true knowledge. After a number of years in the company of Chinmaya, Shaykh Fadhlalla Haeri was encouraged by his guru to return to the valid traditions within the Islamic heritage of his own past. There then followed an enthralling set of encounters with leading masters of the Islamic Sufi tradition, both in the East and the West, as Shaykh Fadhlalla Haeri begins his spiritual seeking in earnest. The descriptions of his various meetings and experiences with these astonishing masters provide some of the most absorbing passages in the book. His first Islamic guide after his departure from Chinmaya's ashram, was Shaykh Abdalqadir as-Sufi, an extraordinary person in his own right, a Scottish-born master who had established centres for his mainly European adepts in various parts of the world. As Shaykh Fadhlalla Haeri matured into a recognised authority, he began to collect around him a growing number of followers, seeking from him the guidance that would assist them in their own life journeys. Several centres for his adepts were established, nearly all focussed on both enhancing the inner life of its members as well as emphasising a strong service ethic to the community and society at large. Village style communities, clinics, schools, and places of worship were organised around the world, from the US, to Britain, Sweden, Pakistan, India, Sri Lanka and South Africa.

"Son of Karbala" is not an ordinary memoir. It is a highly instructive and thoroughly enjoyable book that can benefit the reader at any number of levels. Above all, it is a story of the passion for truth that consumes and then alters a person in ways that are truly inspiring. The delights in knowing, with unalterable certainty, that the subtle breath of an All Merciful God holds the universe together, can bring an immense transformative force into one's life. Each and every thing falls into a pre-ordained place even when one is confronted by a seemingly endless procession of chaotic and meaningless events. Many peoples' lives have been profoundly altered by their encounter with Shaykh Fadhlalla Haeri. In reality, the force of his presence is nothing more than the reflection of a contented self that has made its peace with itself as well as its Creator; and with which its Creator is manifestly contented. The catastrophes that befell his native Iraq did not detract Shaykh Fadhlalla Haeri from his magnificent quest. If anything, the tribulations of his country should be seen also as a salutary warning to all who chose inappropriate paths that strayed far from the divine measure.

It is this property that marks out the "Son of Karbala". It tells a number of stories and carries multiple messages within it. But it is ultimately the sense that serenity and success is assured if one pursues the inner life with sincere determination and purpose. That is the real message of the "Son of Karbala" and we have to thank Shaykh Fadhlalla Haeri for sharing his journey with us.

Ali Allawi
Baghdad,
Iraq

October 24, 2005

Ali Allawi is the Minister of Finance of the Republic of Iraq. He had been prior to his current appointment, the Interim Minister of Trade, and later the Interim Minister of Defence, in the new Government of Iraq.

Introduction

Listen to the reed how it tells a tale, complaining of
separations.

— Jalaluddin Rumi

This book is the journal of a quest. It chronicles my life-long
search for knowledge; a search that was driven by love and
uncompromising passion, in the realisation that conflict within and
with others comes from man's natural drive to resolution. My goal
was to understand the meaning of life and know its Source.

By God's grace and through appropriate applications and
blessings, openings were granted to me. Words, events or books
cannot define my gratitude for this. Yet, when close friends,
students and family requested me to write my biography, I felt
compelled to share the gifts of understanding and knowledge that
have been bestowed upon me.

My experiences may be of particular value to those who have
been displaced from the land of their heritage, especially if they are
from Eastern or Muslim backgrounds. *Insha'Allah* (if God wills),
they will also enable interested people from other cultures and
religions to achieve a better understanding of the Islamic culture
and its way of life, which has undergone such radical changes over
the past decades.

Current world events and conflicts between peoples and nations
add impetus to the usefulness of a book which might show

some order within the chaos and clarify misconceptions and fears Westerners have concerning such issues as Muslim fundamentalism, jihad and terrorism. The reader will share my personal discoveries of how we Muslims lapsed in our socio-economic and cultural development and how our great religion became over structured and ritualistic. I came to a greater understanding and reconciliation with the world situation without compromising my spiritual heritage. I hope the reader, too, may come to terms with difficult events and disturbing global relationships at many levels.

I was born and brought up in the ancient city of Karbala, where Shi'a Muslims, theologians and mystics had lived and died for over thirteen centuries. Apart from its famed date palms and orange groves, Karbala holds great significance for millions of Muslims around the world. It was on the plains of Karbala on the 10th Muharram 61 AH (10th October 680 CE) that Imam Hussein, the grandson of the Prophet Muhammad, along with 71 of his companions, was brutally martyred. Ever since, there is a deep sadness and concern in every Muslim's heart as to why Muslims have often had to endure cruel and hypocritical leaders.

As a European-educated young man, I looked for a home or culture that would reconcile my past with an appropriate future. I had lost Karbala with the continuity of its ancient way of life and Prophetic values, only to find its original blueprint ever residing in my soul, rather than physically in any land – for I looked everywhere without success. The cultural dislocation, eventual statelessness and lack of country or people to belong to, led me to accept wherever in the world I was, as my temporary home. This brought the discovery that the more you identify with your nationality, religion, language and culture, the more difficult it becomes to discover the higher spirit within you. In my case, outer destitution became the door for inner restitution.

My quest and longing for truth has led me to conclude that the end of the search for meaning and purpose in life – the whys, whats and hows of existence – is only the beginning of the enlightened phase of joyful continuity. What I was truly yearning for was closer than I had ever imagined. What I feared and hated lay in my own imagination and mind, veiling deeper meanings and the eternal truth. My desire is now to invite others to the celebration of life through unconditional service and awakened consciousness to the universal Truth, the ever present and perfect ways of the One God.

This book is dedicated to all sincere human beings, who accept the limitations of humanity and seek the boundless delights emanating from the soul. May the wandering seeker be awakened to fulfilled living, surrender in utter gratitude and be content by witnessing the Glorious Creator and His boundless perfections which shine through apparent worldly imperfections.

Oh my son! This world is like an ocean in which many a creation had drowned. Make, therefore, the fear of God your boat in this ocean; your faith the main hull of the boat; reliance on God as its sails; reason as its rower; knowledge as its captain; and patience as its anchor.

— Imam Ali

1

The House of Shaykh Ahmad

Allah makes ample provision for whom He will of
His bondsman, and restricts it for whom (He will).
Lo! Allah is Aware of all things.

— Qur'an (29: 62)

I remember a peaceful winter afternoon in Karbala. The sun brilliant and the breeze cool, the palm fronds swinging with rhythmic ease. I must have been about eleven years old and was sitting on one of the flat-topped roofs of our house. The ancient city spread out before me and as I looked towards the great golden dome of the mosque of Imam Hussein, that had seen so much of the past, I wondered about the future: 'What will become of Karbala, and what will become of me, in years to come? Where and what is my destiny?'

I was in my final year at primary school and preparing to go to Karbala's only and newly built secondary school. That morning the teacher had asked my class to write a composition on what we wanted to be in the future. My friends each expressed their desire to join the professional ranks emerging in Iraq; engineers, doctors and administrators. I could not come up with a desired career. After much thought, I presented one sentence in large letters: 'I could be a doctor, an engineer or a teacher. I do not really mind what or where as long as I am content.'

1

The breeze whispered to me that I would not stay in Karbala for long, although Karbala felt like forever. The town and its people seemingly timeless, an endless repeat of time already unfolded. Somehow, even then, I knew I would eventually leave my home for good. I would leave my people and my country, not to avoid anything, nor to reach anything, but simply to live my destiny.

That which is not meant, the hand cannot reach
And that which is allotted you will find wherever you
may be.

— Saadi

Looking down upon the narrow road, I spotted my uncle's car, one of the first few in Karbala, making its way through the crowd of horse drawn carriages, donkey carts and passers-by. As the sun began to set, orange and red peered through the dusky haze. Over the newly installed loudspeaker, the muezzin sounded the call for the faithful to come to prayer; 'haya alas salat' (make haste to prayer), the oldest of exhortations sounded out from the newest of mediums.

The evening before, my nanny, Mashti, had enthralled me with one of her stories. In Persian she would begin, *'Yeki bood yeki nabood ghayr az khuda kesi nabood'* (There was One, there was no one, other than God there is no one). And in Arabic she would end, 'Wa' llahu a'lam' (and Allah knows best).

'There was One, there was no one, other than God there is
no one.'

'There was a sand storm in which a king, out on a hunting trip, had been separated from his guards. As the lost king wandered, a shepherd boy without knowing the king's identity helped him with food and shelter. The following day, when the storm had passed, the king revealed his identity to the shepherd and invited him to stay at the royal court. The innocence, simplicity and loyalty of the shepherd boy endeared him to the king. Soon, he grew to be an influential vizier, making the courtiers and feudal aristocrats extremely jealous of the king's new protégé.

Now, it was the habit of the young vizier, twice a day, to slip away to the seclusion of his private chambers, where no one knew what he was doing. The courtiers speculated and gossiped about this strange conduct. 'He was stashing away gold and jewels which he has stolen from the royal treasury', one would whisper. 'Perhaps he is performing witchcraft', another would add. When the king heard these speculations, he was determined to find out what his vizier was up to and ordered a small hole to be made in the vizier's wall.

The following day, when the vizier had quietly made his way to his chambers, the king and his retinue gathered by the hole. Looking in, they saw the vizier take off his richly embroidered gowns and put on the patched robe of a shepherd boy. In his shepherd's clothing, he would sit on his prayer mat in deep prayer. The king turned to his courtiers and proudly proclaimed, 'this is the real wealth and magic this shepherd boy seeks. He is a true servant of God.'

And Allah knows best.'

Oh my Son, establish regular prayer, enjoin what is just,
forbid what is wrong and bear with patience whatever
befalls you; truly, this act requires courage.

— Qur'an (31: 17)

With the call to prayer ringing in my ears, lifting above the golden dome of the mosque, my thoughts turned between school and the memory of the shepherd boy. I knew within my heart that it would not matter what professions or roles I would acquire in my future life. It would not matter what clothes I would wear, nor where I would wear them, as long as I was content and secure within myself. As providence would have it, I wore many clothes, accepted various and diverse roles and would come to call different countries and houses home.

The first of these houses was the one where, in October 1937, I was born. It was an old house at the heart of the city of Karbala. The house lay adjacent to the Mosque and Shrine of Imam Hussein and belonged to my father, Shaykh Ahmad Al Haeri Al Mazanderani. The date of my birth was considered most auspicious as it coincided with the 3rd of Shaban (the eighth month) in the Islamic lunar calendar, which was also the birthday of Imam Hussein. My father decided to name me 'Fadhlalla', which means 'the grace of God'.

• • •

Three generations before me, a man named Zainul Abideen (meaning the best of worshippers) had been born in the Iranian province of Mazanderan, on the southern coast of the Caspian Sea. In the early 1800s, his father had fled Shirvan, in present day Azerbaijan, as thousands were slaughtered in the wake of a brutal Russian invasion. Zainul Abideen was sent to the seminary city of Najaf in Iraq where Imam Ali, the fourth Caliph of Islam and the father of Imam Hussein, is buried. Here, he became Shaykh Zainul Abideen gaining an unparalleled reputation amongst his contemporaries for piety and abstinence. For fifty years, he lived the life of an ascetic, without a wife and home comforts.

> *A man will not find sweetness of faith until he is heedless of the fruits of this world.*
>
> — Prophet Muhammad

It is said (legend and truth have mingled) that one night, while in supplication at the shrine of Imam Ali, Shaykh Zainul Abideen let out an exasperated exclamation. 'I have lived my whole life in devotion to God and for years I have lived off nothing but dry bread and vegetables. I am getting old now, I want a home and I want to eat chicken instead of dried bread!' There, at the shrine, he fell into a brief sleep, dreaming the most vivid of dreams. Imam Ali came to him and said that if he had any wish for an easier and more comfortable life, he should pull aside the curtains that manifested in front of him. As the Shaykh opened the curtains, he saw a large tablecloth spread across the floor with several people sitting around it enjoying a sumptuous banquet. The Imam then told him to go to Karbala, for this was the table of his son, Imam Hussein.

Asceticism does not mean that you should own nothing.
It means that nothing should own you.

— Imam Ali

Shaykh Zainul Abideen packed his few possessions and headed for Karbala. At the gates of the city, a wealthy merchant, finely dressed and mounted on a horse, asked the head of the approaching caravan if a man named 'Zainul Abideen' was amongst them. As the Shaykh stepped forward, the man got off his horse, bent down and kissed his hand, introducing himself as Hajji[1] Ali, also originally from Mazanderan, but for many years resident in Karbala. He requested the Shaykh to stay at his home, while in Karbala. He was thanked, but told that accommodation arrangements had already been made at the seminary.

Everyday, a huge tray of food was brought to the Shaykh from Hajji Ali's house. A few days later, Hajji Ali offered the Shaykh his daughter's hand in marriage and money to buy a house and household goods. When Shaykh Zainul Abideen asked the reason for the extreme generosity, Hajji Ali revealed that he too had had a

---

1   A common title in the Muslim world used to designate someone who has been on 'hajj' – the pilgrimage to Mecca, which is a once in a lifetime requirement for all Muslims, who are able to undertake it.

dream. Imam Hussein had come to him and told him that a caravan would be arriving from Najaf on a particular day and amongst the travellers would be a man, who bore the same name as his son. This man was to be served and helped in every possible way. 'Zainul Abideen' was the name of the only one of Imam Hussein's sons who survived the battle of Karbala. Shaykh Zainul Abideen thanked God for this great blessing, married Khursheed, Hajji Ali's daughter, and lived the rest of his life in Karbala. There he established a thriving, internationally renowned seminary.

As Shaykh Zainul Abideen's reputation grew, a group of merchants from India arrived in Karbala looking for a religious leader to whom they could give their zakat, the donation to the poor, which is the obligation of every Muslim[2]. They were first recommended to the house of a well-known cleric, who showed much piety and asceticism. There, they were given the simplest of meals, dry bread and lentil soup, but just before their departure, a cat ran from behind a curtain dragging a chicken in its mouth, which it had stolen from the kitchen. The visitors glanced at each other in puzzlement questioning the cleric's asceticism, and left without handing over their *zakat.*

> **Surely, the hypocrites strive to deceive Allah, but it is**
> **He who deceives them.**
>
> — Qur'an (4: 142)

The following day, the party arrived at Shaykh Zainul Abideen's house, where they were served a lavish lunch with a chicken on every plate; for it was now reputed that there was always chicken at Shaykh Zainul Abideen's house. Impressed with his inner purity

---

2 The word '*zakat*' literally means 'to purify'. The implication being that if you give a portion of your wealth or earnings, you have taken a step towards purifying yourself of your love of wealth. The obligatory *zakat* is the equivalent of 2.5% of particular possessions or earnings, but the word is also used for general charitable donations.

and outer generosity, they handed over their zakat and submitted to him as their spiritual leader. In time, the Indian relationship grew, with the princes and sultans of many states being amongst the Shaykh's followers.

In Shi'a Islam, the principle of guidance is invested in an individual or several individuals who stand at the peak of the religious and scholarly hierarchy and whose authority on matters of Islamic law are accepted by the lesser clergy and citizens in general. Shaykh Zainul Abideen was acknowledged as such a man – a *Marja-e Taqlid* (Source of Emulation). More recently, the term Ayatollah[3] and Grand Ayatollah have been used to designate the same station.

Shaykh Zainul Abideen and Khursheed (meaning sun) had four sons, each of whom were prominent men of their time, all reaching the highest rank of religious or political leadership. His eldest son and my grandfather, Shaykh Muhammad Hussein took over his father's mantle as leader of the Friday prayers and master of the religious institutions of Karbala. He stayed there until his death whereupon, his eldest son, my father, Shaykh Ahmad, took his place; like his father and grandfather before him, he too led the main congregation at the Shrine of Imam Hussein. Shaykh Muhammad Hussein's second son, Shaykh Baqir, went to Iran and became a senior and respected Ayatollah in the Justice Ministry (his descendents are scattered around the world, but a number still live in Iran).

It was on Shaykh Zainul Abideen's prayer mats and with Khursheed's *tasbeeh* (rosary or worry beads) that I grew up. Today, the worn prayer mat and *tasbeeh* sit in my room. The tasbeeh was made of clay pellets fashioned from the earth taken from near Imam

---

3 The word Ayatollah was initially used to denote the prominent clerics who supported the Constitutional Revolution in Iran in 1906. Subsequently, it has become more generalized. As the title Ayatollah began to be applied less discriminatingly, the term Grand Ayatollah gained acceptance to give greater status.

Hussein's burial ground. On each of these beads of sacred earth, a name denoting an attribute of God would be recited.

The use of the rosary in Islam was a foreign custom, probably taken from Byzantium. During the Prophet's time, when something was to be recited repeatedly, they used date pips, as are still used in some places, especially Sufi centres in North Africa. There is a pile of pips on one side and with each recitation one pip is thrown onto the other side. The Qur'an relates, 'To God belongs all the desirable perfections and attributes', and when the Prophet was asked, 'What are these attributes?' he replied, 'He who knows ninety-nine names or attributes of God will be in the Garden.' And so the Muslim rosary traditionally has comprised of ninety-nine beads.

> *Allah's are the most beautiful names, so invoke Him by them and leave those who desecrate His names. They will be repaid for what they do.*
>
> — Qur'an (7: 180)

Off a cobble stone alleyway, across from the *Bab al-Zainabiyyah* (the gate of Zainab[4]), one of the main entrances to the Shrine stood our house. When I was a child, there had been no separation between the Shrine and our house, but in time, a narrow road was built encircling the shrine. There were three entrances to the compound, which actually consisted of a collection of houses, the first lead to my father's home and those of the immediate family and the other two were the guesthouse and my aunts' home.

As you walked into our home, beneath the shade of a tall eucalyptus tree, you would come to what was the first of three courtyards. There, a visitor would sit and wait on one of the benches beside the circle of orange trees in the centre of the

---

4 Zainab was the younger sister of Imam Hussein, whose denunciations of the murderers of the Imam and the ruling king Yazid are famous in Muslim history.

courtyard. Onto the same courtyard opened the three wood and glass doors (the equivalent of French windows) of my father's library. Carpets and cushions lay on the library floor, several thousand books lined the walls, some printed, some handwritten and leather bound, a number in the hand of Shaykh Zainul Abideen and Shaykh Muhammad Hussein. All the books were in the Arabic or Persian[5].

Until the early twentieth century, printing presses were still rare in the country and professional scribes often copied books by hand. It was some 400 years after Gutenberg's invention that the printing press became widespread in the Middle East. The first printing press was established in Istanbul in 1729, but was closed down, only to resume printing in 1784 in a most restricted manner, due to the strong objections of clerics on the spurious grounds that it may defile the Arabic script. It took the direct intervention of a European power, in the form of Napoleon's conquest of Egypt at the dawn of the 19th Century, for the Arab countries to have their printing baptism. The first printing press in Iran only started operations in 1817.

Interestingly, apart from the Muslim countries' general tendency to blindly reject any Western invention that was not directly related to the military, another reason for the prohibition of printing in Arabic was the vested interests of the guild of calligraphers and scribes – the predecessors of those whose inscriptions were written on my father's books. Perversely, their strength was a legacy of the Islamic countries' far greater level of scholarship than that of Europe prior to the Middle Ages.

> *Ignorance is enough for you if you are content with your present knowledge.*
>
> — Imam Ali

---

5 Persian is more correctly called 'Farsi', after the name of an area/province in what is now Iran.

While I was in Karbala, the modern printing presses of Cairo and Beirut were producing increasing quantities of material, but their focus was of a more worldly inclination than my father's interests and so he largely avoided them. From 'Abbas Kutibi', my favourite Karbala bookstore, I would eagerly purchase the latest edition of *Ithnaine* (Monday), the popular Egyptian weekly current affairs magazine, whose owners and editors, like their Lebanese competitors, were zealous Christian freemasons.

It was through these modern publishing houses that the Arabic language subtly began to deviate, reflecting the erosion of the culture of religion in the Arab lands, and its replacement by a more Western and worldly outlook. The Qur'an gradually became less and less understandable to the layman, as a number of key Qur'anic terms took on meanings that were often ironically the opposite of their original. Hence, *da'wa*, originally meaning to invite someone to the religion, came to mean a dinner party; *inzi'aj*, which meant moving the heart towards God, now means to be bothered; *khumul* which used to mean not to show off or be pretentious, now means laziness and sloth; mumtaz which the Qur'an uses as 'to stand out' in the way that criminals do, has come to mean excellent; ratib which meant a repeated litany or regulated supplication, now means a fixed salary; *riyadha* which meant a virtuous and self-disciplined way of life has come to mean sport; and *shahada*, a word used to describe the Muslim profession of faith and which until a generation ago had only religious connotations, is now commonly used for a certified qualification (usually a university degree) that would ensure a well-paid job (*ratib*).

> **There is no good in worship without pondering upon its meaning, and no good in reading the Qur'an without reflection.**
>
> — Imam Ali

Behind the first courtyard in our compound was a second family courtyard, which lead to a third smaller courtyard, and which included my father's small and modest sleeping quarters; barely big enough for his bed. At the other side of his courtyard was the tall wall of my father's alchemy laboratory, whose entrance was from the roof. Next to this entrance were large vats of garlic pickle – my sleeves occasionally bearing evidence of having been dipped in the thick dark liquid as I reached in to sample the product. Every morning after fajr, the dawn prayer, and then again for an hour before maghrib, the evening prayer, my father would retreat to his laboratory. From the upper floor, I would hold on to the banister and tentatively make my way down the precarious wooden stairs, choking and coughing as the sickly smells of sulphur and ammonia would invariably engulf me.

There, on tables or niches in the walls, would be all kinds and sizes of pots, some with burners beneath, crude distillation units, a strip of felt slowly dripping filtered liquids from one container to another and liquids of all colours in unmarked jars. Metal strips would be lying around, copper, lead and silver. There would be animal horns, human hair and chemical compounds. At the end of the ground floor, in an enclosed room, raged a coal furnace. Like his father, and grandfather before him, Shaykh Ahmad was a practicing alchemist.

With a mixture of curiosity and concern, I would quietly sit and watch my father as he worked, totally absorbed in his experiments. Occasionally, he would tell me stories of one of his cousins having an accident, things exploding and pots catching on fire. To my surprise, nothing so exciting happened in his workshop, at least not in my memory. As I grew older, one day he explained to me that the aim of the alchemical process is to enable a base metal to transform into a higher noble metal, from lead to gold, from an unstable to a stable state. 'It is an exercise of being admitted to God's secret of how time and the timeless relate; how thousands of years can be shrunk by speeding up the natural process. Whoever wants to turn other metals into gold for material gain will never succeed', my father assured me.

The alchemist will himself be transformed and will transcend the usual human limitations. This in itself is worth far more than the worldly power and wealth the elixir is meant to provide.

Once I remember, a guest had arrived at our home, from outside Iraq to discuss alchemy with my father. He was a wild looking man with long matted hair, who spoke Arabic with a North African accent. He arrived enthusiastically and left disappointed a few days later, accusing my father of not letting him in on the 'inner secrets' of the craft. When he had gone, my father told us over lunch, 'Whoever is anxious about the end product will miss both the transformation and the product.' Shaykh Ahmad's alchemical pursuits were his struggle to transcend the limitations of reasoning and the mind. Success implies being admitted to a zone of consciousness where you become a conduit for the inspirational Source. 'You must', my father had said, 'unite your will with God's will.' Then there is no 'you' as such, only a soul that is God's agent and a reflection of His knowledge.

> *How can norms be broken for you whilst you have not broken the norms of the self (ego).*
> — Ibn Ata' Allah Iskandari

A few months after I left Iraq, I was informed that my father had stopped going to his laboratory. On my first visit back to Karbala, the laboratory was under a cover of dust, concealing ancient secrets. My mother told me that just before he ceased working in the laboratory, a number of my father's silver rings had gradually became golden in colour. Muslim men are not supposed to wear gold and he stopped wearing these rings.

In my library I have a few of my father's books on alchemy. One in particular, a four-century-old treatise, was his constant companion, always by his bedside. Every now and then, with little comprehension, I read a page or two. It is filled with allegorical references and written in classical Arabic. Typically, the book describes strange mixing procedures, instructing the alchemist to 'heat the mixture until it has become mature and accepted stability'; followed by even more abstract parts to do with the quality of the practitioner's state, telling him to be 'an instrument rather than a manipulator of the event.'

• • •

The second courtyard in our home was spacious and spanned two levels. It was named the *Dakhlani* or inner house. Towering over this courtyard was a tall date palm. It was to this palm tree, one memorable day, that Kareem and two other men came brandishing swords and daggers. Kareem was the caretaker of our family orchard, the *Bagh Jamal* (Orchard of Beauty), situated a few kilometres north of the town. He also occasionally looked into the development of the trees (mainly orange) in our compound. This particular palm was ten years old now and had not yet given fruit.

Failing horticultural persuasion, Kareem turned to more traditional measures. His two associates sharpened, flourished and clinked their swords together as they danced around the tree calling out, 'What use is this palm tree if it doesn't bear any fruit?' Once it was determined that the palm tree was suitably warned and frightened, Kareem interceded, begging the men to give the palm tree another chance. 'Next year', he promised, 'it will bear fruit'. After further prodding, poking and pleading, the mystical troop departed, exhausted, but satisfied.

The following year the palm tree produced several branches of Karbala's finest caramel coloured dates. My mother would climb up the palm's trunk with agility to harvest the dates. She continued to do this for years until her climbing career was cut short by the tree growing tall enough to be exposed to the street outside, which had been recently opened.

Tragically, Kareem's story does not have as happy an ending as the fruiting palm tree's. The old ladies of the house were sure that

Kareem would eventually bring sorrow and the evil eye upon himself by bragging about his good fortune. He would boast about the fruits of the orchard, about his devoted wife, his hard working donkey, and most especially about his military prowess. One night, he heard noises outside his little farmhouse and shouted to the intruder to reveal himself. There was no response, but a shadowy figure continued to move outside. Kareem grabbed his gun, shouted again, and then offloaded several rounds in the direction of the stooping figure a few yards away. His pregnant wife was fatally wounded and died soon afterwards in his trembling arms.

She had slipped out because she was sick and did not want to disturb her husband. She was a shy, modest and soft-spoken lady. Kareem never recovered from this tragic event. A short while later, his pregnant donkey expired whilst giving birth. Kareem was left standing alone and bereft in the 'Orchard of Beauty'.

> *No calamity befalls on the earth or in yourselves, but it is inscribed in the Book of Decrees before we bring it into existence. Verily, that is easy for Allah.*
>
> *In order that you may not grieve at the things you fail to get, nor rejoice over that which has been given to you. And Allah likes not prideful boasters.*
>
> — Qur'an (57: 22–23)

Our home, compound and way of life were part of the evolved Muslim culture. The collection of houses, courtyards and their different functions such as the *Burrani* – the outer house, and *Bayt al Amma* – the house of the aunts were typical of large family homes in the Middle East. As was the habit of the Muslims, each house looked in onto a shady courtyard showing little to the road and passers-by. This was not only to preserve the modesty of the women of the household, but also to contain and shield household contents from praying eyes. Islam frowns on ostentation, but for many of those concerned, more pressing than the chastisement of the hereafter was the possibility of expropriation should a nasty governor or greedy prince thinks his subject's excess wealth could be a threat to his leadership.

> ***Modesty is not present in anything but that it adorns it, and evil is not present in anything but that it makes it ugly. Every religion has its character, and the character of Islam is modesty.***
>
> — Prophet Muhammad

The number of inhabitants in the compound would vary from time to time, but usually there would be seven or eight elderly ladies scattered between the houses attending to the chores; the sweeping, washing and cooking as well as storytelling and child minding. None was paid a fixed wage and all were considered part of the household. Their needs would be taken care of as and when they occurred. Occasionally, visitors and guests would give them gifts of clothes, sandals or special food. The servants in the household acted freely and they could come and go as they pleased. They attended to their duties with the least supervision and were most respected by the younger family members.

First amongst these women was the small, but powerful Nana Sekeena. She had come from Isfahan, capital of the old Safavid[6] Empire, and was very proud of it. Not a day passed without her reminding us, *Isfahan nisfe jahan* (Isfahan is half the universe). Love of Imam Hussein was her first and lasting passion. Her second was to be exclusively in charge of the shopping, storing and safeguarding of the household goods, which were packed away in a room exclusively used for storage and tea making. Boiling water and tea were always available from morning till night, kept simmering

---

6 The ruling dynasty of Iran and for a time parts of Iraq (1502–1736). They were the Ottomans' greatest rivals in the Islamic World.

over small kerosene stoves. This room was on the second floor in the main house and was known as the *sanduq khana*, 'the box room' because it had several black Zanzibari wooden chests with brass trimmings and hinges large enough for us children to hide in.

Incorporated in Nana Sekeena's authority was the maintenance of several ornamental cages for canaries and nightingales, which were hung from the roofs and the feeding of the many cats which looked longingly up at the cages. She was also in charge of insect extermination. During summer, you would hear her pumping away at *Imshi* (go away), the local hand operated insect spray puffing out diluted DDT. She was meticulously clean and fussy, an ancient skinny spinster, inflexible in her ways, but unfailingly loyal to the family and unswerving in her antagonism to my nanny, Mashti.

> **Cleanliness is half the faith and is the key to accepted prayer.**
>
> — Prophet Muhammad

My devoted nanny, Mashti, was a Georgian widow who had come to live in northern Mazanderan where she had married a wealthy landowner and borne him a son. After an epidemic claimed both her husband and their son, the husband's brother, a greedy and ambitious man, managed to acquire his brother's land, leaving Mashti with no inheritance. She was advised to take refuge in Karbala and our family was recommended to her.

When she arrived I was a few months old, about the same age as her deceased child would have been and so she dedicated her life to my upbringing. She would always tell me adoringly, 'You are my reason for living.' She had translucent pearly skin, beautiful blue eyes and long blond hair carefully made up into plaits, which I would often undo and pull. She was always available for my childish demands, some of which in the manner of children who are certain of getting their own way were no doubt unreasonable.

She was so attentive to me that she often pre-empted my wishes, whether it was the olive oil soap I had forgotten before going to our Turkish bath, deep in the cellar of the house, or my favourite fried onions with chicken livers. She was always on hand to do what I wanted making sure no other members of the household competed with her, not even my mother. The poor woman was often reprimanded for such excessive favouritism and was especially picked on by Nana Sekeena.

Mashti's other great quality was storytelling. During the blistering hot summer days, we would spend most of midday in the cellars, being cooled by four *badgirs*, wind-catcher chimneys that funnelled cool air from outside. Then, at night, we would come up to the flat roof exposed to the cool desert breeze and gaze upon the sparkling stars of a desert sky, drifting off into a world of dreams whilst listening to the lady storytellers. Mashti was the acknowledged favourite. Umm al Saadah, and Nana Hussein made up the complement.

> **Surely the heart of a child is like fallow ground: whatever is planted in it is accepted by it.**
>
> — Imam Ali

Umm al Saadah was an old widow belonging to the prominent Arab tribe of *Bani Asad* (Sons of the Lion), the same tribe that my mother belonged to. Saadah is the plural of *Seyyid*, meaning a descendent of the Prophet; thus, her name literally meant mother of the descendents of the Prophet, on account of her husband having been a *Seyyid* [7].

Umm al Saadah had a proud wrinkled face with strong Arab features. She was hard of hearing and sight. We would often exploit these weaknesses for our amusement. We children had a portable

---

7 A conservative estimate would be that there are over 20 million Seyyids stretching across the Muslim World, though there are many more who are unknown or undeclared as there have been periods of persecution against the Seyyids. The wearing of a black turban commonly indicates a Seyyid.

electric lamp with a small bulb and no lampshade. Umm al Saadah had never seen an electric light close up and she had only seen them on ceilings or walls. One night, after she had told us the evening's story, we presented her with the 'candle' to blow out. Blow as she might, it would not go out. We told her that this was a *jinni*[8] lamp and that we had to whisper a secret name before it could be extinguished. We performed the magic of commanding the light to die out, which it did instantly. She was alarmed and concerned about the danger that may result from our relationship with the *jinn*. After several futile attempts to blow the lamp out and our hearty laughter, she came to realise the wonders of electricity.

Nana Hussein was the most devout and eldest member of the household, wise and frail. She ate little and prayed a lot, her black rosary always handy. Whenever one of us complained or expressed discontent, she would answer, *khair, khair* (it is only goodness), then she would produce some biscuits, raisins or nuts to give to us. It was only years later that I realized that the wise see goodness and Divine mercy in every situation and event.

> **My mercy encompasses everything.**
>
> — Qur'an (7: 156)

During summer nights, I would regularly be woken up at dawn by the sound of Nana Hussein unlocking the doors of my aunt's house to go to the Shrine. The doors to the houses had large steel tong-like keys which would jangle loudly as they turned the three or four times necessary before the door opened. My father once overheard me complaining about the annoyance of the early morning noise. He told me, 'it will take you the best part of forty years to realise that the sound you dislike represents for Nana Hussein the opening of the gates to heaven.' I was perhaps then seven years old. The

---

8 In Islamic tradition, the 'jinn' exist in the world of the unseen. Whereas the base elements of humans are earth and water, the jinn are made of fire and air.

sound of my father's teaching still resonates with me, and the peaceful, happy face of Nana Hussein appears vividly before me in my mind's eye.

It was some years later, whilst I was studying in England, that Nana Hussein passed away. My mother wrote to me about how one day Nana Hussein had come to her and cheerfully announced that she will die tomorrow. She was therefore requesting that my mother come and spend the night in her room. 'How do you know you will die tomorrow?' my mother enquired. Nana Hussein explained that the night before she had a dream in which she was taken into a vast garden. In this garden were many beautiful homes and palaces, tendrils of scented flowers cascading over ornate pavilions. She was then directed towards a house and was told that this was her new home. She told her angelic guide that she could not stay there because it had no roof. He answered that 'the roof will be made tomorrow.' From this, she concluded with certainty, she would depart from this world the following day.

Nana Hussein showed my mother all that she had in her possession. Everything was prepared – a few bags of rice, barley and other grains were to be cooked and distributed to the poor for three days following her death and she gave my mother her small pouch containing the sacred dust from Imam Hussein's burial ground. A few drops of the dust would be prescribed for any ailment, mixed in water or placed on the tongue. Throughout her life Nana Hussein kept this small healing pouch next to her pillow. Throughout her life my mother too kept and sparingly used the dust from this pouch.

My mother spent that night in Nana Hussein's room reading the Qur'an until just before dawn. At that time, Nana Hussein turned over towards my mother thankfully and closed her eyes forever. She was buried mid-morning in our family mausoleum, next to the tomb of Imam Hussein, a great and unexpected honour.

*Detach your heart from this world before your body leaves
it, for you are tested in it, and you were created for other
than it. Surely when someone dies, the people say: 'What
has he left behind?' And the angels say: 'What has he sent
ahead?'*

— Imam Ali

In Karbala, whenever anyone died, the corpse would be taken
immediately to one of the few preparation places to be washed and
shrouded. Then, the coffin would be carried by relatives, friends or
porters along the bazaars, alleyways and streets on its way to
burial. As the procession moved along, people would come out
from their shops or houses and walk behind the dead body or help
to lift the coffin whilst chanting, *La ilaha illa 'llah* (There is no God
but Allah). In this way, every death in the town was felt by a large
part of the population – a perpetual reminder as to the fate of us all
and the leap we will make from the stepping-stone of this life to the
eternity of the next.

Every Thursday, this reminder was reaffirmed communally, for
Thursday picnics at the cemetery were a major social event. The
public cemetery of Karbala was vast. Not only did it accommodate
the local inhabitants of the city, but also the many thousands of
coffins that were brought from far and wide, reflecting the dying
wish of many Shi'as to be buried in Karbala's sacred earth.

The picnics would be prepared from before the afternoon, with
the women making *Khubz al Abbas*[9] (the Bread of Abbas). The
bread was kneaded from the flour of wheat and barley, rolled flat
and flavoured with chives, onions, and garlic and then baked with
mincemeat. At the cemetery, the children would run and play, as the
older people read Qur'an, wept and prayed for the dead.

---

9 Abbas was the younger half-brother of Imam Hussein, who was also killed at
Karbala.

Visit graves and by this remind yourself of the next world.
— Imam Ali

Death was very much alive in Karbala. After all, the city was founded on the most tragic of deaths. A death that shook the very foundation of the Islamic world, the shockwaves of which resonate to this day. In 680, on the 10th day of the Islamic month of Muharram, the plain of Karbala became the Plain of Martyrs.

2

The Plain of Martyrs

Muhammad is no more than a Messenger and
Messengers before him have passed away. If then he
dies or is killed, will you turn back upon your heels?
— Qur'an (3: 144)

At Ghadeer-e-Khum, on the return to Medina from his last *hajj* (pilgrimage) to Mecca, the Prophet Muhammad addressed the people, 'I leave behind amidst you two great things: The Book of Allah and my progeny. Should you be attached to these two, never will you go astray from me, for truly, these two will never part company until they both meet me at the Spring of Paradise.' Then he continued, 'The Lord Allah Almighty is my Master and I am the master of every true believer', and taking the hand of Imam Ali, his cousin and son-in-law, he raised it above the crowd. 'He is the master of all those whose master I have been. O Allah, love those who love Ali and hate those who hate him.'

Shortly after this, the Prophet Muhammad died. Yet, on the Prophet's death, his elderly father-in-law and close friend, Abu Bakr was proclaimed as the new Caliph of Islam. The Muslim ranks had swelled dramatically in the last few years of the Prophet's life. Ali was young and there were those who felt he would be unable to hold together the nascent Islamic state. Three times the mantle of leadership passed him by. The borders of Byzantium were rolled back, the Sassanian[1] Empire melted and the banner of Islam swept all before it. Throughout, Imam Ali was loyal, electing not to contest publicly the leadership of Muslims and helping the Caliphs whenever it was in the interests of the people.

One day in June 656, a mob descended on the house of Uthman (the third Caliph) in the capital Medina. They were demanding justice from the misrule of Uthman's governors, and although Imam Ali sympathised with the mob's complaints, he sent his two sons, the Prophet's grandsons – Imam Hassan and Imam Hussein – to protect Uthman. The mob overpowered them and after gaining access to the house murdered Uthman. Upon the news of the Caliph's death, the *Shi'atu Ali*, the followers of Ali – from which the word Shi'a comes – proclaimed Imam Ali as the fourth Caliph of Islam.

Uthman, although a close companion of the Prophet, had come from the Meccan ruling classes, who had bitterly opposed and fought the Prophet in the early days of Islam. As the proceeds of conquests poured in, Uthman was unable to restrain his relatives' greed for wealth and power. Scarcely a generation after the Prophet's death, the rule of money was undermining the rule of God. The bonds of religion, which had held the early Muslims together, began to give way to the bonds of the tribe.

Uthman had appointed many of his relatives from the *Bani Umayya*[2] to key offices. It was against their corruption and nepotism that the mob was protesting. One of these relatives, Mu'awiyah, the son of the Prophet's old opponent Abu Sufyan, and the governor of Syria, refused to acknowledge Ali as the new Caliph.

---

1 Name given to the Persian dynasty and empire, which lasted from 224–651 CE
2 The word 'bani' means 'sons of'. The Bani Ummaya was one of the more powerful clans amongst the larger tribal grouping of Mecca – the Quraish. The Prophet also belonged to this tribe, although he was of the Bani Hashim clan.

*Ali is from me and I am from Ali. No one can
discharge my duty instead of me except Ali.*

— Prophet Muhammad

Banners were raised and the two armies met at the Battle of Siffin on the banks of the River Euphrates. However, just as the Shi'a of Ali had victory in sight, Mu'awiyah showed his guile. Qur'ans were pinned to his soldiers' spears, indicating a wish for arbitration under God's book, and the battle finished indecisively. Shortly after, during the month of Ramadan, as Ali prostrated in prayer in the mosque of Kufa, an assassin struck him from behind[3]. On his death, the people of Kufa proclaimed his eldest son, Imam Hassan as Caliph.

In order to prevent bloodshed, Imam Hassan reluctantly agreed to sign a truce with Mu'awiyah. He retired to Medina to live a life of prayer and devotion until, at Mu'awiyah's instigation, he was poisoned by one of his wives. In the truce with Mu'awiyah, along with other agreements that were flaunted, Imam Hassan expressly prohibited the election of Mu'awiyah's son, Yazid, as Caliph; the latter being a notorious reprobate well known for his public wine drinking and licentious behaviour.

Despite this, on Mu'awiyah's death, Yazid was proclaimed as Caliph. Thus was ushered in the Umayyads, the first usurping dynasty of the Islamic world. It was precisely against this institutionalisation of hereditary leaders that Imam Hassan had fought. Yazid, recognising that his position was precarious, immediately sent word to Medina that Imam Hussein be required to take an oath of allegiance to him. If he refused, he was to be killed.

When asked to take the oath, the Imam suggested that the people should be summoned to the mosque the next day and a consensus

---

3 The assassin was a member of the Kharijites (Seceders), a group that had originally supported Ali, but became disillusioned when he agreed to negotiate with Mu'awiyah.

be taken as to whether he should or should not pay homage to Yazid. This was refused, but the Governor of Medina feared recrimination if he killed the Prophet's grandson and thus spared him. Two days later, with a small group of family and friends, Imam Hussein escaped, by night, to Mecca. From there, he set off on the journey northwards, through the Arabian Desert towards his father's old capital, Kufa. The citizens there had pledged their allegiance to him and had begged for his presence.

On his way to Kufa, he came to a plain on the edge of the desert where some Babylonian villages had once stood. He was told the place was known as Karbala; a name derived from 'Kur Babul' – meaning villages of Babylon. 'Truly', said the Imam, 'this is the land of *karb* (anguish) and *balaa*' (misfortune). There he ordered the tents to be pitched.

> **Hassan and Hussein are the leaders of the youth of Paradise.**
>
> — Prophet Muhammad

Every year, as Muharram approached, hundreds of thousands would flock to Karbala as the city stirred in anticipation. Twenty days before Muharram began, large tents would go up in the open courtyard surrounding the Shrine. The poles of these tents would be some twenty metres high and broad enough for two or three of us boys clasping our hands together to only just encircle one. Inside the tents were calligraphies, rugs and tapestries. Woven on the tapestries were pictures of battle scenes and warriors. There was *Dhu'l Fiqar*, the legendary two-bladed sword of Imam Ali and *Dhu'l Jinah*, the 'winged horse' of Imam Hussein.

In all, six or seven tents would be pitched inside the marble courtyard of the Shrine, each one joined to the next so that sunlight was screened and it was cool inside. My favourite was the Sufi or Dervish[4]

---

4 The words Sufi and Dervish are interchangeable.

tent at the back of the shrine. Although small compared to the others, it was exquisitely colourful and certainly the most enticing and mysterious of the tents. Inside, incense drifted through the air, rose water splashed onto faces, Turkish delight vanished into mouths and men with the most impressive of beards sang and chanted praises of God and the Prophet. They had come from Turkey, Iran, India, Afghanistan and further afield, each one with a staff and each one with his own brand of headgear; turbans of all colours, sizes and styles, scull caps and tall red fezzes.

A dervish is someone who is preoccupied in contemplating the next world and is least concerned about this one. He is intoxicated with the spiritual realm, with its meanings and insights rather than worldly acquisition. The word dervish comes from the Persian word *'darweesh.' Dar* in Persian means door and the true dervish wants to find a door out of the physical imprisonment of the body to the Source of eternal life.

> **Secrets fall from the Sufi's hand, whole kingdoms for the taking. Unlike someone who begs on the street for bread, a dervish begs to give his life away.**
> — Jalaluddin Rumi

'There was One, there was no one, other than God there is no one', so Mashti began her story.

'There was a man who was quietly living out his life, until one day he caught a glance of the princess of his city as she rode through the streets in her carriage. For a moment, her radiant face was accidentally exposed. The man was possessed and infatuated at first sight. From then on, wherever he turned in his mind's eye, he was haunted by the princess' face. He resolved that he could no longer live like this, whatever the cost, he must find a way of obtaining her hand in marriage. There was, of course, a problem. He was an ordinary citizen, while she was the king's only beloved daughter. Her beauty was touted far and wide, kings and princes had come seeking her hand, and all had been spurned, for the old king could not bear to lose her. What could this wretched fellow possibly offer that the princely suitors had not?

Now in this city, there lived a renowned dervish. In desperation, the young man explained his problem, begging the sage for whatever help he could provide. 'I can help you marry the princess' the dervish promised, 'but I need six months of total submission from you. During this time, you must do exactly as I say.' 'Anything', the desperate lover enthusiastically agreed.

The dervish took the suitor high up into the hills overlooking the city. There he was given a patched robe, a rosary and ordered to sit cross legged in contemplation. He was told not to speak to anyone at anytime nor accept any food or gifts. In addition, he was not to be seen eating or doing anything other than meditating or praying.

As time wore on, the young lover's beard began to grow, his hair fell unkempt around his ears and he lost weight. Gradually, he began to look the picture of a wise and Godly recluse. The pure mountain air and sparse food, which the dervish delivered intermittently, were having their expected detoxifying effect. Helped along by the dervish's rumours, our novice also began to gain something of a reputation in the surrounding settlements.

The people climbed up to his retreat with their problems and desires. He would sit solemnly, fiddling with his rosary beads and saying nothing. The profundity of his silence had a remarkable effect on his visitors. Presuming they were in the presence of a greater being, his visitors turned to introspection where they all seemed to find the answers they had come looking for. Soon, the young sage of the mountain was heralded as a great, new saint. From far and wide, presents were brought to him for his services though it was known by now that this man was so holy that all gifts and offerings remained unopened on the ground around him.

After six months of this, and upon the dervish's suggestion, the king decided to see the wise man of the mountain for himself. Accompanied by the dervish and his entourage, he climbed the hills towards the new saint's perch with pomp and ceremony. The king, having heard many stories of the saint's miracles, was in a receptive state to experience miracles as a reward for his strenuous efforts to reach the top of the mountain. The more difficult we consider an achievement, the more we want to believe in its importance.

Sitting humbly beside the young sage, the king asked him numerous questions, all of which were met with wise silence. After a while, the king began to feel that this man was answering his questions without saying anything. He was so impressed by the composure and worldly abstinence of the new saint that he asked him if there was anything that he, the devoted king, could now do for him. The novice silently shook his head. 'I must give you something', pleaded the king, 'you are a blessing to my kingdom and my people, of whom you have helped countless numbers.' Once more, the novice shook his head, signalling his total contentment and disinterest in kingly favours. Then, at length and slowly, the king continued, 'I have one thing which is more valuable to me than anything else. Many great men have begged me to give my princess to them, but you are truly the only one who has proven himself worthy. Will you not take my daughter's hand in marriage?' The novice looked up, smiled at the king and, in refusal, again shook his head.

At this juncture, the dervish was gesticulating ferociously from behind the king's back for his novice to accept, but the novice was unmoved. The king got up and proclaimed, 'Truly, this man is a saint', and set off back down the mountain. As soon as he was out of sight, the dervish pounced upon his student, kicking, punching and cursing. 'You idiot, what have you done! Six months of work! Why didn't you accept the king's offer? You fool! Imbecile!' The erstwhile suitor got up and calmly brushed himself off. In measured words, he addressed the dervish. 'For six months, I pretended to be a pious man and I had the king at my feet. What if I actually was pious?'

And Allah knows best.'

Hussein is from me and I am from Hussein. May Allah love whoever loves Hussein.

— Prophet Muhammad

On the 1st of Muharram (which is also the first day of the Islamic year), the flag flying above the Shrine of Imam Hussein changes colour. The huge blood red flag would come down and hoisted in its place, for forty days, would flutter a jet-black cloth.

The visitors, whether individuals or groups, would percolate throughout the city, the streets would become residences and alleyways toilets. Many houses become overcrowded temporary hostels and the outskirts of the city was a huge campsite. Every night, the people would cook and distribute food to the poor and the passers-by. The kerosene lamps and campfires would be lit, and the lament of Karbala told and retold, fact and fantasy mixing indiscriminately and irrelevantly as each group tried to outdo the next in grief and superlatives. With each passing day, the intensity and fervour of the proceedings would increase. In the first few days, the scene would be set:

Though Kufa was a Shi'a stronghold, Imam Hussein's father and brother had both found to their cost that when the people there were tested by force or bribery, the promises of the majority would come to nothing. Thus, to ensure the sincerity of their requests for leadership, before he left Mecca Imam Hussein had sent his cousin Muslim Ibn Aqil to appraise the steadfastness of the Kufans. Encouraged by the enthusiastic welcome he received, Muslim sent words of encouragement to the Imam.

It was the time of the *Hajj* pilgrimage and Imam Hussein had intended to stay in Mecca until after performing the pilgrimage. When he heard of Yazid's plan to have him killed while he performed *hajj*, he decided to set off immediately so as not to desecrate the Holy Ka'ba[5].

---

5 The square building at the centre of Mecca, which is draped in black during the month of Hajj. It is said that the Ka'ba was built by the Prophet Abraham, as a symbolic house of God and it is towards it that Muslims pray.

Stunned by his decision to leave on the eve of the pilgrimage, the Muslims were perplexed and asked why. 'This year's pilgrimage I have to perform at Karbala', the Imam replied. When asked what animals he would sacrifice, Imam Hussein pointed to his family, his half-brother Hazrat Abbas, his eighteen-year-old son Ali al-Akhbar and his nephews. 'These are my sacrifices', he had said.

As he was making his way to Kufa, the Imam heard word that Muslim had been executed in Kufa. Yazid had sent the murderous Ibn Ziyad to assume the governorship of Kufa and crush the people's insurrection. Many of the Kufans, who were threatened with death and confiscation of property, deserted the cause. The Imam warned those travelling with him of the dangers ahead and told those who wished to leave that they should do so.

> *When they see affliction, there are few who adhere to their religion.*
>
> — Imam Hussein

On the 2nd of Muharram, shadowed by a small contingent of Yazid's army, they reached the plain of Karbala, where the tents were pitched. On the 3rd, the main stay of Ibn Ziyad's army arrived from Kufa, commanded by Ibn Sa'd. The Imam's water supply was cut off and by the 7th, his family and close followers were without water and fully surrounded by a large army. On the 9th, Ibn Sa'd's army marched onto the camp. Imam Hussein asked for one more day to be with his family and supporters for their last prayers and supplications, which was granted.

• • •

Every year in Karbala, on the night of the 9th, the electricity generators would be switched off, plunging the entire city into darkness. On this night of strangers, *sham-e ghariban,* candles are lit as sorrow descends on the city in remembrance of the plight the Prophet's family faced. As Imam Hussein and his companions had done, the night would be spent in prayer and devotion.

Then, on the following morning, *Ashura* (literally meaning the 10th), the story and Battle of Karbala is re-enacted. The tradition of the pageantry or 'passion-play' was probably an import from India and Iran, a few centuries before, but now it had been taken up with gusto by the Arabs.

If you could push your way through the massive crowd to the *mukhayyam*, the tented replica of the Imam's encampment near the shrine, you would see people dressed up as the family of Imam Hussein and his enemies. Whoever played the part of the Imam would conceal his face with a white cloth, for the Shi'a are not supposed to draw or depict the faces of the Prophets or Imams (though this is not always adhered to). The white stallion, which played *Dhu'l Jinah* (the winged one), would be well fed and groomed, ready by now for the great appearance. The unfortunate actors playing Yazid or Shimr (the Imam's killer) could well end up being assaulted as the people's enthusiasm got a little out of hand. The poor pseudo-Yazid could find himself running for his life and often had to be given bodyguard protection. These acts and plays are called *shabeeh* (the like of truth) and had become an important aspect of Shi'a tradition over the years.

Alongside the actors playing out their roles, the declaimers would re-live the legend of the battle through the *marthiyas* or elegies of renowned poets. The poet's[6] words would come to life as with choking emotion through the charged air, the intricate detail of every aspect of the battle flowed out in hyperbole. Starting from the dawn of that fateful day, the poet would begin:

'The sun had run its journey over the night;
Unveiled, the Dawn revealed her glorious face.

---

6 These verses are extracted and adapted from the marsiya of the Indian poet Mir Anis as translated by David Matthews

The king who rides the heaven saw her light
And called his brave companions to their place.
'The time has come at last; to God give praise;
Arise! In fitting prayer your voices give raise.'

The 72 martyrs, ranging from 14 to 70 years old, came out to face the enemy. Dressed in the cloak and armour of the Prophet, wielding *Dhu'l Fiqar*, his father's sword and perfumed in musk, Imam Hussein stood at their head. The time had come.

From the stamping of the horses, sand flew up;
The firmament filled like an hour-glass.
The dark blue sky became a dusty cap,
And blackness spread over valley, hill and pass.
The glow that lights the world was lost from sight;
The afternoon at once had turned to night.

Fighting the huge army of the enemy for most of the day, the desperately thirsty warriors fell, one by one, with grace and nobility. Behind them, in the Imam's camp, the women, children and sick waited helplessly. Sakina, the Imam's youngest daughter, piteously begged for water. Abbas, the bravest of the men, hearing his niece's cry, made for the enemy lines, his sword cutting a path to the river through Ibn Sa'd's army.

The sword of brave Abbas flashed with such power
That Gabriel sought protection from his Lord.
The son of Sa'ad there faced his final hour.
As lions spring to gain the river banks,
Abbas swam through the waves of serried ranks.
The guards of the Euphrates lost their heads
And like the river's current flowed away.
Abbas, dry-lipped, took water back to their tents,
And the Prince of Arabs fought again.

As Abbas emerged from the river to make his way back to the camp, an arrow hit the water skins. Soon his blood was flowing alongside the water, as he lay dead by the side of the riverbank. Meanwhile, Imam Hussein's infant son, Ali Asghar, was also dying of thirst. Holding his son in his arms, the Imam asked the enemy for some water for the baby.

> *He cradled Asghar in his warm embrace.*
> *Outside in ambush lurked black Kahil's son[7]*
> *Who fired a three-pronged arrow from his place;*
> *Its target was the neck of the little one.*
> *The baby cried in pain; the Leader thundered;*
> *The tiny child was slaughtered by his side.*

The Imam put down his murdered son on the desert sand and turned towards the killers.

> *Hussein swooped like an eagle from on high,*
> *As lions in the jungle pounce on deer.*
> *The heavens flashed; the clouds began to cry;*
> *His horse rushed down like water swift and sheer.*
> *The sharp sword cut the foe with thunderous crash;*
> *They fell like mountains beneath the lightning crash.*

Eventually, as the afternoon drew on, all seventy-one of his army of kith and kin lay dead. The Imam was left standing alone to face Yazid's army.

> *Ten thousand arrows dashed upon his chest;*
> *A hundred at one time sought out their prey.*
> *The spears transfixed his side and pierced his breast;*
> *Ten struck for every four he pulled away.*

---

7 Hurmaila ibn Kabil, an expert bowman of Yazid's army.

Eventually, the blessed Imam succumbed to his fate.

> *Hussein falls from his mount – calamity!*
> *His holy foot falls from the horse's girth.*
> *His side is gaping open – misery!*
> *He swoons; his turban drops upon the earth.*
> *The Qur'an has fallen headlong from its stand.*
> *The Ka'aba's walls have crumbled into sand.*

A soldier named Shimr stood over the Imam's body, sword raised. 'I grant you one last wish', he said. 'Give me water', the Imam replied. 'I can give you anything but that', smirked Shimr. 'The water is not for me', exclaimed Hussein, and as he spoke, a spring gathered by his feet. 'It was for you, so that God might find some good reason to forgive you on the Day of Judgment.'

• • •

Through the streets, the human river surged. *Ya Hussein, Ya Hussein*, reverberated between the walls and hearts of Karbala. Stripped to the waist in barefoot procession, the men beat their chests in what is known as the *latum* (beating). Sharpened daggers, attached to chains, were hoisted over shoulders to lacerate the mourners' backs, rising and falling to the accompaniment of drums and cymbals. Dulled swords clashed with bloodied foreheads. Blood and tears mixed in the dust, as the *azza*, the expression of mourning, descended with an avalanche of emotion. My father did not approve of the self-flagellation and discouraged our family from taking part in the upheaval of the proceedings. Nevertheless, whenever any of these spectacles passed, you could not help but let your own streaming tears join the prevailing current. The grief was contagious and the love of remembrance of Imam Hussein's stand against man's vices and injustices always swell in breasts and purify hearts.

*The common people act by imitation, the distinguished
act by love and evidence, and the elite of the elite act by
contemplation and witnessing.*

— Shaykh Ali al Jamal

Three days after the massacre, the bodies of the martyrs were
discovered and buried by the *Bani Asad* tribesman who lived in the
nearby town of Towaireej, about 10 miles from Karbala. In
commemoration, the *Azza Towaireej* would make their way towards
Karbala. It was said that as the Imam's body lay exposed, a lion sat
guard, protecting it from the circling vultures, and so inevitably, a
man in a lion skin costume would be produced, during the *shabeeh*.
Once the growling and swaying lion was removed from the display
platform, the town's people would be fed from enormous trays,
some two metres across, bearing mountains of rice topped with
qeemah (a stew of minced meat with chick peas).

Then, the town quietens until 40 days later when, according to
local tradition, the Imam's severed head, which was taken to
Damascus to be paraded at Yazid's court, was reunited in burial
with his body. In a separate tradition, it is reported that the head was
taken to Cairo and is buried in the famed Mosque of the Head of
Imam Hussein, opposite the Al Azhar University. Under the dome
of that famous mosque is an inscription relating to a Prophetic
tradition that any supplication made under the dome of Imam
Hussein will be accepted. The mosque remains one of Egypt's
foremost places of worship, for the love of Hussein is by no means
limited to the Shi'a world. Many of those who descend on Karbala
in Muharram are Sunni Muslims.

It is generally estimated that the Sunnis constitute around 80
percent of the 1.3 billion Muslims in the world, although they are a
minority in Iraq. The word Sunni comes from *sunna*, meaning the
way or tradition of the Prophet, but the line between Sunnis
and Shi'a is often blurred. Many Sunnis, although not officially
accepting Imam Ali as the rightful successor to Muhammad,

nevertheless hold great love and respect for the Prophet's family and progeny, especially Imams Ali, Hassan and Hussein and their mother of light, Fatima, the daughter of the Prophet. This can clearly be seen in the vigorous *Ashura* celebrations of the Sub-Continent's Sunni as well as Shi'a Muslims. Equally, every Shi'a will strive to adhere to the sunna of the Prophet Muhammad. The lesson of Karbala is for every Muslim.

Every day is Ashura, every place is Karbala.
— Ayatollah Khomeini

In a world where despotic and dictatorial leadership is the norm for most Muslim countries, *Ashura* holds significance far beyond the ritualistic rites that have come to symbolise it. The battle fought between Imam Hussein and the forces sent by Yazid to destroy him has forever linked the name of Karbala to those oppressed by any tyrannical rule. It is so much more than the 'brief military engagement' the Encyclopaedia Britannica dryly refers to. It is to do with the eternal question of what are the qualities of a man that make him worthy of leadership; is it worldly power and political cunning or spiritual insight, justice, wisdom and enlightenment? Saddam Hussein, for this reason, banned the *Ashura* celebrations, fearing that they could become a rallying call against his own despotic regime.

On a profound level, the Battle of Karbala also symbolises the ongoing battle between the higher self or soul and the lower self, the ego. While the lower self asserts its ever-changing indulgences and whims, the soul reflects the Divine light that animates it and calls it to joy, wisdom and harmony.

Today, Imam Hussein is as alive in people's hearts as when he lived. From all corners of the world, millions visit Karbala to pay their respects. Conversely, no one sets off on a journey to pay his or her respects to Yazid or his father Mu'awiyah. No one even knows where Yazid is buried. On one of my latter day visits to Damascus with a friend, Hosam Raouf, and with the help of a local historian, we tried to find out where Mu'awiyah was buried. We were eventually taken to a narrow alleyway and a rather embarrassed guide pointed to a ladies public bath and toilet. As far as he and the antiquities department in Damascus had been able to ascertain, Mu'awiyah's final resting place lay therein.

Some time ago, I was asked to give my first public talk on Muharram to a crowd of British Muslims. I prayed for inspiration, and that night had a wonderful dream. There was a fine black tent, stretching towards the horizon. I was taken inside and saw the Prophet and his family scattered in different parts of the tent. Imam Ali beckoned to me and said, 'You wanted to talk to my sons, and here they are.' Both Imam Hassan and Imam Hussein appeared, as young men, cheerfully exchanging pleasantries. I cautiously approached Imam Hussein and asked, 'Do I have your permission to talk about your martyrdom?' 'Of course you can', he replied, 'but only if you depict me as you see me now; in perfect joy, in timeless bliss – not in any other way.'

> *It rained on the plain of Karbala and passed,*
> *It turned the desert into a blooming orchard and*
> *passed.*
> *He put an end to oppression for all time to come;*
> *He created an orchard by watering the sands with his*
> *blood.*
>
> —Muhammad Iqbal

3

The Last Caravan

You are the best community that has been raised up from mankind. You enjoin right conduct and forbid indecency; and you believe in Allah.

— Qur'an (3: 10)

Like the tribesmen who had buried Imam Hussein, my mother was also from the Bani Asad. Her father was a successful merchant, who had returned to Karbala from Baghdad. His family had been in Karbala for many generations having been sent a few centuries before, from what is now Saudi Arabia, to defend the holy cities of Iraq from a Tartar invasion. My maternal grandfather was called Seyyid Mehdi Hamoudi and had wanted his daughter to marry either a *Seyyid* or an *alim*, a religious scholar. Despite this, as was the common custom amongst tribal Arabs, she was engaged from birth to her maternal cousin. No other man could seek her hand. The proud cousin had already brought gold and other presents to seal the engagement. Before she reached the age of marriage, however, her father died. He had been one of the leaders of the *azza* procession and his family were renowned for their *marthiya*. Due to the exposure of stripping to his waist during one vigorous procession, he had contracted a fatal chest ailment. After his death, my grandmother was not able to cope with the prospect of sending her daughter away to Baghdad where her cousin had his life and business and so, she changed her mind.

Shaykh Ahmad was some 35 years older than my mother. His first wife had borne him five children, but when the children were in their teens, she had died of cholera during an epidemic. He remained unmarried for five or six years, until his sisters and other family members convinced him to marry again. He had known of my mother's family from family friends, so he approached her eldest brother, Abdul Hussein, now the head of the family and asked for her hand. She had only once seen Shaykh Ahmad from a distance as he led the communal prayer at the Shrine. They had never exchanged a glance or a word. Yet, she agreed to marry him. Sherbet was drunk, the marriage was confirmed and the cousin's presents duly returned to him.

The next day, my mother's unhappy relatives in Baghdad heard of the marriage and pandemonium broke out. The cousin, his mother and relatives rushed to Karbala. The dashing young Arab was consumed with anger and felt betrayed and humiliated. He cursed my grandmother saying, she herself should have married Shyakh Ahmad, not her young and beautiful daughter. He threatened to come with his relatives from the *Bayt Thalatha* (House of Three) tribe and steal my mother away from the roof. 'Don't imagine we're just going to leave things as they are,' he warned everyone. Then, he stormed to Shaykh Ahmad's house. 'You're sitting in front of the Prophet's prayer mat, you pray towards the Ka'ba, they call you a Shaykh, but you've taken my right, you've usurped it!'

'On no account have I taken your right.' Shaykh Ahmad firmly replied to the young man, 'I asked her guardian and brother, in case I didn't come forward to marry her, would they marry her to her cousin or to someone else? The mother and brother had assured me that under no circumstances did they intend to marry her to her cousin. When this was said, your rights ceased to apply.' The cousin left Karbala hurriedly feeling slighted and shamed. He then packed up his belongings and left Baghdad, his home, family and work. He moved to Kermanshar in Iran, as if in exile. There he remained, unmarried and unwilling to return to the country and places where he would be reminded of the cousin that he was desperately in love with.

> *This world afflicts whoever puts his trust in it and spares whoever is weary of it.*
>
> — Imam Ali

Despite half the population of Karbala having come from a Persian background, my mother knew nothing of the Farsi language and customs when she married[1]. Within a couple of years, however, she could speak Persian and even took to writing Persian poetry. Her father, like most of the Arabs of his time, disapproved of girls writing, although my mother had of course been taught to read the Qur'an. At Shaykh Ahmad's house, most of the women could read and write and seeing this, my mother asked her husband to teach her. He gave her a line to write out, *'Ta'lam ya fata fa'l-jahlu 'arun wa la yarda bihi illa'l-himaru'*, 'Take on to learning, oh young one, for ignorance is indeed shameful and none will accept such a state except an ass.' Then, he brought her a book of short stories in Arabic, and by copying the whole book out, my mother learnt to read and write.

> *The ink of the scholar is holier than the blood of the martyr.*
>
> — Prophet Muhammad

When she first arrived at Shaykh Ahmad's house, my mother faced numerous difficulties, including resistance from paternal aunts and

---

1   There was a similar demography in Najaf. But, before the Iran–Iraq war, in the early 1980s, Saddam deported at least 250,000 people of Persian origin from Iraq and killed many others.

other 'elitist' relatives. However, after giving birth to my brother, her first son Fazel, she gained appropriate status, settled down in the household, and established her role as the Shaykh's wife. Her mother would often come to visit and within a few years, my aunts' initial coldness thawed into the warmest of friendships. Soon a circle of friends developed around her and she was much sought after amongst the leading families of Karbala.

One of my earliest memories of my mother is her coughing from tuberculosis. On one occasion, she was in the palm tree courtyard, when she started coughing violently over an open drain. When I saw that she was spitting blood, I became very frightened. I remember being so concerned that, following this incident, when she took me to the public bath or '*hammam*', I gave her most of my roasted almonds thinking it would give her strength. A year or so later, she was cured, but her left lung was much weakened.

Almost every Friday, my mother would go to the *hammam* with a few lady friends. Some seasonal fruits and other snacks would accompany them, and they would sit and chat for hours before emerging with hair and nails hennaed and with lips reddened from moistened walnut skins. Every other week there was a '*qabool*', a women's party, alternatively held at the different ladies' houses. From the early afternoon, they would arrive and remain for several hours feasting off a diet of sherbet, cake, tea and gossip. It was always a jolly gathering of between twenty to fifty women, all nicely dressed up with only the married ones wearing lipstick. In an effort to get at some of the cake, I would often find an excuse to make my way into this exclusive club, often with rewarding results. This included a hug or two from a few of the ladies. My favourite was the wife of the guardian of the Shrine of Abbas who was close to my mother.

Then, there was the regular '*qaraya*' or recitations. The ladies gathered in formal black clothing. Mullah Zakiya, the chief female Qur'an teacher of her time, who was a serious spinster and was living in my aunts' house, would read about the life of one of the prominent religious leaders of the past. The Prophet's daughter, Fatima, was a favourite subject. As Muharram drew nearer, the frequency of meetings and number of attendees would increase. Then, the recitations would focus on Imam Hussein and his sister Zainab, who had bravely confronted Yazid, when the survivors of Karbala had been dragged in chains to Damascus. The women also had their own *azza* activities, where men were excluded. I remember on several occasions looking down into the courtyard and seeing the ladies decked in black nightdresses, hair flowing long and loose around them as they wept standing in line swaying from side to side and forward and backward.

The women of Karbala had a full social life, which in no way resembled the picture of oppression which detractors have tried to paint of women in Islamic countries. The headscarf or '*hijab*' was not considered an instrument of subjection. Indeed, it was considered a liberator by most ladies I knew. It was a unifier, stretching across class, designed to provide both modesty and safety. The Karbala *hijab* was not the tent like burkah that is worn in Afghanistan, but a simple *chador* (or aba as called locally) covering from the head to the ankles and made mostly of thin hand woven cotton, dyed black.

> *Say to the believing men that they should lower their gaze and guard their modesty: That will make for greater purity for them. Verily, Allah is All-Aware of what they do. And say to the believing women that they should lower their gaze and guard their modesty; that they should not display their beauty and ornaments except that which must ordinarily appear.*
>
> — Qur'an (24: 30–31)

Mashti considered me as her son and so did not always wear *hijab* around me, but the other ladies of the household, who were not of my immediate family, observed the strictures scrupulously as I grew older. Often, several ladies would be sitting in the courtyard with their heads uncovered as they cut vegetables or cleaned rice. When they heard us young boys coming around the corner, immediately and dexterously they would reach for whatever cover was handy. One day one of the older maids, toothless, almost hairless and not as nimble as the others was taken by surprise as my friend, Sahib Mohsin, and myself came running into the courtyard. Swiftly, she lifted the hem of her long dress to her head unveiling, in the process, most of her wrinkled body. Sahib and I choked with laughter before disappearing shamefacedly.

• • •

Sahib was a handsome Arab boy and the son of a tailor in the local garment bazaar. Throughout my early teens, he would often stay the night in our house and together we would explore Karbala and its surrounds. On the main road that links the city's two principle shrines, those of Imam Hussein and his half-brother Abbas, we would visit our favourite ice-cream parlour; a most popular hangout during the *Ramadan*[2] evenings.

It was customary that if you were already in a teahouse, or public place, and somebody you knew came in after you, you would pay for that person. It was the same if you were at the public baths. The cashier at the baths would even expect and anticipate this custom. You would automatically become the host. This custom would cause some confusion for the poor ticket collector on the Baghdad buses, who could not easily identify who had called out '*wasil*' - meaning already paid for, when somebody new got on the bus. I would imagine this custom has its roots in the desert, as part of the obligatory hospitality of the tent dwellers towards the new arrivals.

---

2 The Islamic month of fasting.

The Garden is the abode of the generous.

— Prophet Muhammad

Arab generosity is famous and it would regularly work its way into Umm al Saadah's stories, particularly in the legendary character of Hatam Tay, the man who was never known to refuse anyone anything – the archetype of boundless Arab generosity.

'There was One, there was no one, other than Allah there is no one.'

'One year there was a severe famine and a needy man had walked for days to Hatam's house to ask him for help, feeling sure that Hatam would not refuse him. On his way up the hill to the house, he met another, who was on his way down. The poor man eagerly asked the other if he had been given what he had asked for. 'Yes, of course', the other replied as he sang out Hatam's praises, 'Hatam is such a generous man he gave me all that I asked for and more.' But when our man reached the top, he found Hatam distraught with grief. 'What is wrong', he enquired. 'I am ruined', Hatam explained. 'With the drought, so many people have come to ask me for help that I have given everything away. Just now I had to turn a man away empty handed, for I had nothing left to give him.'

The confused man consoled Hatam, then quickly made his way back down the hill to catch up with the fellow who had misled him. 'Why did you lie to me?', he demanded from his fellow petitioner, on catching up with him. The other replied seriously, 'Hatam's reputation is such that had I told you I got nothing, you wouldn't have believed me. On top of getting nothing, I would have been considered an ungrateful liar by you.'

And Allah knows best.'

• • •

The short road that linked the shrines of Imam Hussein and Abbas, the same one our ice-cream shop was on, was called 'between the harems', and along this road and its tributaries were the bazaars. Shops of the same type would cluster together. The rosary stalls were a distinctive feature. At the textile bazaar, busy young assistants scurried to and fro, sewing and measuring; at the metal works bazaar, the cacophony of the clang of pots, plates and cauldrons in the making would drown any conversation; the leather bazaar was fully stocked with cow, sheep, goat and the especially popular camel skins, fashioned into any number of items: water skins, belts, pillows and tents. The awful smell of this bazaar was only rivalled by the meat, poultry and fish market near the slaughterhouse. However, amongst the herb, perfume, oil and incense markets, one could bask in delightful smells. Nowadays, of course, aroma chemicals have replaced the old delicate bouquets.

Each bazaar was distinct, engulfing the senses with the unique sounds and smells of the master craftsmen at their time-honoured professions, working in perfect rhythm to the old songs of the guilds. These were not the guildsmen of the West, whom Adam Smith noted, 'seldom met'; these men lived side by side as extended families. This was not the individualistic capitalism of the West, for it was not uncommon for a shopkeeper to tell you to buy from his friend next door, if he had sold enough for the day. This was particularly the case with the fruit and vegetable market. Each shop would recommend the other rather than compete with or criticise their competitors.

It was in this market that Gertrude Bell[3], the British archaeologist, adventurer, spy and diplomat that some historians have dubbed the architect of modern Iraq, recorded her delight when she first visited Karbala, during the early years of the twentieth century. 'The shops were heaped with oranges and pale sweet lemons. I stopped at every corner to buy more and yet more, and ate them as I went along the

---

3 See Gertrude Bell, 'Amaruth to Amaruth.'

streets, hoping to satisfy the inextinguishable thirst born of the desert. Side by side with the oranges lay mountains of pink roses, everyone in town carried a handful of them and sniffed at them as they walked.'

The Prophet said, 'When your path leads you into the Garden of Paradise, eat of the fruit of these gardens. Gather the roses of these gardens and smell their scent. When they asked, 'What is the Garden of Paradise, Oh Messenger of God?' He replied, 'The circle of remembrance (of God) is the Garden of Paradise.'

Gertrude Bell went on to hold regular afternoon tea parties in which she dictated to Faisal I, the first king of modern Iraq, how to run '*her Iraq*'. She went on to establish the Museum of Archaeology and filled it with the wonders of ancient Babylon and Assyria – so that they could be looted some eighty years later in the wake of the American invasion of Iraq in April 2003. In the end, she died of an overdose of barbiturates in her Baghdad bed.

• • •

When the weather was suitable, Sahib and I would fly our kites from the rooftops of our home. Along with the pigeons, which a number of the young men kept, kites were a common sight in the Karbala skies. An enthusiast could get his paper kite from one of a few specialists' kite shops in town; the standard size was about 40 cm square with a thin wooden spine. They came in all colours, some with tails and others without, the length of the tail depending on the extent of stability desired.

Although kite flying took place all year round, it was in the winter months that the skies would be full of them. Hundreds of kites, flying high and low, would swoop up and down from the early morning. Just outside the town, you could see young *seyyids* and *mullahs*[4] casting aside their turbans and cloaks, as they propelled their kites to the heavens.

> **And do not forget your share (of pleasures) of this world.**
>
> — Qur'an (28: 77)

By nightfall, the amateurs, such as me, would retire to make way for the lantern-flying professionals. The lanterns comprised of a candle enclosed by a cylindrical frame made of thin paper and light hardboard. A champion could fly ten lanterns dangling from his kite, spaced a few metres apart. The lanterns however, did have the tendency to occasionally fall on a tree or a roof. As people often slept on the roofs, bedding would typically be lying around. It was most unfortunate if a lantern fell on the bedding, doubly so if someone was sleeping in it. Although these pyrotechnics were rare, they happened every now and then, spectacularly.

Where there are kites, there are also kite fights and so the dedicated enthusiasts extended their interest to 'combat strings'. Jawad Kaar, 'One-eyed Jawad', the town's top kite shop owner, whose workshop was next to the Shrine of Abbas, made the most prestigious 'combat strings.' The secret of Jawad's prestige was the gluey paste of powdered glass with which he treated his strings. If a Jawad string were to touch another, it would instantly cut it. Jawad would even produce a double-coated string for special fights, if requested. The increased weight might reduce manoeuvrability, but ensured triumph and victory on the first encounter. A spindle of string would be wrapped around a protected arm, so that you could easily take in or release string. Even though only the fighting part of the string would be treated with Jawad's paste, it was common to cut one's fingers on the normal string. This was, however, the least of the kite-flying perils.

---

4 A religious teacher.

As kites were often flown from rooftops, especially by the younger participants, to manoeuvre a kite optimally, it was sometimes necessary for a kite flyer to cross the small gaps that separated the roofs of the various houses. Most people tolerated the youngsters jumping from one house to another. Those who were not kite enthusiasts were noted and their roofs avoided. However, in the intensity of a challenging fight, concentration on the sky could make one less aware of the ground below. Back-peddling from the threat of a 'Jawad string', one might find oneself in someone else's courtyard with a broken arm or leg. Such unfortunates would make their way to Nana Raheem, one of our maids and the acknowledged bonesetter of Karbala. Just after distracting the person by inquiring about the finer aspects of kite manoeuvring and just before they yelled, Nana Raheem would give the patient's limb an almighty tug. Several generations could testify to her bone-setting competence, which was always performed free of charge, but for which she was often gifted a present.

> *If you do good, you do it for your own souls.*
> — Qur'an (17: 7)

From Estes Park in Colorado, USA to Bucklebury Common, Berkshire, England, I have tried to recreate my childhood kite flying experiences without it ever being quite the same. The no longer accessible roofs of Karbala have remained the favourite spot in my mind. The indelible imprints of childhood memory cannot be replaced. It is said that your early memories are like etchings on marble – not easy to erase.

Along with kite strings, 'One-eyed Jawad' sold another highly desirable commodity – '*pootaz*', small homemade grenades. About four centimetres in diameter and tightly wrapped with string, they would have in them tiny steel pellets and some form of explosive. To produce the perfect effect, Jawad would experiment with different chemicals and it was presumed that he had lost his left eye from one such explosion.

There were two options when detonating a *'pootaz'*. Either, you threw it hard on the ground or high underarm so that it landed near the target. One popular method of disposal was, while riding on a horse drawn carriage, to casually throw a pootaz over your head so it landed at the feet of a teacher or an obnoxious *mullah*. You could then look back and admire your handiwork as the shaken victim struggled to normality, looking around for the culprit. By then, the carriage was at a safe distance away and unsuspected.

I generally managed to avoid reprimand for misdoings, but on one occasion, I remember being scolded by someone outside my family. I was walking to school with my brand new leather satchel along the alleyway. The novelty of the long strapped satchel was too much to resist and I took great pleasure in liberally swinging it around until accidentally it chanced upon a pedestrian, whom I must have hit in a sensitive place. 'Who are you', he demanded. I told him I was Shaykh Ahmad's son. 'In that case, I'll have to take you home to tell your honorable family of its son's misbehavior in public.' He took me home where my father's manservant, Baba Mahmood, met us at the door. The man related my misconduct and then left courteously. Baba Mahmood looked at me disapprovingly and then allowed me to run back to school so that I missed no class.

In this way, Karbala's social and moral norms were constantly reinforced by its inhabitants. The city was in many ways self-governing and self-monitoring. It had a feeling of coziness and security. People would care for each other in a considerate and neighborly way, informally, but effectively.

> ***The people of this earth will be treated with mercy as long as they love each other and carry out their work (service) sincerely.***
>
> — Prophet Muhammad

Baba Mahmood was a Turkoman from Azerbaijan, a small, wiry man with blue eyes, neatly trimmed beard, full of energy, determination and blind loyalty. He was very devoted to our father and treated us as if we were his own. I do not think he had ever married, although he was already in his 50s when I was a child. He chain-smoked local cigarettes, ineffectively rolled, any movement of his hand ashes would drop, and burn holes in one's clothes. The only time I did not see him smoke was when he was asleep or roasting coffee.

Every other day, the wafting aroma of fresh coffee would drift through the houses with Baba Mahmood presiding over the operation in the Burrani. It was typical Arabic coffee, brewed over a long period of time with the old constantly being blended in with the new. No sooner would the smell reach me and I would run to grab a handful of hot black beans, filling my pockets, to keep me going through the day.

Sahib, myself and a few of our friends would regularly go on bicycle rides along the rivulets and water channels that fed the date palms and orchards surrounding the town. At the edge of the desert, there might be gypsies and we would take care to peddle hard when within biting distance of their mangy dogs. Along the bridges, there was an occasional water buffalo. On the scrub lands and salt flats, a few kilometres out of town, was the Shrine of Hurr. Before my elder brother had gifted me a shiny 'Hercules' bicycle, Hurr had been a favourite destination for my walks with Baba Mahmood.

Hurr was the commander of the initial force of Yazid's army that had met up with Imam Hussein before he reached Karbala. When they reached the Imam, they were in desperate need of water. The Imam ordered his caravan to provide them with what water he had. Soon after, Ibn Sa'd arrived with the bulk of the army and on the night of the 9th, Hurr came to the Imam's camp with two of his deputies and begged forgiveness for his part in the impending tragedy. The three asked permission to fight alongside the Imam.

Although facing certain death, these repentant warriors stood beside the family of the Prophet and were amongst the first to die.

If anyone does evil or wrongs his own soul, but afterwards seeks Allah's forgiveness, he will find Allah Oft-Forgiving and Most Merciful.

— Qur'an (4: 110)

Hurr's shrine was an hour away by donkey. One day, Baba Mahmood hired a particularly obstinate beast. We barely managed to get out of town when the donkey decided he had had enough and tried several times to throw me off its back before pushing Baba into the river. Occasionally, it darted away with me on it, quite dangerously, as we were close to the desert. This was my last experience of a donkey ride. It was also the last time Baba took me to Hurr, but we did make excursions elsewhere.

The local *zurkhana* (house of strength), located next to *Bab al-Khaymah* (the district of tents), was one of the popular destinations. In a circular pit, half a dozen large men, young and old, would juggle heavy wooden clubs, throwing them higher and higher in the air at the beat of drums. On the way there, Baba would buy some raisins, almonds and dates and I would munch away as I watched the thick clubs rise and fall, while the stout men chanted their admiration for the great Imams of Islam. The drum would be next to an open fire to ensure the skin remained tight and dry. The atmosphere evoked an ancient past.

The *zurkhana* performance was always spectacular. I especially liked the kettledrums and the fragrance of incense in the air. In Iran, the *zurkhana* tradition is still kept alive in many cities and towns. Originally, it had been an exercise to promote chivalry in Persian culture, the equivalent of Zen martial arts. More recently, it has become a tourist attraction in a similar way to the whirling dervishes of Turkey.

• • •

Karbala is not only a city of pilgrimage, but also an extensive market town. While Basra is Iraq's port to the sea, Karbala was one of its ports to the desert; linking the migrant and the settled, the nomad and the townsman, the '*bedouin*' and the '*hathar*'. Every week or so, an extensive bedouin caravan would arrive with hundreds of camels to buy, sell and barter. They would come for grain, sugar, tea, dates, pots and pans, gold, silver and perfumes. They would leave behind them salt, yoghurt, leather, wool, livestock, saddle bags and carpets.

Just outside *Bab al-Khaymah*, on the same spot where Imam Hussein's tents had been pitched, the bedouin would camp. Spilling out onto the desert, the open caravanserai would move to the sway of the camel. I loved watching these noisy creatures rising and falling, growling and snapping. After a *zurkhana* session, I would do my best to convince Baba to take me there, but he was always hesitant.

The most conscientious of guardians, he would anxiously watch, afraid that I might get lost in the bustle as I investigated and drank in the spectacle. There were Bedouin children with long plaited hair and women in colourful clothes, adorned with large nose rings, earrings and ankle bracelets that jingled exquisitely as they emerged and disappeared behind waves of sand. Many of the women, like my mother's relatives, had green henna tattoos. Many of the men had pistols and other weapons. Tribal feuds and fights were common.

One of our neighbours was from the Al Kamouna clan, a well known leading tribal family with vast tracts of land and considerable influence amongst Arab leaders and landowners. Once, this family had a feud with another clan, which exploded in violence and killings. Eventually, the two clans came to my father for arbitration.

On that day, as I returned home from school, I was shocked to be faced with a dozen armed Arabs, lined up along the entrance and inside the *Burrani*, our guesthouse. Along the corridor, grim looking men with pistols and rifles stood facing each other. Some were bearded, some not, but all had stern Arab faces and thick moustaches. There was shouting and threatening, something entirely alien in our household. After much animated discussion, my father brought about an acceptable resolution. With a shower of hugs, kisses and blessings for my father's wisdom, the feuding Arabs left. Muhammad Ali Kamouna, the chief of the clan, was always one of my father's favourite companions. I had great respect and admiration for this most noble man.

> **It is preferable to me that I reconcile two people than I give away (much money) in charity.**
>
> — Imam Ali

The tribal Arabs particularly revered the Shrine of Abbas. Abbas' loyalty and bravery epitomized Arab chivalry. Normally, an Arab could swear blindly and unscrupulously on anything, but it was never known for someone to swear an oath on Al Abbas unless it was true. Such was the respect and fear of reprisal with which Abbas, nicknamed 'the hot head', was held. Even the government's legal department used the Shrine's oath when serious testimony was necessary.

The Karbala of my youth was the last in the train of human caravans that had stretched back into the invisible past. In my early teens, things were starting to change rapidly as the westerly winds gathered momentum. These were the last few years of the old days of local self-government and consensus – the days of the Burrani.

4

The Burrani

Sitting with people of the path means honour in this world and the next.

— Prophet Muhammad

The Burrani was the second of the three houses in our compound and used exclusively for male guests just as the third house, *Bayt al Amma*, my aunts' house, was used for female guests. It was a three-floored house looking onto a large rectangular courtyard, which was dominated by an old Cedar tree, prolific in its tasty aromatic berries. On the roof, several goats, domesticated birds and the occasional desert gazelle resided. The house itself was in the charge of Baba Mahmood.

Visitors from all over the world had stayed there, princes of the old Qajar[1] royal family, dervishes and special dignitaries from distant lands. They were guests, but would always follow the traditional courtesy of reciprocation in gifts. Most of the guests would stay for few days, but close friends of the family stayed longer, especially during the month of *Ramadan*, which precedes the *Hajj* (Karbala is a major *Hajj* terminus) and of course during the

---

1 The dynasty, which ruled Iran from 1794–1924 CE, until its members were ousted by Reza Shah.

month of *Muharram*.

Every morning, from around 9:00 to midday, my father would go to the *Burrani* for his '*majlis*' or 'public hours'. Visitors and friends would all be treated to some of Baba Mahmood's coffee. I would occasionally slip into this august congregation and settle down in a corner, quietly chewing on my coffee beans; Baba Mahmood's piercing blue Turkoman eyes were always on me to ensure that proper etiquette was observed.

The company at the *majlis* would be drawn from all levels of society. There were wise old men, steeped in the ancient scholarly traditions, visiting dignitaries, tribal leaders as well as young politicians and professionals. Several of my father's close friends – members of families resident in Karbala for many generations with orchards, properties or trade to support their comfortable lifestyle – would be there. On occasion, a lady would come in to ask a question or make a request. Clerics abounded, transacting and discussing both current issues and ancient texts. One cleric might be an academic and esoteric, another legalistic and functional, a third might be more politically inclined.

I recall well how people would be slotted into different categories according to their profession or trade. A government official would be regarded as a truly unfortunate person. People who had to do a job that was undesirable or businessmen and traders were looked upon with some puzzlement. Poor people, the truly destitute, were the most respected. 'True worth belongs to Allah!' they would call out in the alleyways. In other words, 'who do you think you are? Nothing is yours to own.'

Amongst the visitors to my father's gatherings would be people who were pointed out to us as *arifs* or gnostics. 'You children better watch out!' my father would say. 'This man knows the states of the innermost, the heart.' And truly, there was something to distinguish these men from the others. They would always be courteous and correct, but there was an X factor or another window in their life that was open to the unseen. The people who came to sit with these men were also of a different quality from the other visitors; perhaps an unusual dervish with his plain, rough clothes and his *kashkool*, a simple wooden or metal bowl attached to a chain round his neck.

There was no talk of mysticism or mystery. It was normal to expect to reach a point in your life when you knew the higher purpose of your existence. 'May Allah not remove us from your shadow,' was how they were addressed, implying that these men were of the light and being in their shadow meant partaking of some of their luminosity. But, of course, where there is light, there is also darkness.

During one of my *Burrani* visits, when I was about eight years old, I overheard a discussion between a vocal and rather shallow *mullah* and two other men. One of them wanted to borrow some money, but the other was reluctant to lend without a good interest rate in return. Usury is forbidden in Islam, but such a matter was not about to deter the deal-making *mullah*. In addition to the principal loan, it was decided that the lender could sell the borrower a cigarette for an amount that reflected the desired interest rate. Thus, the mullah concluded, the transaction would be permissible, 'halaal'. I turned to the *mullah* and said, 'In the same way, on the Day of Reckoning, Allah will put you in a barrel and as He throws it on the fire he'll say, 'I didn't throw you into the fire, I only threw the barrel.'" The *mullah* turned bright red and with twitching eyebrows would doubtless have reached for his cane had I not been the Shaykh's son. This was one of the very few instances when I said anything at the *Burrani* to my father's visitors.

They think they deceive Allah and those who believe,
but they only deceive themselves and perceive (it) not.
— Qur'an (2: 9)

Occasionally, the *Burrani* would have a distinguished visitor. When I was a teenager, the second Pahlavi Shah of Iran, Muhammad Reza was one such visitor. In Iran, he was facing a populist national movement. The Prime Minister Muhammad Mossadegh had gained such popularity that when, in August 1953, the Shah attempted to dismiss him, Mossadegh's supporters took to the streets and the Shah was forced to flee the country. He went first to Baghdad and then headed for Karbala and the Shrine of Imam Hussein, to ask the spiritual leaders of the city to pray for his return.

There was a special reception organized for him, but as was my father's custom, he declined to attend the public occasion. The Shah and his wife, the beautiful Empress Soraya, then came to our house with their small entourage. He asked my father to pray for his return and my father assured him that it would happen soon. But, my father also predicted that unless he checked his arrogance and love for popularity, he would eventually lose his kingdom.

> *The most dreadful of man's shortcomings is that he is unaware of his own faults.*
>
> — Imam Ali

Thanks to a British instigated, US led coup, the Shah did return and Iran suffered for twenty-six more years of an insensitive and repressive dictatorship. A high-ranking CIA agent, Kermit Roosevelt, grandson of President Theodore Roosevelt, was responsible for orchestrating the Shah's return. Suitcases stuffed full of dollars were liberally distributed to mullahs and local thugs who demonstrated against the legitimately elected government of Prime Minister Mossadegh. The print media spewed anti-government propaganda and pressure was put on foreign countries to boycott Iranian oil. Mossadegh's only crime was that, by popular demand, he nationalised the Anglo-Iranian Oil Company and took control of the world's largest refinery in Abadan. Eventually, Mossadegh was arrested and he spent the rest of his life under house arrest.

In this operation lie the roots of much of the discord, turmoil and conflict from which the modern Middle East suffers today. The rise of Mossadegh was an authentic expression of nascent democracy. It had within it the seeds of the homegrown, representative and constitutional rule that the Middle East is always accused of lacking. The truth is, however, that whenever legitimate and popular attempts were made to install democratic regimes in these countries, they have been repressed, if they were not totally in line with western stakes — evidence of the double standards of the west. It is much harder for a foreign power to impose its wishes on an accountable and representative parliament than on a despot who draws most of his power from the west.

As the extent of the CIA's involvement became apparent, the initially pro-US Iranians began to realise that perhaps the ideals of liberty and equality may not extend to them. Indeed, it was no accident that when the Iranian Islamic revolution erupted in 1979, the jubilant crowds carried pictures of Mossadegh alongside those of Khomeini.

After the coup and until the revolution, Kermit Roosevelt continued to visit Iran regularly, acting as a consultant for American multinationals that wanted to do business there. His special friendship with the Shah was undoubtedly invaluable. As Kermit was fond of saying, the Shah had told him that he owed his throne to four things: 'God, my people, my army and you.' One still wonders whether the order should be reversed.

In a different world and altogether for different reasons, Reza Shah, the 1st Pahlavi king of Iran, had said he owed his throne to a man. This man's name was Shaykh Abdullah Haeri Mazanderani. He was my father's uncle and the youngest of Shaykh Zainul Abideen and Khursheed's four sons.

• • •

When the great master of the dervishes, Mullah Sultan of Gonaabad, visited Shaykh Zainul Abideen on his way back from

Mecca, young Shaykh Abdullah had avoided meeting him out of disrespect. Historically, the Sufi movement was rooted in the Sunni tradition of Islam, although many of the Sufis claim spiritual descent from Imam Ali. What is more, the Sufis developed a reputation for being lenient on matters of Islamic law. As such, they were often derided by scholarly orthodox Muslims, especially amongst the Shi'a. This was then Shaykh Abdullah's general stance.

One day, when Shaykh Abdullah was returning from the public baths, he came face to face with the Sufi Master, but walked on pretending not to see him. 'I am sure you'll finally come to me', the Shaykh called out after him. These words rang in Shaykh Abdullah's ears, until eventually, he did go to visit the great dervish. What he saw impressed him so much that he eventually abandoned his parental home and formal religious status and left for the secluded village of Gonaabad in North Eastern Iran.

> **Harmonize with destiny, or it will break you.**
> — Shaykh Abdul Qadir al Gilani

Because of joining this Sufi movement, Shaykh Abdullah was largely shunned by his family and particularly by his elder brother, my grandfather, Shaykh Muhammad Hussein. My father, however, had a great love for his Sufi uncle and when Shaykh Abdullah came to visit Karbala, he stayed with him. In time, through my father's mediation, Shaykh Muhammad Hussein met his brother and came to recognize his spiritual qualities. The two were fully reconciled with the discovery that their apparently different roads took them to the same destination.

It so happened that at some time along his journey, Shaykh Abdullah's path took him to the small and remote town of Arak, in Western Iran. It was there, at a Sufi gathering that his eyes fell on an unhappy young soldier who, though not a religious man, had come to seek comfort in the food and warmth of the Sufi's, '*khanaqah's*' offerings.

Many years later, that subaltern sat in a Tehran palace as the new, all-powerful Shah of Iran, known as Reza Shah. Now, it had been Reza Shah's habit to hold daily court in the early afternoons with several of his close confidants. One day, as his confidants waited, he walked straight in and without explanation asked, 'What is the meaning of the word '*esteghna*'?' '*Esteghna* ... *esteghna*', he repeated thoughtfully, 'What does it mean?' *Esteghna*, he was told, is an Arabic word roughly translated as self-containment, sufficiency. If someone is '*mustaghni*', they are enriched or content. 'Ah, now I understand', he whispered audibly, and went on to tell the extraordinary story of an extraordinary Shaykh. This story was retold by the recorder of those meetings in a popular Persian book on the two Pahlavi Shahs, entitled 'Father and Son[2]':

When Reza Shah (then known as Reza Khan) was still a subaltern stationed in Arak, he was at the lowest ebb in his life. He was struggling with a miserly salary and no prospects or hope for any future. 'It was', he said, 'the worst time of my life. I never thought I would leave that town alive.' Then he chanced upon the aforementioned Sufi gathering and saw Shaykh Abdullah, who beckoned the tall soldier to come forward and sit next to him on the carpet. Shaykh Abdullah then asked him a few questions about his life. There was a pause and suddenly he looked straight into Reza Shah's eyes and told him, 'You will be a powerful future king of this country!'

Reza Khan was shocked and thought the man was joking. He had no such thought, as his only concern was how to feed himself and his young family. He didn't know what to say, so he kept quiet. The Shaykh spoke again, 'Do you understand what I am telling you? You will be the king of this country.' This time Reza Khan

---

2 The story, which follows, is largely taken from this book, Father and Son by Mahmoud Taloui, p. 349–359. My father and several family members also knew it.

replied irritably, 'I don't believe you and I am surprised a person such as yourself would make fun of me in this way.' The Shaykh looked back at him seriously, 'I am not joking with you, whatever I tell you is the truth, you will be the king of this county and you will remember this meeting.'

This time Reza Khan decided to play along. 'Alright, if I become what you say, what do you want from me. Let us get that problem out of the way now!' 'I want only one thing from you', said the Shaykh, 'For you to have kindness and love for Allah's creation, especially the poor and the needy.' After he had said this, Reza Khan got up and left. Reza Shah told his confidants that 'This meeting was the light for the future.' 'Every bad thing went out of my mind and hope came to me.'

> *And in the earth there are signs for people of certainty.*
> *And in yourselves. Do you not see?*
> *And in the heaven is your provision – and what you*
> *are promised.*
>
> — Qur'an (52: 21–22)

Ten years later, Reza Shah accidentally came across Shaykh Abdullah in the streets of the town of Ray just south of Tehran. By then, Reza Shah's situation had improved dramatically. He was a senior military commander with great prospects and hopes for the future. 'Do you remember what I told you in Arak?' Shaykh Abdullah asked him. 'That time is coming near.' Reza Shah laughed, 'So, when I become king, what do you want from me?' Again, the Shaykh replied, 'I only want you to show kindness to Allah's creation.'

Five years later, Reza Shah ascended the Peacock Throne. He called one of his aides and asked him to locate and arrange a meeting with the Sufi Shaykh. It was discovered that Shaykh Abdullah was staying in Tehran and the Shah arranged to meet him on a Friday at the popular shrine of Shah Abdul Azeem, south of Tehran.

Reza Shah went alone and in disguise to the Shrine, where Shaykh Abdullah was sitting waiting for him in the corner. The Shaykh got up to greet and hug the new king without congratulations and fanfare. For an hour, they talked, 'and that hour', confessed the Shah, 'was the happiest in my life.'

'I am at your service', he told the Shaykh. 'I have come to meet you so that I may grant you whatever you want.' But, the answer was the same as it had been before, 'I don't want anything for myself; I just want you to be kind to Allah's creation.' 'Alright', said the Shah, 'but aside from this, humans have problems they need to solve. Maybe you don't want anything for yourself, but you have family and friends. Whether near or far, if you want anything for them, please tell me. I never thought I would be a king and your prediction had given me drive, energy and hope. It transformed me from a hopeless soldier. You woke me from my sleep and pushed me to the brightest future. How can I not thank you?' 'Imam Ali is my master', the Shaykh replied, 'and so I don't need anything. I am lucky that he is also the master of my relatives and so they will not expect anything. If I do anything contrary to this faith, trust and reliance, I am then not worthy of Allah's way.'

The Shah then became insistent, 'Are you such a rich man that you don't want anything. If you are rich, nevertheless, you have other needs. If you or your relatives want any position, I am ready, even if it is difficult.' 'I am not rich,' replied the Shaykh, 'but I have *'esteghna.'* The Shah begged him to the point of shouting at the Shaykh, who only answered slowly over and over, 'I have *esteghna'*, I am *mustaghni.'* The Shah could not understand what was more important than money and power that could make this humble man more satisfied than a king.

Surely, this world is the furthest that the blind can see.

— Imam Ali

Then the Shah asked Shaykh Abdullah if they could at least meet again so that the kingdom could benefit from his knowledge and advice. But as he asked this, he saw the Shaykh becoming agitated and uncomfortable. 'If you excuse me from meeting you again, that is the best you can do for me,' responded the Shaykh.

The Shah had already met many clerics and religious leaders, but they would always tell him what they thought he wanted to hear. Most were hypocrites and desired worldly rewards or they were simply sycophantic 'yes' men. This Shaykh was different. What was more, 'He and I are originally from the same town,' the Shah told his confidants, as the Shah was also from Mazanderan. 'This man,' the Shah insisted, 'was a real dervish.'

One of the confidants who heard the Shah's outpouring also knew Shaykh Abdullah well. Immediately, he went to tell him about what the Shah had said and asked him why he had not met the Shah again. 'I thought about what is good for him and Allah's creation' replied the Shaykh, 'and decided not to waste his time.'

'There was One, there was no one, other than God there is no one.' [3]

'There was a kindly man who saw a snake fighting with a bear and went to the bear's assistance to save it from the snake. The bear was so moved by the kindness of the man's act that it followed him about wherever he went and became his faithful slave, guarding him from everything that might annoy him and providing him with anything that he might want.

Then one day, the man was lying asleep and the bear, according to its custom, was sitting by his bedside driving off the flies. But the flies became so persistent in their annoyance that the bear lost patience. It seized the largest rock it could find and threw it at the

---

3   As was often the case with Mashti's stories, this one is based on the work of the great Persian sage, Jalaluddin Rumi.

flies to crush them utterly. The flies escaped and the stone landed
upon the sleeper's face and crushed it. The moral is, 'be careful who
you make your friends.'

And Allah knows Best.'

Sit not thou in the company of those who do wrong.
— Qur'an (6: 68)

The story of Shaykh Abdullah and the Shah does not end here.
There is a fitting epilogue. In later years, two of Shaykh Abdullah's
nephews (one of whom was also married to his daughter) became
prominent in Reza Shah's government. Together with a few others
who were discontented with Reza Shah's despotism, they were
caught planning a coup against him. However, as the Shah knew of
their relationship to Shaykh Abdullah, he exiled them from Iran
while all the other conspirators were executed. When Muhammad
Reza Shah (the son) came to the throne, he invited them back to Iran
and in subsequent years many members of the family, including
the sons of the two exiled men, became prominent in the Iranian
government as ministers. Until Shaykh Abdullah's death, Reza
Shah, without disturbing him, always made sure he knew where
Shaykh Abdullah was and what he was doing.

The uneducated, barely literate Reza Shah ruled Iran for sixteen
years with an iron fist. He could not and did not heed Shaykh
Abdullah's request. Witnessing how far behind his country was
compared to the West, he dreamt of a day when it might once more
be great and so, in line with Turkey and a string of other aspirant
countries, embarked on 'westernization', believing somehow that
this was inextricably linked to 'modernization'. Also like many
others, he made the mistake of throwing the baby out with the bath
water. He rejected everything from the past, including Islamic
culture. This was exemplified by his instituting on the wearing of
what was called a 'Pahlavi', in imitation of his hero, Kamal Ataturk,
who had banned the *fez* in Turkey. The 'Pahlavi' cap was like a

baseball cap with a long peak, making it impossible to prostrate in prayer while wearing one. Neither he nor Ataturk went so far as to ban prayer, but by making the Western hat or cap compulsory in public for at least government employees, they set up an impediment to prayer. A new saying entered the Persian vernacular, '*kularo sar gozasht*', 'to put a hat on one's head', meaning to cleverly cheat someone. In Turkish, there was a similar expression, '*sapka giymek*', 'to put on a hat', meaning to be a turncoat or a renegade.

One of the old servants in my family household had refused to wear this new hat, leaving Iran in disgust for Karbala. He was a pious landowner in Iran, but exiled himself to Karbala rather than be 'cheated with the cap'. In Karbala, though, things were also changing. Iraq had now become a country with an uncertain and confused future. The westerly winds had been gathering strength and there were dark and ominous storm clouds on the horizon.

5

Westerly Winds

Those people have passed away. Theirs is that which
they earned, and yours is that which you earn. And you
will not be asked of what they used to do.

— Qur'an (2: 134)

The ancient Greeks had called it Mesopotamia, the land between
two rivers, the Tigris and the Euphrates. It was the cradle of
civilisation, the lands of Sumeria, Babylon and Assyria. At Ur,
Abraham was born, and from beneath his 'hanging gardens'
Nebuchadnezzar directed the building of the Tower at Babel.
It was the battleground for the Romans, the Parthians, the
Byzantines and the Sasanians. It was the capital of Islam and
Baghdad (meaning the gift of God) was at one time the wealthiest
city in the world. It was the glory of Harun ar-Rashid, the home of
'A Thousand and One Arabian Nights.' Yet, it was not until 1921
that, to the tune of 'God save the King', Faisal 1 was crowned its
first king, and the British Empire gave birth to the modern nation
state of Iraq (an ancient name that means origin or root, and which
was used to define the area).

The land that was to become Iraq was ruled by the Ottoman
Caliph from Istanbul for three and a half centuries as three provinces
of the Ottoman Empire: Mosul in the north, Baghdad in the centre
and Basra in the south. When the Ottoman corps was finally

vanquished in the First World War, the British, with the help of their loyal Indian troops, seized control of 'the land between the rivers.'

At the beginning of the war the British, to facilitate the demise of the Ottomans, had instigated an Arab rebellion against their Turkish overlords. This rebellion came to be known as the Arab Revolt and, thanks largely to T.E. Lawrence (better known as Lawrence of Arabia), his self-serving search for adventure and a journalist's fertile imagination, it was subsequently immortalised in the Western media.

The revolt had initially been instigated from Mecca by Sharif[1] Hussein. He was originally the Ottoman governor of the Hijaz[2], but with characteristic treachery had turned to the highest bidder, in this case the British. Sharif Hussein thought his promised reward for participation in the Revolt would be the crown of an independent state incorporating all Arab lands. The British and French thought otherwise. In 1916, an Englishman and a Frenchman had drawn lines in the desert, dividing the Middle East into English and French areas of influence and control. This was known as the Sykes–Picot agreement and was the blueprint for the modern Middle-Eastern states. The Sharif was thrown the Hijaz as a pacifier.

The most competent of the Sharif's sons, Faisal, had been proclaimed King of Syria, but this was in the French domain, so he was soon ejected. At the same time, the British were looking for a suitable king to rule the cobbled together Protectorate of Iraq. Various names were suggested including, absurdly, the Aga Khan, but helped along by Gertrude Bell and Lawrence, Faisal got the nomination. He was hardly known in Iraq and had had little to do

---

1 'Sharif' literally means noble, but like 'Seyyid', implies descent from the Prophet. Seyyid is a more commonly used in the East, Persia and the Sub-Continent, whereas Sharif is commonly used in North Africa, Turkey and parts of Arabia.

2 The Ottoman province runs along the west coast of the Arabian Peninsula and incorporates Jeddah, Mecca and Medina.

with the country until then. One popular story of the time highlights
this. It involves Faisal and the Ottoman educated Nuri Sa'id who
dominated Iraqi politics for the duration of the monarchy.

Faisal and Nuri Sa'id were on Nuri Sai'd's boat crossing the
Tigris river. As was prone to happen, the boatman was serving them
some wine. Faisal was dictating to Nuri Sa'id various matters of
state and what he wanted done. Nuri Sai'd had been punctuating
the conversation by regularly telling the boatman to fill up
Faisal's glass, and Faisal was subsequently getting more and more
animated and dogmatic. Eventually, after several such requests, the
boatman refused. Nuri Sa'id was astonished and demanded that
Faisal be given more wine. 'I cannot Pasha', said the boatman.
'Look he is already bossing you around, if I give him any more, he
is going to start thinking he is the King.'

> *They ask you concerning alcohol and gambling. Say, 'in*
> *them is a great sin and some benefit for men, but the*
> *sin is greater than the benefit.'*
>
> — Qur'an (2: 219)

The borders of the new Iraq were political and created for
expedience. In many ways, they are peculiar, not least in
that they fixed a border on a tribal and nomadic desert
people unaccustomed to European cultures of state governance
and law. The boundaries of the Arabian Peninsula had always
been porous and moved like the rivers and dunes that defined
them. As late as 1933, Faisal acknowledged that there are 'no
Iraqi people', but rather: 'unimaginable masses of human
beings, devoid of any patriotic idea, imbued with religious
traditions and absurdities, connected to no common tie, giving
ear to evil, prone to anarchy, and perpetually ready to rise against
any government whatever.'[3] Such is the inevitable conclusion of

---

3 See Thabit Abdullah, A Short History of Iraq p. 134.

instilling arbitrary national borders on a people, which until then had defined themselves by their religion not their nation.

Not only did the British redraw borders, they also created new ones, carving out countries that did not exist. The country of Jordan was carved out from a stretch of desert, prudently created as a buffer state in the time honoured tradition of divide and rule. It is said that Winston Churchill, who was Head of the Colonial Office at the time of Jordan's birth, bragged that he invented Jordan while 'drunk in the back of a London taxi.' Faisal's younger brother, Abdullah was without a throne. He had originally laid claim to Iraq and so he was given the Jordanian throne to appease his filial jealousy at having been usurped by his elder brother. It is a historical misfortune that a man such as Churchill, who is reported as proclaiming 'Arabs were savages and they ate nothing but camel dung', should have been in a position to so dramatically impact on the life of the Arabs.

Like Jordon, Kuwait, on Iraq's southern border, was another invented country. It was a Sheikdom with no more claims to be declared a country than the many other settlements that littered the Arabian Peninsula. It was, however, fortunate enough to be strategically situated on the Persian Gulf and have oil potential. The first steps towards statehood were taken in 1899 when to thwart German proposals to extend the Berlin–Baghdad railway to Kuwait and the Persian Gulf, Britain concluded an agreement with the local Shaykh, whereby it took over the Sheikdom's foreign policy. In time, Kuwait asserted its nominal independence, but events like the 1991 Gulf war have exposed the extent of its foreign dependence.

• • •

The south of Iraq was largely Shi'a Arab and the north a mixture of Sunni Arab and Kurd, with a few enclaves of Turkomans, Assyrian Christians and other ethnic and religious groups. Kurds formed a substantial minority (about 20%) and Shi'as constituted over 60% of the population. However, as had been the case with the Ottomans, the British maintained and strengthened the hand of the old Sunni Arab families in government.

The government of Iraq, like those of its Middle Eastern counterparts, was considered a product of British colonial policy. To the masses, it was viewed as illegitimate, and so many would have nothing to do with it. This was particularly the case with the Shi'a, who had long since earned the epithet, '*rafida*', those who refuse, on account of their opposition to virtually every government; the reasons for this are found in the Shi'a concept of leadership.

> *If a man excuses an oppressor for his oppression, then*
> *Allah will put a ruler over him to oppress him.*
> — Imam Ja'far as-Sadiq

In the early 1920s, as the British were trying to consolidate their control over Iraq, the Shi'a's were characteristically insurgent. Typically, Karbala was the epicentre of this insurgence. My grandfather, Shaykh Muhammad Hussein had inherited the support of the Shi'a Indian Muslims from his father. This included large donations and dues (particularly from the old ruling families of Oudh and Mahmoodabad), which the Shaykh would receive via the British offices in Baghdad. One day, as he was returning home from his evening prayers, an assailant came from the dark of the alleyway and stabbed him in the abdomen. The Shaykh firmly held the man's hand and took him into his house. He asked the would-be assassin the reason for the attack upon which the nervous man confessed that he thought the Shaykh was a British agent. The Shaykh then explained the reasons for his receiving money from the British and the assailant realising his mistake begged forgiveness. The Shaykh never fully recovered from his wounds and died a few years later at the relatively young age of sixty-three. Until then, the reformed assailant stayed with the Shaykh serving him with great loyalty.

And if you pardon and forbear and forgive, then surely
Allah is Forgiving, Merciful.

—Qur'an (64: 14)

The Shi'a were equally obdurate towards the Ottomans as they were towards the British and throughout Ottoman rule, they rose several times and were duly suppressed with brutality. Karbala was always a popular target. Regularly, the *Wali*[4] of Baghdad would attack Karbala. In 1842, there was a particularly effective massacre with some 20,000 men (many of them Seyyids) being killed within a couple of days and then unceremoniously buried behind walls, hastily built where resting houses and seminaries had once stood. There was once a small earthquake in Karbala and some of the walls of our house collapsed. Exposed beneath were the skeletons of dozens of men, lined up and standing upright; a favourite Ottoman burial practice. Pillaging and abuse of power became institutionalised amongst the Ottoman *Walis*. The system of Wali appointment, whereby the post is given to a favoured bidder, did not help. Thievery was necessary and expected in order to get a return on the initial investment.

One 19th Century Ottoman *Wali*, Midhat Pasha, was held in high esteem for being different. His modernizing reforms included registering property rights, establishing Iraq's first newspaper (in 1869), building a hospital and establishing a military college in Baghdad. He asked many well-known families to send their children to the academy, but the response was sceptical. He warned them that he would then have no choice, but to recruit children from Baghdad's streets and in time, these would be the ones to rule Iraq.

---

4 The title given to the Ottoman governors, but is also used to denote one who has attained the spiritual status of a friend of Allah.

It was an ominous prediction and one that was to be fulfilled not just in Iraq, but also in almost every Arab country.

> *Do not oppose the changes that are coming nor fill your hearts with hatred for them, for then you must retreat as they advance.*
>
> — Imam Ali

The Ottomans were of course not the first or the last to sweep down on Karbala. In the 9th Century, the Abbasid Caliph Mutawakkil set the precedent deciding to forbid pilgrimage to the city and to flood the Shrine of Imam Hussein. However, as the waters approached the shrine, they suddenly began to recede and it was said they became confused – '*ha'ir*'. So, the precinct around the Shrine, which unbelievers are not permitted to enter, is known as the '*Ha'ir*'. It is from this root that my family took their name of Ha'eri.

When the Wahhabi tribesman of Muhammad Ibn Sa'ud sacked Karbala in 1802 (an act the Wahhabis were to repeat in 1923) and flooded the Shrine, the waters were not so confused; neither were the Shi'ite, who assassinated him two years later in reprisal. Wahhabism is an austere form of Islam, born out of the teachings of Muhammad Ibn Abd Al-Wahhab (1703–1791), whose dour creed of puritanical Sunni Islam embraced a particular dislike of Shi'a rituals and emotionalism. In the mid-1700s, the House of Sa'ud had converted to Wahhabism and imbued with proselytising zeal managed to take over much of Arabia, until the Ottomans eventually checked their expansion.

The Saudis, at the turn of the twentieth century, were revived by the extraordinary and admirable character of Abd Al-Aziz Al-Sa'ud. Not yet 22, and with just 40 men, he retook his ancestral capital of Riyadh, in the central Arabian province of Nejd. Over the next 30 years, he extended Saudi authority east to the Persian Gulf and then west to the Red Sea. In 1924, he sent the senile Sharif Hussein scurrying from Mecca, his fleet of cars laden down with pillaged gold, heading for an ignoble exile in Cyprus. Even Hussein's sons were unwilling to host him. It was a pathetic end, following in a long tradition of ineffectual rulership in the Muslim lands, one of the few enduring legacies in the Middle East today. With the Sharif's removal, a new political reality was created, and in 1932, proclaimed to be the Kingdom of Saudi Arabia.

> *Those are the days that we place them in the hand of people (to rule)*
>
> — Qur'an (3: 140)

The constant fear of attacks left an indelible mark on the psyche of Karbala. The years of the raids were very much remembered and retold to us children by Nana Hussein and Umm al Saadah. The attacks on the city also left their marks on the Shrines of Hussein and Abbas. After each attack, there would be repairs, upgrades and new endowments from devotees all over the world. Great crystal chandeliers, magnificent Persian carpets, gold inlayed calligraphies and numerous other objets d'art with religious symbolism would return to fill the mausoleums. It was the job of the *killidars*[5] , whose families had held the positions for generations, to watch over these treasures and maintain the upkeep of the Shrines.

> *Whoever remembers our suffering and weeps for the crimes which have been committed against us, will be within our rank on the Day of Resurrection. Whoever remembers our suffering and weeps and makes others weep, his eyes will not weep on the Day when many eyes will weep. Whoever attends gatherings where our situation is kept alive, his heart will not die on the day when many hearts will die.*

---

5 Means 'holder of the key.'

— Imam Ali Rida

In my time, the Shrine of Imam Hussein had a large marble paved courtyard, crisscrossed with corridors and alcoves leading off to various tombs, with the tomb of Imam Hussein in the centre. It was covered with a silver screen, adorned with metallic Qur'anic inscriptions, with much gold, silver and rare wood. Kings, rajas and merchants would vie with each other to bestow the most generous gifts. Storage rooms had to be used to keep the valuable antiques, but following in the footsteps of many a predecessor, Saddam Hussein was to relieve the Shrine of much of these. There was a curtained section cordoned off for the ladies and other wings where men and women supplicated together, asking for anything from good health to a child. Intricate mosaics and mirrors adorned the high ceiling that hung above the Shrine. The huge gilded dome radiated an ethereal majesty.

The faithful came through one of eight cedar doors from the bazaar and roads outside. Shoes could be worn around the main shrine building except, of course, during prayers. During the five daily prayers, long one-metre wide cotton carpets were rolled out into lines. Several thousand men would fill the courtyard, often spilling into the streets outside. They would stand up straight and to the punctuation of 'Allahu akbar' – God is greater – bend in prostration and sink to their knees, their foreheads to the earth. One day, a particularly mischievous cousin wondered if the worshippers remained bowed long enough for him to run from one end of the congregation to the other on their backs. Alas, he discovered the line too long, was caught halfway in mid-stride and subsequently given a good lesson not to disrupt worshippers.

During the day, a number of men with decorated elongated brass pitchers could be seen in the Shrine's courtyard decanting cold water into shiny metal drinking bowls. You would pay the '*sagi*' (pourer of drink) to distribute water, in memory of a deceased relative, free to anyone who was thirsty – a popular custom especially in the light of the thirst the dying martyrs suffered from. Other men had trays balanced on their heads filled with *halva*, rice pudding, rose water and treacle-like desserts.

Just outside the main gate, scribes sat at their wooden boxes, paper, inkpot and steel pointed pens ready. These were the professional petition or letter writers. I remember once seeing Nana Sekeena sitting there in the corner dictating a letter to her family in Isfahan. Obviously, she did not want anyone in the household to be exposed to the contents, so I quietly walked away.

· · ·

Much as their predecessors had done, the new British installed government of Iraq left Karbala mostly to itself. The unofficial council of several elderly learned men, such as my father, continued to influence and guide the city's affairs. The adhan – call to prayer – from the minarets of Imam Hussein and Abbas remained the focal point of social, as well as religious life. If there were important announcements, they would be made after the *adhan*, such as the burial time of a prominent person who had died or even prayer requests for the sick or those having difficult pregnancies.

> **Remember Allah at times of ease and you will be
> remembered at times of difficulty.**
> — Prophet Muhammad

The clocks on top of the entrances to the Shrines and mosques showed Muslim time, with 12 o'clock denoting sunrise and sunset. Thus, every couple of days, it would change slightly. I barely remember seeing policemen in Karbala. There was no prison, except for a small detention centre near the government central office. Besides the occasional tribal killing, there was hardly any crime. An Arab would kill if he came to know his sister or daughter was shaming the family with an illicit relationship. Tradition and custom were the foundation of conduct and ethics. I do not remember a single theft. Umm al Saadah would tell us about 'Abbas the Thief,' blind in one eye with a pronounced limp, the consequence of having jumped off a roof in rather dubious circumstances. Despite our best efforts to be introduced to him, we never saw him and concluded he may have been invented by Umm al Saadah to bring in some mischief to her storytelling repertoire.

There was no mental asylum, and the two or three mad people in town were tolerated and assimilated. 'Layla Deweenah', 'Mad Layla', would come to visit our house at odd times demanding food, occasionally selling some eggs as an excuse. If we did not run to pacify her, she could get quite upset, resorting to shouts and hysterics. However, she, like the others, was accommodated. In this way, the town looked after itself organically. Central government involvement was largely limited to garbage collection and the provision of water and electricity in the town. Over time, however, the impact of the central government and modern foreign ways and customs began to increase. As they became more noticeable, they were often criticised at the Burrani meetings.

European goods, which were available in the market, were associated with quality and desirability. Far Eastern goods were also available, but did not enjoy such a reputation, perhaps because they had not colonized us. From a young age, I enjoyed the pleasure of Kraft's tinned cheese. I was also the proud owner of more than one pair of 'Bata' shoes, fitted for me at Aziz Ali's shop – a well-known personality on Iraqi radio (one of his more memorable monologues focused on the superstitions of the Iraqi villagers, who to relieve the moon of its dark monster during a lunar eclipse banged on their pots and pans).

Karbala even boasted of a photography shop courtesy of Baqir al Akkas – 'Baqir the Photographer', another *Burrani* regular, who doubled up as a dentist – though one of my aunts did her best to ruin his reputation after he pulled out the wrong tooth. Seyyid Baqir taught my mother the art of the black box camera and the dark room and she soon became an accomplished photographer. Inside the compound, she would take pictures of her lady friends, who were relaxed and confident in the knowledge that no man would see them with loose long hair – not even in a photo. Today, these old pictures still exist and they are occasionally circulated amongst her four children in remembrance of those sheltered Karbala years.

When the Singer sewing machine shop opened in town, it enjoyed a spectacular boom and effectively announced the industrial supremacy of the West. It was a modern shop, different from all the others. It did not spill onto the street; one had to enter the shop through its own door. Even in the town's bookshops, one dealt with the owner as he sat behind a counter overlooking the street. However, at Singer it was different, there were sliding glass doors, sales representatives and the novel concept of 'hire purchase'. It was the first time financial intricacies came into the people's lives. It was Karbala's indoctrination into the world of institutionalised borrowing. Although, culturally, it was considered degrading to be in debt, the new habit prevailed. The slippery path of ease and convenience is attractive to all, especially when there is a lack of awareness that it takes you along the road of indebtedness and greater future difficulty.

> **The Garden is surrounded by fires and the Fire is bordered by gardens.**
>
> — Prophet Muhammad

Bankers and moneychangers, *'sarrafs'*, of course, did exist. My maternal uncle, Abdul Hussein, was the town's most famous *sarraf*. People would give him money to be transferred to others in Iraq and abroad. He also operated cheque accounts, savings accounts and acted as a trade financier. Although most transactions were recorded, there were those that were not and depended only on trust. He became very wealthy and his car, at one stage, had the honour of 'Karbala 1' as a license plate. The head of the great Arabian tribe of *Anayza*, of which the Saudi ruling family is a part, was based just outside Karbala. He had 'Karbala 2' and 'Karbala 3' and so asked my uncle if he would give him 'Karbala 1'. My uncle obliged and thus it was in 'Karbala 6' that I once had an adventurous journey with my uncle on our way to Baghdad.

Half way along the 90 km to Baghdad, the car broke down. My uncle managed to wave down a bus to arrange for a taxi from Baghdad. Abdul Hussein and his faithful driver nervously passed up and down alongside the stranded car on the side of the narrow road. Only when the taxi arrived did I realize why. The two men lifted the back seat of 'Karbala 6' to expose bags of gold and silver coins, which were hurriedly transferred to the taxi.

• • •

Baghdad was very different from Karbala, for it already had Western style homes and amenities. Baghdad even had the famous or notorious 'Abdullah's night club' (Abdullah was a common name for Middle-Eastern Christians) replete with locally brewed 'Diana' beer, and Paris-style cabaret shows. In Baghdad, you could see the new Coca-Cola advertisement, the first in the country, and for 14 fils (the price of a worker's daily wage) indulge in the exotic beverage, which had the reputation for being thirst quenching and a digestive.

Such luxuries were not available in Karbala, but outside the old town, far from the Shrines, the newly built Municipal offices and government club could boast the town's first proper restaurant, an industry which until then had been the monopoly of the street vendors. I was quite upset to discover my brother would occasionally eat there, for it had generally been considered something only a friendless or homeless person would do. There was even an expression, 'he is like the donkey driver who has to eat out.' Years later, even in Beirut, such attitudes still existed. I was visiting an Arab Christian friend of mine who suggested we eat out.

His mother, who overheard this offer, was horrified. 'Do you have no home that you have to eat out?' she scolded.

> *You must not eat any food unless you know who has prepared it.*
>
> — Shaykh Ikram

When the government club leased its restaurant to an enterprising man from Baghdad, a little of the Baghdadi decadence reached Karbala. Adjacent to the restaurant, he built a secret gambling room. This, together with a government-introduced lottery, was too much for a number of the *Burrani* regulars. 'The lottery of the hospital', as it was called, was justified because the proceeds would be used to build health facilities; some clerics had even sanctioned it, despite gambling being forbidden in Islam. The Burrani faithfuls were having none of it and asked my father to interfere, but he declined. This was for him only a symptom of unstable foreign poisons and he had the wisdom to take a longer view. The Western avalanche could not be turned back. The Muslim world would have to be submerged before it could emerge, ready to re-implement the Prophetic values anew. Each action has its appropriate timing and at that time, my father recognized the pointlessness of preaching to people who would hear, but could not listen.

> *'There was One, there was no One, other than God there is no one,'*

Mashti began one of her stories on Hodja Nasradeen[6]. 'One day, Hodja came to a town whose Mullah had recently died and on account of Hodja's large turban, the people asked him to preach to them. He was reluctant, but upon their insistence, he eventually rose

---

6 The fictional character Hodja or Mullah Nasradeen is the subject of amusing and moral laden stories from Turkey through to the Sub-Continent.

to the pulpit. 'Oh people, oh people', he called out, 'do you know what I am going to teach you today?' 'No', they cried back. 'Well', he said 'if you are so ignorant I am not going to waste my time.' With that, he abruptly stepped down and left.

The next week, Hodja returned to the town, which still had not found a Mullah. Once again, they insisted he give a talk. Hodja ascended the pulpit and again called out, 'Oh people, do you know what I am going to teach you?' 'Yes', they eagerly replied. 'Well', he said 'if you know, then what is the point in me telling you.'

When Hodja came back the third week, the people formulated a plan, which they were convinced could trick him and so again asked him to preach to them. Standing on the pulpit, Hodja repeated his question. 'Oh people, do you know what I am going to teach you?' Half of the congregation proclaimed they did, and the other half that they didn't. 'Well', Hodja smiled 'in that case, those who know should teach the ones who don't.'

Allah knows Best.'

> *You can only make hear those who have faith in Our Signs.*
>
>   — Qur'an (50: 53)

Across from the government club, the Ministry of Agriculture was trying to industrialize. A vegetable canning plant was built, part of a broader export-orientated effort, with the ultimate result of numerous defunct factories across the country. The gap between the simple peasant farmer and technology was just too wide to be instantaneously bridged by a decree from on high. One tragic incident highlights the broader pattern of third world failures in industrialisation. The government imported hybrid seeds impregnated with certain poisonous chemicals and designed for high yields. Officials warned the farmers that these beans were exclusively for planting. Alas, the illiterate peasants did not heed. Hundreds ate the beans and died. Goodwill based on ignorance is often as bad as ill will.

Beside the government club, the new, westernised professional class had started to build European style houses, looking out onto the street rather than into a courtyard. New styles of furniture were made and there was the novelty of en-suite bathrooms. My brother, Fazel, who had recently graduated from the new engineering college in Baghdad, was responsible for building many of these houses and eventually moved into one himself. He and his 'suit wearing' friends represented the new generation of educated 'modern Iraqis'.

On the weekends, they would go to the Bagh Jamal, our family orchard, a few kilometres north of the town, along the road to Hur. Although the climate in Karbala was generally hot, the shade of tall palm trees provided cover under which a wide variety of fruits and vegetables could flourish. Beneath the trees, beside one of the two ponds used as water reservoirs, and away from the attentive ears of Karbala's residents, they would listen to gramophone records. In Karbala, radios were still treated with suspicion and when my sister sold a bracelet to buy a small radio, she was most careful to keep the volume so low that she had to put her ears next to the speaker.

As 'the modern Karbalais' cooked their kebabs, the tango, Latino beats, and the ever-popular Umm Khulthum would mix in to the accompaniment of bullfrogs, which lived in large numbers, amongst the pond's algae. Umm Khulthum was a favourite, not just for my brother and his friends, but also for a whole generation of Arabs. For many years, two hugely popular Egyptians dominated the radio waves of Cairo, Arabia and the Gulf. It was a predictable program. In the day, the charismatic oratory of Gamal Abdul Nasser[7] would break into a mammoth political discourse. At night, the rotund Umm Khulthum would launch into one of her drawn-out love songs.

I would often go to Bagh Jamal for a picnic with friends and

---

7 President of Egypt (1956–1970).

cousins, especially those from my mother's side of the family. At one end of the orchard was an extensive wilderness, thick with tall reeds and bamboos. On occasions, we would penetrate deep into the thickets in the hope of stumbling upon a boar, which every now and then, Kareem, the orchard-keeper would excitedly report he had shot.

The bright sun and flowing river water ensured that the Bagh Jamal remained resplendent, but there was always the danger of a cloud, not of condensation, but of locusts. The sky would turn black. A tree that was verdant in the morning would be bare by the evening. The swarms would move through the grape vines, the plum, peach and pomegranate, the apple, the apricot and the fig trees. A few young boys would make the best of the epidemic by frying locusts on Karbala's street corners and, for a few days, provide the market with a new delicacy.

> *And certainly we shall try you with something of fear and hunger and loss of wealth and lives and of crops. But give glad tidings to the steadfast.*
>
> — Qur'an (2: 155)

The other natural but detested phenomenon was sandstorms. Not a year would pass without the desert reminding us of its proximity and mobility. When the sand settled, and the azure colour returned to the sky, and the birds had once more begun to sing, my father would climb to his rooftop. From atop, he would call the family to bring buckets of water to pour over his beloved orange trees and to wash off the sand-sodden leaves and branches until green and orange once more emerged from their sand encrusted coating.

6

Student Times

Acquire knowledge. It enables its possessor to distinguish right from wrong; it lightens the way to heaven; it is our friend in the desert, our society in solitude, our companion when friendless; it guides us to happiness; it sustains us in misery; it is an ornament amongst friends, and an armour against enemies.

— Prophet Muhammad

Centuries ago, Islamic academies had led the world in philosophy, logic, theology, artisanship, mathematics and the sciences. The translations into Arabic and thence into European languages of the classical Greek texts provided the fuel for the Renaissance. In the traditional academic gown (which derives from the Middle Eastern *'aba'* – cloak) and in the design of the cloisters of Oxford and Cambridge can be seen traces of the Andalusian courtyards and teaching centres. Yet, in my time, whether in Cairo, Damascus, Tunis or Baghdad, little remained of the glories of the early Islamic universities. The closest modern university to Karbala ironically was the American University in Beirut.

I had attended a local Karbala primary school, aptly named 'The Sibit[1] School', housed in a rambling two-story building ten minutes

---

1 'The son', meaning Imam Hussein.

walk from where we lived. Then I went on to Karbala's only
secondary school. In 1918, there were about 200 students enrolled
in secondary-level schooling across Iraq[2], but the British and
early Iraqi governments had quickly moved to improve this. The
curriculum in the school was a western one, but the teachers were
mostly Iraqi. The exception was our English teacher, a subject we
started in the last year of primary school, who was a Palestinian
called Shukri Samarah.

We had no uniform at school, but wore western style clothes. The
dress code was modest and simple. Modesty and temperance were
key considerations in all aspects of life; luxury and waste were
always shunned. I would be fitted out at 'Hamid the Tailor's'. We
were taught to supplicate with each new item of clothing: 'Oh
Allah, make me content in your adornment.' I was shocked one day
when a woman came into the tailor's shop and Hamid took her
behind a curtain to be fitted. I was most relieved when, after
confronting my mother, she assured me she had had only women
seamstresses, who would do their work at our home on her
cherished 'Singer'. My puritanical outlook was common amongst
the Karbala boys of my generation.

Religious studies were taught at school, but were never taken
seriously, and did not count towards our final marks. In fact, a stage
was reached in the Middle East where the ultimate threat a father
could make to a difficult son was to send him to a religious school,
or traditional '*madrasa*'. Here, a ferocious Mullah would teach
Qur'anic recitation (which he did not fully understand himself)
assisted most often by the rap of a cane on open palms or
more severely on the soles of the feet[3]. As for girls, primary and
secondary education was beginning to take root in the face of much
opposition from ultra conservative mullahs and ignorant parents.

---

2 See Thabit Abdullah, A Short History of Iraq, p. 123.
3 This is known as 'falaqa'.

There is no compulsion in religion.

— Qur'an (2: 256)

After matriculating from secondary school I was all set to go to the Medical College in Baghdad which, like the Engineering College, was founded and largely run by British staff. These were the first practical higher education colleges in Iraq, established soon after the Second World War. I had befriended the chief surgeon in Karbala, whom I would visit in the town's Ottoman built, but recently expanded hospital. Sometimes, I was the only assistant available to him in the operating theatre and would help with minor surgeries, such as appendicitis. The new doctors and modern medicine had already displaced the traditional *'hakims'* and herbalists. Even the poor peasants were spellbound by western medicine. Queues developed around the modern doctors' practices, the patient never quite happy unless he or she received some form of an injection – the bigger and more painful the needle, the better. Because of this, some doctors occasionally resorted to injecting placebos.

Then came the tempting offer of a scholarship to England. Every year, the top few students in the country would be sent on a government/oil company scholarship. My friend, Sahib, who was a year ahead of me got the second top marks in the country in his year and had already gone on scholarship to England. The following year, I also got the second highest marks in the country and like him, was offered a scholarship.

Initially, I was indifferent to going. If I were to go, I wanted to study analytical chemistry, partly due to an investigative nature and perhaps subtly influenced by my father's alchemy work. The scholarship board, however, was keen on sponsoring engineering graduates to fill in the requirements of the fast growing oil industry. The head of the scholarship board at the time was Nadeem Pachachi, who was also Director of Petroleum in the government (and became Minister of Economics). He later became my friend

and would joke with me that all the other scholarship candidates
had been nervous and readily accepted to do their degrees in
engineering. I was the only intransigent one and the only one who
didn't really care if he went or not. Accordingly, I was allowed to
do my degree in Physics and Chemistry.

My father recognized the superiority of the West's secular
education and their civil societies. He also knew that culture and
life in the Middle East had stagnated and unless it was radically
reformed both in style and content, social collapse was inevitable.
The Muslims had fallen short of uniting their hearts and heads to
balance the rational and spiritual teachings of their religion. Most
Muslim societies did not have Islamic justice or wisdom. Often
leadership was incompetent, despotic or ruthless with men of
religion caught by theological hair-splitting. For this reason he
supported my going abroad. He knew that my future did not lie in
the traditional religious education, which he and those before him
had received. Times had changed radically and the Muslims had to
alter their attitudes instead of making futile attempts to preserve
old habits and norms, even though they may have contained
much goodness.

The encouragement of my father and some of his friends to take
up the offer, together with the prestige of the scholarship and the
subtle pressure that came with hearing my name on the radio
amongst the selected few, encouraged me to go. The scholarship
students needed guarantors to ensure they returned to work for the
government or the oil company. One of my father's closest friends,
Hussein Dallal, immediately offered to do this for me.

It was often the case with the established 'ulema' families that a
close friend or relative of the family would take a young son under
his wing. Hussein Dallal filled this role for me. He was my mentor
and role model, a lawyer from a landowning tribal family of central
Iraq. He was a most noble and generous man. He lived in a simple
room, overlooking the Tigris, in one of Baghdad's small old hotels.
The room had a steel bed and mattress, an old leather suitcase under

the bed and a small cupboard with clothes, nothing else.

Hussein was well known and respected as a courageous man who always took up the case of the poor and the destitute without payment. Modern in outlook and always dressed in a handsome western suit, he was, nevertheless, traditional and uncompromising in Islamic values and culture. Before I left for England he gave me one piece of advice I would always adhere to. 'Do not ever be involved in any of the modern political ideologies, whether Communism, Socialism or Nationalism.'

Sadly, it was in the name of such ideologies that Hussein Dallal was brutally murdered. In the early 1970s, he stood up against the atrocities committed by the Ba'th government against the Kurds in the north of the country. He was condemned for treason, tortured and executed. His slumped figure was displayed on national television as a warning to all others who may have had his courage or conviction.

> *The most excellent jihad is to speak the truth in the face of a tyrannical ruler.*
>
> — Prophet Muhammad

The summer of 1954 saw me at Baghdad airport boarding a Range KLM propeller plane bound for London and a strange world I could not have imagined. I was not yet seventeen and eighteen was the minimum age to be allowed to go on a scholarship. Thus, my age was falsified on the newly issued passport. I had not been on a plane before. In fact, I had only once been outside Iraq, when all the family members who were living in Karbala had gone on a trip to Iran to stay with my elder half-brother, Muhideen. Now, I was leaving all that was familiar to embark on a journey I probably would not have made, if I had known what awaited me.

> *Do not force your children to behave like you (in outer manners), for surely they have been created for a time*

which is different to your time.

— Imam Ja'far As-Sadiq

Baba Mahmood boycotted the event in a rare display of disapproval and refused even to take my luggage to the taxi. Mashti warned, as she had many times before, that should I leave, she would die, for she would have no more reason to live. I tried to remain steadfast and matter of fact and told her not to be so silly. My mother had 'tears frozen on her cheeks' for months after my departure (my sister, Fodhla, later related to me). She had stoically backed my departure, but afterwards, my father wrote me a letter telling me that had he anticipated the extent of her grief, he would have thought twice about the wisdom of sending me abroad.

A man came to Prophet Muhammad saying, 'Oh Messenger of Allah, whom should I treat kindly?' 'Your mother', he replied. 'And then whom?' 'Your mother' 'and then whom?' 'Your mother' 'and then whom?' 'Your father.'

During my early teens, two Englishwomen had come for a visit to Karbala. Although non-Muslims were considered 'unclean' by many of the townsfolk, my family welcomed them. My father said he considered them cleaner than most of the people in town and was happy to have them in our house. He even wanted them to be allowed into the Shrine, but the uproar this would have created prevented them from doing this. They left behind them, as gifts, two picture books of England. Thus, prior to leaving on scholarship, my only images of England were of Victorian nannies pushing prams in Hyde Park, a scant preparation for the chilly, damp and clouded skies that awaited me. I had naively expected the Christians of England to be like the Christians of Iraq, of which there was a sizable number, and who were largely indistinguishable from the Muslims in their mannerisms and value system. I was to have an unexpected awakening. My feeling of alienation was total. My understanding of the language was limited. My understanding of and ability to relate to the culture was non-existent.

The flight to England stopped a couple of times to re-fuel with a one night's stopover in Beirut. The strange sight of attractively dressed female airhostesses, an occupation a respectable Arab girl would have considered most dishonourable, but which western girls viewed with envy, amazed me. The high-rise buildings and glitzy hotels of Beirut were equally overwhelming.

In England, I was sent to a technical college in Weybridge, Surrey. The Iraqi Baccalaureate was considered equivalent to O-levels and thus I needed to take A-levels. I was initially put up, together with another Iraqi, in a rather gloomy eight-room guesthouse. The pungent smell of grilled bacon drifted through the air and had already saturated the dining room furniture. On our first evening, my fellow Iraqi and I came down to supper in our pyjamas, as we would have done at home. Our landlady was horrified, immediately sending us upstairs to change. This was the first in a string of cultural misunderstandings that I was to encounter and often had to yield to, albeit reluctantly.

My mother had bought me a brass jug for my ablutions from Karbala's copper bazaar. This was stored behind my suitcase, to be taken out when I went to the bathroom. One evening I invited some of my Arab friends to come up to my room for a visit. There, to everyone's amusement and my embarrassment, the brass toilet jug was neatly displayed on top of my new radio. On discovering the shiny brass object, the landlady obviously thought it was an ornament worthy of a prominent place.

Thankfully, I soon discovered other lodgings, and for three pounds ten shillings a week, the kindly Mrs. Cubico (an Englishwoman with a French husband) made me sandwiches for lunch and did her best to supply me with whatever fruits she could to compensate for the withdrawal symptoms I felt. I would dream of the fresh fruit of Karbala and would imagine Kareem every morning offloading his donkey cart of the fresh fruit and vegetables for our house. Meanwhile, in an England still not fully recovered from the ravages of the Second World War, I would save up for one orange or a neatly cut quarter of a cucumber. Often, I would shut my eyes to smell the aromatic cucumbers and the sweet oranges of the Karbala market.

At the Iraqi embassy in London, the genial Mr. Pierce, an English educationalist, was assigned to look after the Iraqi scholarship students. Our monthly allowance of 40 pounds a month was more than adequate for all our needs and was always paid on time. A number of students from poorer families would even remit some money back to their families in Iraq. Until then, I had had very little to do with money. When I wanted to buy something in Karbala, usually stationery, I would just pick it up and charge it to my father's account.

When I got to England, one of the first things my friend, Sahib, did was take me aside to warn me that should a girl smile at me, it did not mean she was making immoral advances. The European women and their participation in every aspect of society were disconcerting. In Iraq, women seldom ever pursued professional careers (although Iraq was the first Arab country to have a woman cabinet minister[4]) and in Karbala, they never did. When I left Karbala, there was not even a secondary school for women. No respectable family would allow their women to be exposed to males other than their relatives. In the Iraq of my youth, if a girl so much as looked at a man attentively or with a faint smile on her lips, it would be considered reprehensible or even punishable behaviour. Once when I was with my younger sister on our house's rooftop, I noticed two young men on the pavement below looking up at us. My immediate response was to accuse my poor innocent sister of attracting their attention. She had done nothing wrong,

---

4 Her name was Dr. Naziha al-Dulaymi appointed in 1959 as Minister of Municipalities.

yet immediately she apologized and stepped back out of sight

And lower your eyes in the presence of women (other than family) and others will lower their eyes.

— Prophet Muhammad

Another adjustment I had to make was in general behaviour and conduct. In Karbala, there were certain standards which had to be adhered to. By emulation and from an early age, my grandmother, mother and the women of the house would instil in us what was and what was not appropriate conduct. In Arab culture, it is shameful to ask for anything, only the food in front of you is taken and then only when offered. If I had done that at the college canteen, I would have probably starved. As offering is central to Arab culture, when somebody asks for something, they usually do so in a circumscribed way, which is pre-empted; this extends to things other than food. I recall the total puzzlement of an English student who had commented on my attractive necktie when I took it off to give it to him. He was just being complimentary, but for me the appropriate thing to do was to gift it to him wholeheartedly.

Occasionally, when I felt particularly homesick and wanted some escapism, I would go to the cinema, but this only made things worse as the movies championed all the characteristics I had been taught to shun – individualism, ostentation, frivolous pleasures and personal aggrandizement. Elvis Presley's hip gyrations were particularly difficult to reconcile with my notions of Christian modesty. I had seen my first movie in Baghdad a number of years before. It was a typical Egyptian melodrama called. 'My Heart and my Sword', a rich city boy discovers a poor peasant girl, rescues her from her mud hut in the village and takes her to his modern villa in the city. Together, they live happily ever after. Soon after seeing this movie, Mashti had told me a story.

*'There was One, there was no one, other than God
there is no one.'*

'There was a prince who was constantly tempted to do what was not
approved of. His teachers were unable to place any moral or ethical
boundaries upon him. Then one of them had a wise idea. 'I'll know
exactly what you are doing', he told the Prince. 'I have a fly which
will follow you and report to me when you do something wrong. No
matter how much you try to hide, the fly will be there to see you.'

The following day, the prince stole a piece of special cake
and, remembering the fly, hurried to the bathroom, making sure
he locked the doors and window so that the fly couldn't get in. As
he started to tuck in, he was horrified to discover a fly perched on
the ceiling.

The prince went back to his teacher repenting and apologizing.
'More than my fly', the teacher explained, 'it is Allah who sees
you.' Wherever you go, Allah is with you and He knows what you
are doing. What you know is a small part of what Allah knows.
What you see is a small aspect of what the All Seeing God sees.
Now, you can forget about my fly and be concerned about Allah's
presence. His angels are recording everything that you do, the good
deeds written on your right shoulder, the evil on your left.'

At this point, the young prince started to cry, 'I have done so
many bad things that I am sure to be doomed.' The teacher shook
his head. 'No.' Allah has promised that good deeds will wipe out the
vices and all good deeds are multiplied tenfold whereas bad deeds
will only bring about their equivalent.

And Allah knows best.'

*And to Allah belong the east and the west, and
wheresoever you turn is the face of Allah.*

— Qur'an (2: 155)

This story had a lasting impact on me. The movie reinforced my picture of an Ever-watchful Divine eye. It gave real life to Mashti's story. Often, when I was tempted to do what was incorrect, the moral code of Karbala flashed through my heart and reminded me that all my actions were being recorded. Nevertheless, towards the end of my stay in Britain, most of my religious duties had been reduced to a ceremonial shell. Cultural identity and values became blurred. In an environment where all those around you act as mirrors for approved or normal conduct, most of my thoughts and efforts had turned to the existential needs such as my studies and future career.

• • •

Overall, my initial baptism in the west was a messy and miserable affair. I suffered from a homesickness and cultural alienation that was clearly felt by most of my Arab friends and other students from Muslim countries, who studied in England. We all experienced jarring dislocation and misunderstandings, some of which were humorous.

There was the case of Kareem Ferman, from Baghdad, who with each passing week was becoming progressively more homesick and distraught. He presumed that his family had forsaken him for a reason he could not understand. Every week since he had arrived in England he would write a letter home, but in over six months, he had not received a single reply. One day, while walking in town with him, his futile faithfulness became most comically apparent. Brandishing a stamped letter, he purposefully crossed the street and deposited it in a neat mounted box with the word, 'LITTER', written across the side. After we pointed out his mistake, he laughed with relief and cursed the Iraqi educational system for not teaching us enough English before sending us to such a different land and people.

Then there was Yusuf, who sung the praises of the wonderful chicken sandwiches he would regularly buy from a small café in town. Most of us Arabs had been to that café regularly, but none of us had seen any chicken sandwiches there. One day, I went to the café with Yusuf. When he went up to the counter and asked for his usual 'hen sandwich' he was given a sandwich with suspiciously pink flesh. The proprietor, unable to differentiate between 'hen' and 'ham' when spoken through Yusuf's thick Iraqi accent, had been feeding pork for weeks to the innocent Muslim boy. For months, poor Yusuf felt dreadful for having wolfed down pork with so much enjoyment.

> *He has forbidden you the dead animals, and blood,*
> *and the flesh of swine and that, which is slaughtered*
> *as a sacrifice for others than Allah. But if one is forced*
> *by necessity without wilful disobedience, not going to*
> *excess, then there is no sin in them. Truly, Allah is*
> *Ever Forgiving, Most Merciful.*
>
> — Qur'an (2: 173)

After I had spent a year at the College in Surrey, the Embassy decided to spread us more widely across Britain due to the growth in their Iraqi student population. I was not really settled and so was happy to be relocated to Wrexham, North Wales, only to find it colder and wetter than Surrey. We stayed in a grim college hostel, which the formidable Mrs. Davis ran like a juvenile detention centre. During the weekends, all the English students would go home leaving six homesick Iraqi Muslim boys. For us, Sunday represented leisure time, but for the devout chapel going Mrs. Davis, it was 'the day of rest.' The ping-pong nets were removed, the dartboard taken down, and the inmates prohibited from doing anything 'unchristian'. Welsh lamb for lunch was the only compensation.

Over one such Sunday spread, I took my revenge on Mrs. Davis. She asked me if I could say grace. 'Could I say it in Arabic,' I answered. Certainly I could, after all, I was thoughtfully reminded

'God belongs to everyone.' So, bowing my head solemnly, I prayed in Arabic; '*Bismillah ir-Rahman ir-Raheem...*' – 'In the name of God, the Beneficent, the Most Merciful, deliver us from these miserable and wretched people. Oh Allah, save us from this hostel, from Wales and Britain. From the affliction of its weather and the torment of its food.' A gleeful, unanimous and emphatic 'amen' resounded from my fellow Iraqis.

Mrs. Davis was second in charge of the hostel reporting to the blind Mr. Roland, a kindly soul, from whom we got a heavy dose of proselytising. Endlessly he would talk to us about Jesus. Yet, Jesus the Prophet was not at all unfamiliar to us. Indeed the Qur'an refers to him and describes his qualities numerous times. Muslims believe in the immaculate conception of the Virgin Mary, and venerate the great miracles Jesus performed. Like Mohammad, he was a Prophet of God.

What was more difficult for us to understand than the teachings of Jesus was the role of the Queen of England as the Defender of the Faith[5]. One wondered how much the bare-footed Middle Eastern ascetic would have approved of the pomp of the British monarchy and the decadence of the aristocracy. How would he be received at the pretentious gates of Buckingham Palace?

> *It is not befitting to (the majesty of) God that He*
> *should beget a son. Glory be to him. When He deter-*
> *mines a matter, He says only to it, 'Be' – and it is.*
> — Qur'an (19: 35)

It is difficult to exaggerate the difficulties and confusions of those first few years in England. I was an alien in a strange world. There was no call to prayers to punctuate the day, no minarets from which

---

5 The Pope initially bestowed this title on Henry VIII for his opposition to the Protestant movement. Following Henry's change of heart and the founding of the Church of England, the British Monarchs, nevertheless, continued to use the title.

to make the call, no rooftops to fly kites or courtyards with palm trees. During Ramadan, nobody would walk through the streets before dawn, as they would in Karbala, to awaken the faithful for 'suhur' – the pre-dawn meal before the beginning of the fast. In the Ramadan evenings, there were no 'tea shops' where I could go with my friends to play one of our favourite Ramadan games. In place of home familiarities, I was faced with mini-skirts and Christmas trees with advertising boards pronouncing the benefits of this or that pet food. It was a culture of materialism.

Thankfully in time, albeit gradually, I began to understand and even enjoy Britain more, especially the countryside. With my friends, we travelled around the country visiting museums, churches and town centres. The liberal use of incense at the Orthodox Church on Moscow Road, London, made it particularly appealing. I would sometimes visit London with friends and other times I'd go alone to visit my brother, Danish, in his Kensington office or his Wembley Park house. The Christmas turkey his wife prepared was especially enjoyable. On the *Eid*[6], some of us would go to the Woking Mosque, where after prayers, we would secure a hearty Middle-Eastern meal, sometimes with second servings.

The alienation of language, because of radio and practice, rescinded as my English improved. The cultural alienation can never be fully removed, but understanding goes a long way in diluting its impact. Anthony C. West was a big help in improving that understanding. One day, while on one of my customary walks in North Wales, I came across this friendly looking man and his Labrador. He was an Irish writer with great talent, but limited popular appeal. Although his books received literary acknowledgment and awards (critics favourably compared him to James Joyce), he struggled to support his ten children. I enjoyed my long walks with Tony and the strong black tea with thick slices of homemade buttered bread that we would share afterwards. Through

---

6 The Muslim festival that follows the month of fasting.

his influence, I began to discover more about the philosophy and literature of the West and to appreciate it. There was much wisdom therein. I became particularly fond of the existentialists and Camus. Tony's tutelage helped me to build bridges and initiated me into the European socio-political evolvement, from the Reformation to the coming of modern society. Our meeting point was much more on the level of the soul and the discovery of the truth within oneself than on the material or cultural plane. I felt that he understood me, and the predicament I was in. He did not give me sympathy, but a reflection of the higher values that all human beings share.

He who seeks the truth should be of no country.

— Voltaire

During my first summer holiday, I decided to take up a temporary job and came across an advertisement for a 'smart petrol pump attendant'. Accordingly, one of my Iraqi friends and I dressed up in our smartest clothes and went confidently off to be interviewed. 'I didn't mean smart dress, I meant smart in the head', growled the owner. I assured him that we were also smart in the head and he hired us. The owner came to like me so much that just as the holidays were ending, he approached me. 'Look, you people believe in arranged marriages. Give up this studying nonsense, you can marry my daughter and I'll give you my garage and petrol station.' I was flattered, but politely turned down his offer.

I bought a 'Lambretta' scooter with the money I had earned at the garage. The following summer holidays, I subscribed to the youth hostel associations of a number of European countries and with my scooter set off for Baghdad, travelling through France, Germany, Switzerland and Italy. I disembarked at Genoa and took a boat to Beirut from where a bus took me on to Baghdad. From Dover to Venice, I gave a lift to an English architectural student. On the boat from Venice to Beirut, I enjoyed the company of a young Lebanese Jesuit Priest, who was studying in Paris and later corresponded with me sharing his love of God and the human drive towards enlightenment.

It was 1956 and the Egyptian President, Gamal Abdul Nasser, had just nationalized the Suez Canal. The 1950s were before the massive influx of foreign immigrants had made itself felt in Britain. I never experienced any racial or religious animosity. Easterners and Muslims existed in far too few numbers to be a considered a threat or a nuisance to the British. We were curious, exotic, but harmless specimens and thus were tolerated, in the same way that the British accommodate eccentrics – with patience and amusement. Indeed, I felt I was pandered to and pitied with a measure of condescension, here from the colonies to learn something about civilisation. The British had not quite got to grips with their role in the post-war world and the patronising psyche of a great power still prevailed. This all changed with the Suez crisis. It was a reality check and a wake up call to the world, and especially to the British.

The Suez crisis was also the first time that Iraq became a significant news item. Nasser's blocking of Suez disrupted oil exports from the Gulf. No longer were we from some obscure country. Now, we were from some obscure country that had lots of oil. In Suez, the British and French governments had achieved the exact opposite of what they set out to do. They had inadvertently consolidated Nasser's power and worsened their standing amongst the countries of the Middle East. They had shown what little respect they had for the sovereignty of other states and increased the suspicion with which they were already held in the Arab lands.

Political necessities sometimes turn out to be political mistakes.

— Bernard Shaw

Upon arrival in Karbala, I was informed of Mashti's death two years prior. From long periods exposed to the heat of open stoves in the kitchen, she had developed eczema. During my first few months in England, I would regularly buy her a special eczema cream, that I had seen advertised, and send it to Iraq. Then I received a letter from my mother telling me Mashti would not need any more cream. I thought the cream would be effective, but not to such an extent. I suspected something was wrong, but had no idea she had died.

On the day of my departure from Karbala, she had slipped away to hire a taxi to take her to Baghdad, so she could see me off at the airport. Having taken her money, the unscrupulous taxi driver dropped her off halfway to Baghdad. In the mid-summer heat, poor Mashti had to find her way back home. Her pale Georgian skin could not take the exposure to the searing summer sun and she died of sunstroke a few days later. Her loving presence and unconditional devotion are deeply ingrained in my memory.

This visit was also the last time I was to see my father. On New Year's Eve, 1957 he passed away. He showed no sign of illness during the day, then after the sunset prayers, he retired to his bedroom saying he was feeling a little weak. At midnight, he collapsed on the veranda just outside his room. My mother stayed with him as my brother, Fazel, rushed to call the doctor. When they returned, my father was still lying on the veranda. It was a cold winter night and the doctor recommended they take him inside. As my brother tried to move him, Shaykh Ahmad turned to him with a serene smile on his face and calmly said, 'There is no point, it is over'.

> *You ask me the marks of a man of faith? When death comes to him, he has a smile on his lips.*
>
> — Muhammad Iqbal

There were a number of indications that my father foresaw his own death. The day before he had given Baba Mahmood a list of shops where accounts were to be settled. In all the years Baba worked for my father, he had never settled all his accounts at the same time.

Some time before he died, he had been tending to his favourite orange tree, which adorned the courtyard, standing at the centre of a ring of trees. Try as he might to revive it, the orange tree has become increasingly barren. As he vainly tended to it, he turned to my sister who was standing by his side. 'It is a sign', he said.

A few weeks before, he took Fazel on a trip by horse drawn carriage[7] half an hour into the desert. When the carriage was well beyond the sprawling public cemetery, he pointed out a spot and said this was where he wanted to be buried. He told my brother that he had already shown the undertaker (from whom he had also bought a shroud). It was considered a strange place for my father to want to be buried. It was of great prestige to be buried close to the tomb of Imam Hussein and our family had a beautiful mausoleum at the entrance to the Shrine, which was well known to the local population. There were only two other private mausoleums next to the Shrine, but with the expansions, they had already been partly incorporated into the public areas.

On the day of his funeral, Karbala closed down. Thousands came from all over; religious leaders, tribal chiefs, government officials and the King's representative, as well as merchants, shop owners and street vendors. He was truly loved and respected by all. For forty days, the traditional mourning period, relatives came to our house. The women dressed in black and Qur'anic recitation filled the rooms.

I flew to Iraq six months after he died and wanted to go alone and visit his grave, but when I got there, I found a large cemetery had sprung up around where he was buried. There were so many graves that I could not find his. I even had to go back to town to get Baba Mahmood to take me to my father's grave. At the time of his burial, there was not a single grave in that area. The people obviously felt something special about the place that such a man wished to be

---

7 The carriages were known as 'Doroshka', a Russian/Persian word used in some parts of Iraq.

buried there. Indeed, next to his grave, a water spring had sprung up. Until recently, it was known as 'the fountain of Ahmad', in honour of my father.

My father left this world with complete ease and readiness. He had settled his accounts outwardly and inwardly. He had acted appropriately in whatever he did, always faithful and cheerful to the needs of the moment. His memory is forever with me. In my mind's eye, I see myself walking behind him, in the late afternoon, as he did his occasional maintenance work around the house. I helped him plaster walls, mix the gypsum and knock in nails. It always gave me a great sense of pride to be his apprentice while he was alive.

> *And give glad tidings to those who believe and do good*
> *works; that theirs are Gardens underneath rivers flow;*
> *as often as they are regaled with fruit thereof, they say:*
> *This is what was given to us before; and it is given*
> *to them in resemblance. And therein they have pure*
> *companions; and therein forever they abide.*
>
> — Qur'an (2: 25)

The year of my father's death was also the year I finished my A-levels in Britain. I went on to do my degree in Physics and Maths at the University of Wales at Bangor, as I had grown used to Wales, and liked the North Welsh coast, especially the beautiful Isle of Anglesey. Bangor was a small, pleasant seaside town and the university had a number of Arab and Iraqi students, whose presence and companionship greatly alleviated my sense of isolation and loneliness. There was even an Arab Student's Union with its head office in London. Faris Glubb, the son of Sir John Bagot Glubb, better known as Glubb Pasha[8], was a very active participant in

---

8 The British Commander of Jordan's Arab Legion who transformed it into a disciplined army that supported the Allies in WW2.

this organisation.

It so happened that the Bangor town council had raised some money for the plight of refugees and organized a forum to determine whether the cause of the Palestinians was worthy of their donation. Various members of the Arab Students Union, including myself, were invited to talk to the town council.

For centuries, the Jews had lived in Muslim lands and were respected and influential members of society. The periodic persecution of the Jews that scars European history has no equivalent in the Islamic World. In Muslim Spain, the Jews were an integral and respected part of the cultural flowering that took place there. One prominent historian, Bernard Lewis notes, that even the Ottomans offered 'a degree of tolerance without precedent or parallel in Christian Europe. Each religious community – 'millet' – was allowed the free practice of its religion. Had their own communal organizations, subject to the authority of their own religious chiefs, controlled their own education and social life, enforced their own laws to the extent that they did not conflict with the basic laws of the empire…non-Muslims controlled much of the economy, and were even able to play a part of some importance in the political process'[9].

The Jews of Iraq traced their ancestry from the Jews whom Nebuchadnezzar had exiled to Babylon in biblical times. Iraqi Jewry represented the largest and strongest of the Eastern or Oriental Jewish Diaspora. Jews were especially important and influential in Baghdad. At the start of the British Mandate, it was estimated that they were numbered fully one-third of the city's population. When King Faisal 1 first came to Iraq, he was accommodated in the Jewish quarter, both his house and car bankrolled with Jewish money. The Jews owned much of the best property in Baghdad and controlled a significant portion of trade. In many matters, including education, they led. Their influence was

---

9   See Bernard Lewis, What Went Wrong, p. 33–34.

such that in the early Iraqi governments, Jews were often in control of the Ministries of Trade and Finance. In Karbala, I remember the frequent visits of Khatoon, a Jewess merchant, who would come to our house with a huge bundle of cloth for my mother and the ladies of the house to buy and sew from. There was a great feeling of warmth and friendship towards the Jews as well as Christians throughout the land. My good friend Saad Jabr (whose father Salih Jabr, a friend of my father, was the Governor of Karbala province and the first Shi'a Prime Minister of Iraq) remembers going to his Jewish neighbours on most Sabbaths to light up their stoves.

The lead up to and the eventual creation of Israel gradually fractured the ancient symbiosis. The ordinary people began to view the Jews increasingly as British or Zionist collaborators. The rising nationalistic tide together with British suppression of the Palestinian revolt (1936–39) led to some disgruntled people making attacks on Jews, particularly, in 1941[10]. Incidentally, during the attacks more Muslims died trying to protect their Jewish neighbours than Jews[11]. The Jews of the Middle East were distinct from the Ashkenazi[12] Jews of Europe, for they had shared many commonalities with the Muslims, the main differences being in the places and method of worship. The Iraqi Jews were reluctant to leave the country in which they had prospered. Then with the birth of Israel came greater harassment of the Jewish community, aided by covert Israeli secret service activity. The intention of the aforementioned was to fuel the anger of the Iraqi mob and precipitate the exodus of wealthy Iraqi Jews, who were needed to boost the fledgling Israeli state. The mob obliged and in 1951 all but a handful of Iraq's Jews left – a great loss to the country's cultural

---

10 This was during a period when Rashid Ali al Gilani, an Arab Nationalist, became Prime Minister. He refused to allow British troops to cross Iraqi territory. The killings took place in the interlude between when Rashid Ali was removed and British troops arrived.

11 See Thabit Abdullah, A Short History of Iraq, p. 142–143.

12 Askhanazi Jews make up more than eighty percent of the World's Jews.

diversity and economy.

> *Do no argue with the people of the book [Jews and*
> *Christians] unless it is in the kindest way except when*
> *they do wrong, and say, 'We believe in that which has*
> *been revealed to you. Our God and your God are One*
> *and we submit to him.'*
>
> — Qur'an (29: 46)

Back in the town hall at Bangor, the Mayor introduced me to a sizable audience before settling down into his seat to catch up on some sleep – doubtless induced by the weight of the colossal chain hanging from around his neck. I tried my best to explain to the audience how the Palestinians had been terrorized and expelled from their land, not voluntarily displaced. I tried to convince them that despite their numerical superiority, unlike the Israelis, they had not been formed into heavily armed military units. I tried to highlight the ineffectiveness of the Arab governments, whose incompetence and pursuit of their own short-term interests had exacerbated the misery of the Palestinian people. If there was a worthy cause to support, it was the cause of the Palestinians, who otherwise would end up destitute in refugee camps, breeding a homeless and disillusioned people from where popular discontent would eventually erupt violently in every direction.

Doubtless disturbed by the audience's polite claps at the end of my speech, the Mayor awoke and rose to the rostrum. He thanked me for my most informative talk adding that 'my' Prime Minister Ben Gurion[13] had already greatly impressed him when he explained the political situation on television the day before. With the pronouncement of Ben Gurion as Prime Minister of the Arabs, I realised the Palestinians could not, at least for a long time to come, win the war of the Western media. I also realized, simultaneously,

---

13 Israel's first Prime Minister (1948–53) and (1955–63)

that Hussein Dallal was wise – I should not pursue a career in politics!

The only problem with not entering politics is that you end up being ruled by someone stupider than you.

— Socrates

Ben Gurion had come to tour England while I was a student. He was extensively on the radio and television and made an excellent case for the state of Israel. The mantra, however blatantly absurd, 'a people without a country for a country without a people', nevertheless resonated lyrically. Jews were part of the Judaeo-Christian culture, much more understandable to the Westerner. The Zionist propaganda machine moved into full swing backed by influential and wealthy Jews in Europe and America. Anyone who criticized Israeli policy was simply branded as anti-Semitic. A ridiculous accusation when one recognizes that Arabs are also Semites. It is inevitable that whoever has the power and political-will will prevail.

• • •

The Arab Students Union in London took part in protests and demonstrations to relay their frustrations over Israel, the Algerian War of Independence and the Suez Crisis, but to little avail. Therefore, they turned to supplementing their agenda with social activities and competitions, such as the amusing and highly competitive sleeping competition. After three days without getting out of bed, Ghazi Ayub, one of my close friends, emerged the victor. As he accepted his prize, he modestly proclaimed that he slept like everyone else, only slower.

Ghazi was a great practical joker who occasionally wore mismatched shoes. On one occasion, when he went to get them cleaned, the polisher pointed out that the shoes did not match. 'I have another pair just like them,' Ghazi sighed. 'My father is a very simple man and they cheated him at the shop in Baghdad by selling him two mismatching pairs. The strange thing is, in one pair the left shoe's black and the right is brown. In the other pair it's the other way around.'

Ghazi went on to marry a Welsh girl who accompanied him back to Iraq, where he became a senior member of the Ba'th Party and the Director of Industry. In the late 1970s, during a difficult period for Saddam, as he tried to consolidate his power, a referendum of senior party members was called to consider whether he should temporarily step down from office. Ghazi and a few others voted in favour. They were charged with treason and executed. His wife and three children were kept in Iraq under surveillance before eventually managing to flee the country. Such was the fate of many of the intelligent and capable potential leaders. Most of the political systems in the Middle East made a mockery of democracy because there was never any room for dissent or even differing opinions.

One day, Ghazi, a few others, and I strolled into Speaker's Corner, in Hyde Park. We were listening to a communist ferociously attacking the government and the Royal family. Ghazi had a scooter with him and kept it running, fearing a police raid, as would certainly have been the case back home. One policeman indeed did approach us. He asked Ghazi if he could kindly turn his scooter's engine off as people wanted to hear the speaker. I learnt to admire much about the West's respect for freedom of expression. It was strange to see how a government respected people's opinion and allowed criticism, and how this helped to strengthen the fabric of society, rather than weaken it, as most Muslims believe. In the East, dissent is associated with treason. Public opinion is of no importance and an unknown concept. The ideological 'righteous Caliph' of Islam which, following the death of Imam Ali, had ceased to exist had, nevertheless, ingrained in the Muslim psyche the concept of a divinely guided ruler. The ideal of the model Prophet King, ended up giving the king all the profit and his people nothing.

As you are so will you be ruled.

— Prophet Muhammad

The by-product of these unjust rulers in the Arab world was the stifling of natural human development and creative potential. In order to secure their rule, potentates would eliminate every remnant of the preceding regime and its power base, thus eradicating systematic and sustainable development. There was no continuation or preservation of what came before. We called ourselves conservative, yet we conserved little of the past in terms of institutions or values. It is sad but perhaps a fortunate reality that all the best records of Middle-Eastern manuscripts, artefacts and history sit in the West. After all, archaeological discoveries were largely pioneered and maintained by Westerners.

• • •

After finishing my degree, I was eager to go back to Iraq and so left before the graduation ceremony. The Iraq I returned to, in 1960, was rapidly changing. On July 14th 1958 there had been a military coup. It was a popular protest against a pro-British government. This expression of frustration due to the failure of high expectations was driven by the rising tide of nationalism, brought to the fore with the creation of the United Arab Republic (the short-lived political amalgamation of Egypt and Syria) earlier in that year.

Faisal I had died in 1933, the year after Nuri Sa'id had negotiated nominal Iraqi independence from Britain (though Britain maintained a veto on all foreign policy). His rash son, Ghazi, took over. Ghazi's pan-Arab sympathies and support for the Palestinian cause endeared him to the population, but not to the British. The possibility of World War II made him a liability and, in 1938, he died in an automobile accident in which it was widely believed the

British were involved. Since Ghazi's son, Faisal II, was still a minor, until he reached maturity his uncle Abdul'ilah ruled as regent. Faisal I, it was said, was able but unpopular. Ghazi was popular but unable. Abdul'ilah was neither.

Faisal II was my age and when his mother, Queen Aliya, died. School delegations from across Iraq had been sent to Baghdad to give condolences. I was selected to lead the Karbala group. The Harrow educated Faisal was nice looking, polite, hesitant and dominated by his uncle. He stood no chance when a group calling themselves the Free Officers of Iraq, in imitation of Nasser, descended on the royal palace (not much more than a modest villa), the radio station and a few other strategic installations. Faisal, Abdul'ilah, Nuri Sa'id and several others were murdered. Thus was born the bloody Republic of Iraq and it has been bleeding ever since.

Following the 1958 coup, the responsibilities of the President were taken over by a three-man Sovereignty Council, comprising of a Shi'a, a Sunni Arab and a Kurd. The Shi'a, Abdul Majeed al Kamouna, was a member of the same Kamouna family who were our neighbours and regular visitors to the *Burrani*. Real power, however, was with the leader of the coup, General Abdul Karim Qasim, who assumed the role of Prime Minister.

The revolution introduced compulsory military service in Iraq, but after my medical examination, I was exempted because of 'flat feet'. Later, I found out what I actually have is 'fallen arches', common enough and in no way a hindrance to military service. I was, however, grateful for the ineptitude of Iraq's military medical examiners. Within a couple of months, as expected, I was employed by the Iraqi Petroleum Company (IPC) and so set off to take my place in the burgeoning oil industry with the largest, most efficient and most prestigious employer in the country.

Shaykh Zain ul-Abidin seated centre with his sons.
Shaykh Armad, the author's father is to his right.

Above: Shaykh Armad, the author's father.

The author with Sufi Barkat Ali of Pakistan

Above: Bibi Fadhela, the author's mother.

Shaykh 'Abdalqadir As-Sufi and the author

Above: A typical old courtyard.

Below: Old part of the city of Baghdad.

An arched covered street in Nejaf.

Karbala street scene.

Kufa street scene.

Above: The Great Mosque of Imam Husain.

Bedouin woman and child on a camel

A main street leading to the Shrine of Imam Husain.

Exterior and interior of the Shrine of Imam Husain.

7

The Curse and Blessings of Oil

And We shall afflict you with something of evil and
good as a trial. And to Us you will return.
— Qur'an (65: 63)

In 1927, at Baba Gurger, well number two, near the town of Kirkuk, northern Iraq, oil gushed from the earth and has been flowing ever since. A clever Armenian, Calouste Gulbenkian[1], had brokered the concession for oil exploration with the Ottomans on behalf of a consortium of oil companies. The concession had been agreed upon just before the outbreak of the First World War, but when war broke out, the Ottoman Grand Vizier had not as yet formally recognised the claim. The outcome of the war scarcely made this a problem.

In anticipation of Iraq's oil potential (and strategic position), the British prepared to invade Iraq, even before the Ottomans entered the war. The Mosul area, in which the initial oil explorations were situated, had already been designated as being within the French

---

1 Gulbenkian took 5% ownership in the Turkish Petroleum Company (eventually the IPC) for his efforts – and was subsequently known as Mr. Fivepercent. An interesting anecdote on this colourful character was the case of the world's most expensive chicken as related by his son, Nubar, in his autobiography. In June 1939, Calouste took his son to court, angry at Nubar having charged a chicken to an expense account while he was working at his father's office. The long and convoluted court case eventually ended when Nubar withdrew a court action and Calouste paid his son's legal costs, amounting to some 30 000 pounds.

sphere of influence. But at San Remo, the French and the British Prime Ministers, Millerand and Lloyd George, hammered out an agreement whereby France, in the form of the national French oil company *Compagnie Francais des Petroles* (CFP), agreed to relinquish Mosul to Iraq in return for a stake in the oil.

The initial consortium morphed and the company that emerged from this agreement was the IPC – the Iraq Petroleum Company. It had four main shareholders, CFP, Royal Dutch Shell, a US consortium (that included Exxon) and British Petroleum, each with an equal share of 23.75%, with responsibility for the management resting with BP.

Throughout the Middle East, the Western multi-nationals and governments were clamouring for the prize of the century – 'black gold'. In 1952, *Time Magazine* described how[2]: 'On a lonely stretch of sandy, salt encrusted coastline ranging from Oman to Iran, in lands so parched that clear drinking water is a luxury, the greatest treasure hunt of modern times goes on.' But as *Time* warned, 'This is no gold rush for amateurs.' Already the West had invested $2 billion in the Persian Gulf area; it was the biggest overseas venture of US big business. The US and Britain competed feverishly, if covertly, for a Sheik's favour, each Cadillac presented by a friendly US company seemingly met by a Rolls Royce coming from London.

Nothing prepared the Middle East for its destiny as the source of vast oil reserves that the west coveted so voraciously. Had there been no oil, it seems highly unlikely that the west would have shown much interest in the politics of the region. It is primarily due to the massive scale of oil explorations in the early part of the twentieth century that the people in the area came under the direct influence of the western powers.

In Iraq, petroleum exploration and extraction had been approached with a degree of caution and was initially slow. Time

---

2 Time Magazine, March 3rd, 1952.

had noted, 'Iraq's oil is a big 'if'. The oil is there alright and it has been since recorded in history. Noah caulked his Ark 'within and without with pitch' taken from bitumen springs in the Tigris and Euphrates Valley. Just few hundred yards from where, Nebuchadnezzar cast Shadrach, Meschach and Abednego into the fiery, oil-fed furnace. Yet, Iraq's past output has been paltry compared to its potential. Moreover, its future seems hazy and filled with portents. The jinx of Iraqi oil is an incredible series of double-dealings, involving the British, Germans, French, Americans and the Dutch'.

By the time I joined the IPC, the future of Iraqi oil was not so hazy. The blue flames of the wells burned as a bright prospect for the future. Oil revenues were climbing exponentially. Oil revenues that accounted for 7.5% of state revenues in 1948, accounted for 90% of revenues by 1980. The centre of the oil industry was Kirkuk and it was at the IPC compound near Kirkuk that I was stationed.

> *Two starving men cannot be twice as hungry as one;*
> *but two rascals can be ten times as vicious as one.*
> — Bernard Shaw

Cut off from the realities of the world around it, several hundred modern houses lay nestled in the IPC camp surrounded by hills and valleys that were crisscrossed with rivers and matted with scrub. Inside the camp were all the amenities of suburban England. Impeccably sculpted lawns adorned bungalow-lined streets, with names like Essex Lane, Norfolk Road and Somerset Avenue.

Beyond the perimeter fence, Kurdish herdsmen tended their sheep and goats as their ancestors had done since pre-Biblical times. At night, the cackle of the hyenas reminded one's ears, even when the eyes could not see, of the incongruity of the camp. This was a world apart from the world outside.

Only in spring, when the valleys burst with blossom clothing, the earth with crimson, violet and indigo and the heady scent of the wild tulips and narcissus wafted over the mountainside were we reminded of what lay beyond the camp. Then, the searing sun would scorch the munificent soil, the delicate flowers would return to dust and their fleeting fragrance would wane into a lost memory. Then, the familiar sulphur saturated air prevailed and petroleum reclaimed its ascendancy over one's senses.

For several years, the camp was home and my newly wed western wife had joined me there after my return from England. The company had its own infrastructure: telecommunications, aircraft, a huge fleet of cars, shops and restaurants. It was an efficient mini-state within a dysfunctional state.

Life was made comfortable for those staff members such as me who were grouped as 'covenanted staff' – the top stratification in the 10-tier employee categorization. As one of the British educated Iraqi elite, my salary, even as a junior engineer, was as much as a government minister's in Baghdad. Life had a hypnotic and secure rhythm about it. The camp had a cinema, hospital and a nursery school, but when my eldest two daughters were of the appropriate age, they were not allowed to attend the school, as it was for expatriate children only. Thus, I sent them to a Catholic school in nearby Kirkuk.

The town looked up to the company as its wealthy benefactor. Regularly, the company would help with the supply of water, electricity and fire fighting assistance. The camp had an exclusive club where a Lebanese Christian manager organised the entertainment and the well-to-do people of Kirkuk would do whatever they could to gain entry. The camp even had a Freemason Lodge.

Although very much a Western institution, Freemasonry had its roots in the Middle East, beginning at the time of the brief Crusader colonisation of the Levant coast. With the subtler, but far more extensive re-colonization of Eastern lands, a number of Muslims from the upper echelons of society became Masons.

Several prominent Islamic leaders and reformers were

Freemasons – people who were at the forefront of bringing about changes in governance and education in their societies. Men, such as Amir Abdul Qadir (1808–1883), the Algerian resistance fighter who for 15 years opposed French rule, and Jamal al-Din Afghani (1837–1897), an Iranian who spent time in India during the 1857 Mutiny, which made him hate the British. He promoted pan-Islamic schemes and the political education of Muslims, campaigning strongly against the corruption of the then Iranian Shah Nasiruddin. Mohammad Abduh (1849–1905), a famed legal reformer, *mufti*[3] of Egypt and close friend of Afghani was also a Freemason; as was Malkum Khan (1833–1908), an Armenian Muslim, born in Isfahan, who was Persian ambassador to Istanbul and London and a vocal commentator on the economic and political backwardness of Iran.

It was men like Malkum Khan and Afghani, who encouraged the transition in the Muslim world from a focus on religion to nationalism. They questioned the prevalent blind obedience to authority. They advocated emulating western society, even as they opposed the western powers, and ascribed Muslim backwardness to a lack of reasoning and not adopting scientific rationale.

> ***Trust in God, but first tether your camel.***
>
> — Prophet Muhammad

Some of my relatives had become Masons, one of whom, my cousin, Ali Majeed Khan, held the prestigious job of the Iraqi Secretary of the State Railways. He would occasionally come and visit me in Kirkuk to add some colour to our sleepy camp life. When I asked my relatives why they became Masons, the answer was similarly convincing to the one I got from Ismailis in Karachi many years later, 'The brotherhood amongst the members was better than what one finds amongst many Muslims within the same

---

3 A legal functionary, usually in Sunni Islam, who is empowered to make decisions of general religious import, called a '*fatwa*'.

family.' This brotherhood extended to numerous services and Ali Majeed had even gone to the Royal Freemason hospital in London for medical care. There was no equivalent safety net available to any Muslim group.

• • •

My upward progression at the IPC was swift. When I first got there, the company's senior staff was overwhelmingly foreign, mostly British with a few other Europeans and Americans. The repercussions of Mossadegh and Nasser's nationalism and nationalisation, and the emergence of a class of western educated people such as myself, hastened the 'Iraqisation' process – replacing expats with Iraqis. The company was, of course, hesitant and would often warn the government against a speedy transformation.

Despite this, the results were better than expected. Within five years, the number of foreign senior staff was halved whilst productivity and efficiency increased. Interestingly, a somewhat similar improvement had occurred when the Suez Canal was first nationalised and Egyptian engineers and managers operated the canal.

The new Iraqi graduates were well qualified and motivated. We had a unique identity as the burgeoning elite and shared a warm camaraderie. We were eager to perform and impress. It was a period of great hope and expectation, not just in Iraq, but also in the entire 'Muslim world'. It was when 'the rest' were going to start catching up with 'the west'. The potential was vast and my generation was supposed to fulfil it. On a practical level, the expatriates were experienced and competent, even though very few of them had university qualifications, but their loyalty was first to the company and their country. They were not committed in the same way as we were to an emerging Iraq.

It is the nature of men to be bound by the benefits; they confer as much as by those they receive.

— Machiavelli

The IPC regularly sent me abroad and my trips outside Iraq gave me a gauge by which to judge the changing political climate inside the country. After the first military coup in 1958, the country began to disintegrate under repeated coups, each promising much and achieving little. In 1963, Qasam was killed in a coup staged by his deputy Abdul Salam Arif, with the help of the Ba'ath party, which was led by a military officer, Ahmad Hasan al-Bakr. There is a suspicion that the CIA may also have lent a helping hand.

Ba'athism was a political ideology that had been developed in Syria by an Arab Christian, Michael Aflaq. It entwined Socialism (or state dominance) with Arab nationalism, but the glue that bound it was anti-colonialism. Primarily, it spurned foreign influences. It was a direct result of the impotence and emasculation which colonialism had reared.

The Ba'ath made a mess of their original stint at ruling. Its militia were so disliked that Arif had no problems in getting rid of them. Three years later, Abdul Salam Arif died in a helicopter crash and his brother Abdul Rahman took over. Then in 1968, the Ba'ath came back with a vengeance using their thugs to take advantage of the power vacuum that had emerged in Iraq and helped along by a new surge of nationalism born of the humiliating defeat of the Arabs in the Arab–Israeli War of 1967.

The Syrians were beaten back to the Golan Heights, Jerusalem and the West Bank fell and the Israeli Army once more took control of Sinai. Nasser's airplanes had been neatly lined up in Gaza as an inviting target. Within a few hours the Egyptian air force lay shattered, along with any illusions the Arabs had held that their numerical advantage was a match for Israel's solidarity, competent organisation and technology.

When Arif had first expunged the government of Ba'athists, there was a backlash with many Ba'athists being imprisoned. Sunni Ba'athists, however, managed to survive with light or no prison terms thank to their contacts within the army. The army officers (including Arif) were mainly Sunni, courtesy of the Ottoman and British legacy and the 'refusenik' attitude of the Shi'as.

Thus, when the Ba'aths regrouped, one faction from the Sunni district of Tikrit emerged dominant. Ahmad Hassan al-Bakr was amongst them and he became president. His young relative, Saddam Hussein, who had controlled the Ba'ath militia, was made his deputy. He was the same age as me.

Several of my friends knew Saddam well and some of them were close advisors to him in the early years. He had been brought up in the poverty stricken and harsh peasant environment of Tikrit. Smart and quick to learn, he was guided by his own ideological amalgam, which he perceived vital for the Arab cause – a mixture of historical nostalgia, searching for identity, Nasser's populism and Stalin's iron fist.

> *There are some people who say: We believe in Allah,*
> *but when they suffer harm in Allah's way, they take*
> *people's persecution for Allah's punishment. When help*
> *comes from your Lord they say: we were with you. Is*
> *Allah not fully aware of what is in every person's heart?*
> — Qu'ran (29: 10)

For a while, I was seconded to CFP in Paris. The CFP also sent me for a visit to their magnificent oil camp in the remote gas fields of the Algerian desert. This exposure to Algeria encouraged me to tour the North African coast and Turkey. The political winds were changing direction in North Africa and particularly Algeria and I wanted to see it first hand. I bought an Opel station wagon and together with my wife and two young daughters, set off from Paris, through Spain to Morocco and then on to Algeria.

For 132 years (from 1830 to 1962) Algeria had been subjected to brutal French colonial rule, the longest of any of the Arab countries. Some 300,000 died to secure independence. When I got to Algeria, you could see the fabric of society had disintegrated. The Algerian people were shattered without a clear identity or direction. They did not know whether to look east or west. I found the country like a mansion in which the original inhabitants, having disposed of the unlawful tenants, had no idea how to operate the plumbing or electricity.

The city of Algiers was eerily silent. Just before I arrived, the first independent Algerian government had been overthrown and a military regime imposed. There were beautiful cafes and boutiques, partially empty, wide tree-lined boulevards, but hardly any cars. In the city, amongst civilians or officials, Arabic was scarcely spoken. There was barely an Islamic presence.

I stopped for a couple of days in a town on the Algerian coast called Mostaganem and felt myself drawn to the '*kasbah*', the citadel area that is in the old part of the town. There I found the tomb of a Sufi Shaykh by the name of Ahmad al-Alawi. He had died in 1934 and his '*zawiya*' or centre had been built by his followers out of love for their Shaykh, taking no money for their labours. The reward of his discourses and '*dhikr*'[4] were enough. This man had been a torch for the Algerians in their great difficulties, shedding light on the darkness of his time. Some twenty years later, I came to love and respect this great Sufi, learning by heart many of his odes and expressions of Divine love.

> *'Oh my friend, remember Allah and journey to Him,*
> *Seek the ultimate Truth and know that all creation will*
>   *vanish,*
> *He appears by the multitude of creation and thus his*
>   *people miss Him,*
> *Make sure you remain on the Path and persevere to the*

---

4 Sufi invocations and supplications, often interspersed with Qur'anic recitations.

> **abode of perseverance,**
> **And thus you return to the Beloved, Who is above the**
> **throne and the pen.'**
>
> — Shaykh Ahmad al-Alawi

In Libya, the straight road was endless, desolate and always near the coast running between Tripoli and Benghazi. The ancient Roman ruins of Leptis Magna were still echoing with life, as though the inhabitants had vanished overnight. Further along, the road was strewn with the relics of the Second World War. Battles that dictated the future of millions waged on a desolate expanse of sand – another scene in what appears as God's great comedy. When I got to Libya, the head of the Sanusi Sufi brotherhood was still the king. Soon after, in 1969, Colonel Qaddafi, an idealist from a bedouin background, staged a coup and Libya became yet another Arab casualty of military dictatorship, espousing some hybrid of pan-Arabism and socialism.

In Egypt, I came face-to-face with the legendary stifling Egyptian bureaucracy over the car transit and its German registration plate. My resourceful lawyer cousin, Haider, who was living in Egypt and knew the system well rescued me by taking matters into his hand. He took me along with the documents to the traffic police headquarters and marched straight to the chief of traffic police's office. He walked open armed into the large office and hugged the traffic chief with typically friendly Arab gesticulations. The chief immediately proceeded to sign all the relevant documentation. Upon leaving the office, I asked my cousin how he knew the police chief so well.

'Never met him before', he replied, 'but I made him ashamed that he had forgotten me!'

• • •

Before my North African excursion, I had visited Turkey. There I had wandered through palaces, museums and cities, ancient and modern, reflecting upon victories and defeats past and present. The spectacle of the monumental Imperial Ottoman palaces in Istanbul stood in strange contradiction to Islam's advocation of modesty and humility for its rulers.

Everywhere in Turkey, Ataturk's exaggeratedly youthful pictures beamed out at me. He had been the historical agent who put an end to the outdated decaying edifice of the '*Ottmaniah*'. The 'sick man of Europe' died of the combined ailments of despotism, feudalism, corruption and impoverished ignorant masses. It was replaced with nationalism and the hope of instant emancipation from centuries of denial, hypocrisy, religious confusions and unjust rule.

When the 'Young Turks' and Kamal Ataturk had finally removed the last of the Ottomans, they were left with a country where feudal families ruled, whilst a group of merchants and businessmen influenced events, both bolstered by an official class of clergy whose shallow Islamic sentiment centred on the notion of a historic Caliphate.

During Ottoman rule, the Turkish masses had looked towards their rulers as the vice-regents of God on earth and expected them to bring about worldly success for their people. Yet, for the last two centuries of their rule, the sultans had looked towards the Europeans to fulfil military, financial and even administrative needs.Complicated hierarchies and rituals had been attached to Islam with no real light, except by the Sufi groups that maintained the inner meanings of the rituals. Ataturk later banned such groups.

The Muslim people's lack of progress can partly be attributed to incompetent and corrupt rulers who were obsessed with power and love of this world. The sanctioned clergy kept the people under a frigid time warp, while the sultans lived cocooned in their luxurious palaces.

Whoever presents himself as a leader to people should begin by instructing himself before instructing others, and he should correct by the example of his actions

before he corrects by his words. The one who instructs
his self and corrects it is more entitled to be respected
than the one who instructs people and corrects them.

— Imam Ali

It was just after the Arab–Israeli war and just before the Ba'ath came to power that, I left Iraq, never to return. There was a disturbing echo of something deep, like a volcano rumbling before it erupts and I had a strong feeling that the system was about to topple over. I could not see any possibility of stability in the near or distant future. I was desperate to get away and requested official permission to further my studies abroad, which was granted. Birmingham University had recently begun the first MBA programme to be offered in the UK, and this was my excuse.

Ostensibly, Iraq was still a country of great promise and my family, friends and colleagues were all shocked at my sudden decision to leave. I had a good job and a most promising future in the company. The IPC had recently got its first Arab General Manager, a Palestinian, Dr Hilmi Samarah, coincidentally the brother of my old English teacher in Karbala. Hilmi took me into his office, sat behind his desk and asked me to reconsider my resignation. I told him if he needed an example of how our society was degenerating, he should look at the guards at the Camp's entrance. Usually an Arab man would be shy to look a woman in the face, but the guards of today shamelessly ogled every woman that went through. However, Hilmi tried his best to get me to stay by telling me what a great future I had in the company. 'One day', he said, 'you could be sitting in my chair.' 'I am not so sure', I responded 'that you will be able to keep that chair for long.'

Within three years of my leaving, a broken Hilmi Samarah arrived at my office in Beirut. He had been released after two months in an Iraqi prison that specialised in interrogation and torture. They had wanted him to join the Ba'th and he had refused. I offered him to join an oil consulting partnership I had recently formed and he accepted.

8

New Horizons

*There is no fixed abode or station for the one with
intellect. Thus, roam the earth as a stranger. When
the water stops flowing, it becomes a swamp, unfit for
drinking. And unless the arrow leaves the bow, it will
not hit the target. And if the sun does not set, life would
be monotonous.*

— Sayings often related by Shaykh Ahmad Haeri

The fall of 1967 marked the dawn of new horizons in my life on an
outer, existential level as well as on an inner, spiritual one. I was at
a major turning point and there was to be a substantial shift in my
inner and outer understanding of reality. With this shift came a
desire to comprehend the role of a spiritual objective in one's life
and the part religion plays in the lives of individuals and nations, in
the Middle East as well as elsewhere.

Having escaped Iraq on the brink of chaos, Britain seemed
less austere and much friendlier than before. My time in
Birmingham exposed me to the best of Britain's academics in
business, economics and statistics. Nonetheless, for several months
after graduation, I was without a suitable job. I had applied
for dozens of posts and with each rejection I sent out seven
new applications. I was determined to persist as I had a wife and
daughters to support and at one stage not enough money for the next

month's rent.

It was at this point that I was invited to the IPC's London headquarters by Dr. Samarah, who was on a visit to the UK. He served me a lavish lunch in the directors' dining room and offered me a salary, three times as much as anyone with my qualifications could hope to get in England. I would be given the contract out of Britain and treated as an expatriate with an annual return fare to the UK. I was flattered and tempted, but my inner conviction persisted that my future did not lie in Iraq.

> *None of you will believe unless he believes in the decree*
> *– its good and bad, its sweetness and bitterness.*
>   — Prophet Muhammad

Soon after rejecting the IPC offer, I got a job in a small prestigious recruiting with offices in London. The senior partner, William Key, was also the managing partner and after having interviewed me for an oil company client, offered me the opportunity to join his firm instead. After a year of professional exposure to international consultancies, more doors opened.

I was rewarded for my patience and determination by being offered a director's position with a large computer-consulting subsidiary of BP. While at the IPC, I had had a stint at IBM and this proved useful for working at the cutting edge of computer technology. I was soon assigned to open up offices and markets in the oil producing countries of the Middle East from a Beirut base.

> *One prospect lost, another still we gain;*
> *And not a vanity is given in vain.*
>   — Alexander Pope

For a couple of years, I was preoccupied in setting up consulting offices in Beirut, Tripoli, Tehran, Kuwait and regularly visiting other emerging oil producing countries looking for appropriate computer related work for the company. This included bidding for the tender for Saudi Arabia's first comprehensive population census.

Although I was the most senior member of the six-member team designated to carry out the negotiations, I quickly realised that the Saudis, like most Arab government officials, put a premium on European '*ex-er-perts*', as they were called. Sadly, Arabs could not trust one another on technical or scientific matters. How could I be an Arab '*expert*'? They felt it was best to entrust the programme to western, blue-eyed boys, the 'real' specialists.

The 'foreign expert' attitude in Saudi Arabia was echoed in other Arab countries, proving how far our people are from trusting themselves and other Muslims. Arabs and Muslims pay lip service to brotherly feelings, but in truth, many trust outsiders more. A glance at the history of Muslim countries reveals that non-Muslims were often in charge of finance, military security and other sensitive matters. A deep cultural and religious malaise has brought about a confused identity and lack of confidence and self-reliance.

The most ignorant people are those who leave the certainty of what they have for the assumption of what other people have.

— Ibn Ata' Allah Iskandari

Saudi Arabia in the 1960s was very different from the Saudi Arabia of today. Riyadh was a small dusty town with mud houses across from date orchards. There were a couple of uncomfortable, cockroach-ridden hotels and shabbily built government offices. This was the beginning of its transformation from a small medieval desert citadel into a bustling and polluted capital. By the mid 1970s, the municipal authorities of most towns or cities in the country had brought in Korean, Filipino or other cheap imported labourers to sweep streets and clear garbage as the vanguard of the 'cleanup'.

The state of Saudi hotels was an indicator of the ineptitude of the early transformation. In Jeddah, the largest hotel was the Red Sea Hotel, consisting of a few dozen grubby rooms with cheap synthetic curtains and dusty, stained carpets. The situation was even worse in Dhahran, the main town in the east of the country, where most of the oil is produced and where Aramco's headquarters is located.

On a visit in 1971, I had booked in advance at the only hotel. It was midnight when I arrived from the airport to be met by locked doors at the hotel's main entrance. After some loud banging, a sleepy Sudanese face greeted me and offered me a choice of any of the twenty rooms on either floor.

I discovered my initial choice had no glass panes in its windows and swapped with the room next door.

'Is there any food in the hotel?' I asked hopefully.

In a kitchen crawling with cockroaches, the friendly Sudanese man pointed to a refrigerator and told me to help myself, as he headed back to bed. A plate of stale bread and an opened tin of cheese accompanied me to my room.

An hour or so after I had fallen asleep, I wakened to the shattering of a fallen plate. Turning on the light, I was confronted by several terrifyingly large rats fighting over my leftovers.

• • •

Beirut, by contrast, was a far cry from Dhahran. Here, east met west with successful and symbiotic understanding. The bustling seafront, near the old port, had become a stylish pleasure spot on the Mediterranean Sea. Beirut had developed into the hub of Middle Eastern business, finance and recreation. The 'Paris of the East' was abuzz with international oil companies eyeing the emerging Arab world with cash in hand and a desperate urge to buy a position in the oil rush.

Everywhere in the petrodollar Arab world, new roads, schools, universities, hospitals, housing projects, airports and ports were being built at breakneck speed. Million dollar contracts soon became billion dollar mega projects.

It was in Beirut that many of these projects were hatched and negotiated. Huddled together in luxury hotel bars, oil consultants, company executives, business spies, bankers, entertainers and crooks drank imported wine or spirits and plotted their moves. The city was the playground for the rich of the east and west and an arena for every imaginable (and unimaginable) mischief. With money and the right contacts, you could do practically anything you wanted and many did.

> ***Love of money brings about additional desires and concerns, which increase proportionally with the increase in money.***
>
> — Sufi Abu Ahmad

My position as a western educated Arab put me in an advantageous position. I was at home in the east and understood the west and this is where they met. Beirut offered me the right business exposure and opportunities. Thus, after two years of consulting activities and having obtained a few contracts for my employers, I decided to leave my cosy salaried position to take on new entrepreneurial ventures on my own. My old firm retained me for a while as a consultant, but within a few months I had set up, in Beirut, one of the first Arab oil consultancy companies.

• • •

It was early morning in Kuwait airport, on a routine business trip, that I caught a glimpse of a distinguished looking man who would transform my perspective on life in a dramatic and long-lasting way. He had a long beard and wore saffron robes, with the Hindu *vibhuti* mark on his forehead. His regal yet humble bearing intrigued me. We boarded the same plane and I was immediately drawn to him. I went over.

'What is that coloured dot on your forehead?' I asked.

'Sit down, sonny', he said.

I was quite taken aback by his response. Here I was, after all, my own boss and a successful consultant in the booming oil industry and this slim figure in saffron appeared clearly unimpressed.

'You are not asking about the dot', he continued, once I had regained my composure and sat down.

'You are asking about happiness, truth and life's purpose, about really deep joy and being in a state of constant well-being and contentment.'

'I was just curious', I protested.

'Your curiosity hides a deeper search', he responded confidently. 'This sign on my forehead brought you to me. Unless a human being is rubbed like sandalwood, the oil will not come out, the truth within will not yield its essence. In our culture, if a person emerges after the morning meditation without this mark, it means he is so disturbed that he is disconnected from the One and is left alone.

'If there has been a bereavement or some other shock for the committed seeker, he is permitted to go without this ritual for three days, no more. On every other occasion, we apply it on the forehead to seal off the fact that we have totally submitted to our essence. Then we begin to seek who we are, why we are here.'

This man's charisma, frankness, humility and freedom of soul captivated me and left me hankering for more. My heart yearned for him. His name was Swami Chinmayananda, an Indian Brahmin, Sanskrit Master and Guru.

Little did I realize then that I too had left quite an impression on the great teacher.

'You stormed into my life and I feel I am still reeling from its effect', he wrote in a letter shortly afterwards.

Swami Chinmayananda was in my heart and mind all the time after our meeting. I did not undergo a 'spiritual crisis' that often seems to follow such momentous meetings, but I felt moved and touched in ways that were new to me. Until then, I had been a restless soul, always moving on in my existential situation, seeking community, a home. On a deeper level, though, I was contented with whatever state I was in, whether it was ignorance or stupidity or restlessness. The love of my family and the early years of close-knit community life in Karbala gave me a solid inner confidence.

I became aware, to my amazement, that as long as Chinmaya was alive I would be challenged. I would not be able to rest in peace until I realised the source of peace within myself, through his companionship. For me, he was an emancipated soul.

I had met and grown up with a number of people who were truly enlightened people, especially my father, but seldom had I seen one being who I sensed knew fully what I did not know. I felt love in its most wholesome form. Suddenly, it was like looking in the mirror; the closer I looked, the more I could see.

Swami Chinmayananda's basic teaching was to do with making people aware of the interconnectedness of mind, body, spirit and the environment they inhabited. I learned from him that we have this overriding impulse to match, harmonise and balance all these elements, which then leads to heightened awareness. With increased awareness, we could see ourselves more clearly.

From then on and for several years, as often as I could, I visited India or wherever Chinmayananda was to be in his joyful company. The nature of my consultancy work gave me the luxury of being able to spend time in self-discovery and awakening to truth. My earlier visits included sightseeing tours to Hindu temples – the Ellora cave temples in Aurangabad and other great monuments, all works of art with spiritual meaning, purpose and dedication.

Much of the organised life in ancient India revolved around religion. The ultimate goal was to evolve towards higher consciousness and pure awareness and, thus, constant connection to the Divine source. The great temples, caves, and spectacles of pilgrimage were all means of shedding images, to realise the Divine light that permeates creation. Although different gods and idols proliferated, worship ended up at the altar of One Atman, the One Soul.

Chinmaya's ashram, called '*Sandeepany Sadhanalaya*', was in a beautiful park, an hour's drive from Bombay (now Mumbai), later to be engulfed by development and housing estates. I learned many fundamental lessons at the ashram. During my second prolonged visit there, one of the lessons was taught by a family of local monkeys.

On arriving at the ashram, I had told myself that I would only eat the food available there. But I soon found this increasingly difficult to do. I especially longed for some decent fruit. Then one day as I was sitting and listening to a talk, I saw a big bowl of fruit being carried past. I presumed correctly that the fruit was a gift for me from a friend and so I excitedly started to visualise what I was going to do with the fruit. I saw myself eating all the choicest pieces and distributing the rest. After the talk, I hurried up to my room, but when I got there I found monkeys all over the place – there was scarcely any fruit left.

Each one of us is in the right atmosphere and environment for our evolution. Don't try to be more intelligent than universal intelligence – stay where you are and start opening.

— Swami Chinmayananda

Chinmaya's relationship with me and my family was very close. He loved my two young daughters, who had visited India with me several times. He had told them that whenever they were upset and things were not working out to 'put a chocolate in your mouth, then look at the world, and you will find it agreeable.' He called them his 'chocolate girls' – able to see perfection through a layer of chocolate.

My mother constantly feared that I would convert to Hinduism. No amount of assurance could reduce her anxiety and concern. It was only years later when I took up teaching and writing about Islam in the US, that she felt reassured about my loyalty to Islam.

I never denied Islam or my heritage. But up to that time, it had not given me spiritual fuel like my time with Chinmaya had. Our relationship was founded on an understanding of subtle realities and entirely based on grooming the self for enlightenment. It was never an issue of religion or conversion. Now and then, he would make a passing remark as a joke about the religiosity of a pious Hindu pundit or a Muslim mullah, pointing out that they were both ignorant, with which I agreed. There was never any glorification of Hinduism or any other 'ism.' He always spoke about the One and opened for me windows and doors to tawheed (the Oneness of God).

When I met Chinmaya I was not a practising Muslim, but a ceremonial one – praying only the Friday prayers or prayers for other special occasions. I was not in the grip of the rituals of Islam. It was he who nudged my return towards them. Every time I arrived in his presence, he would almost shout out to me, *La ilaha ila'll'ah!* (There is no god but God) or *Assalamu alaykum!* (Peace be upon you). Unknown to me at the time, every such exuberant greeting by the master was turning me to my own heritage and traditions.

> **To teach the common people bare truths without the aid of fables, stories, allegories and the like is almost an impossibility.**
>
> — Swami Chinmayananda

I knew Chinmaya to be a true teacher because he was very faithful to the path of transformation from the Divine light, found within the self. The path is about awareness of the higher in you and about pure consciousness, which is the key to all levels of enlightenment. When you are centred in your heart, there is no need to remember what you said – it will not be 'on the one hand this and on the other hand that.' The self, which is the shadow of the soul, will then totally follow the movement of the soul and the appropriateness of the moment.

The perfection of the moment can only be understood if you look at it through the light of the soul, which is the Divine gift to humans. Being with him, I became aware of how reflective we can be and how forgetful, too. If I was away from Chinmaya for longer than usual, I started to feel confused and broken. On meeting him again, I would explain wearily:

'I have kept to all your prescriptions of meditation and outer practises to maintain my inner hygiene and still I feel shattered.'

He would reply: 'You are talking like a driver on the highway who says, 'I was fully awake for five hours, but fell asleep for a minute,' he said.

In an interview on Beirut television, early in 1975, Chinmaya was asked his opinion on Lebanon and the situation there. He simply said the country was beautiful. When pressed to comment on society or people, he reiterated softly and slowly that its mountains, land, sea and nature were beautiful. Privately, however, he was clearly concerned.

In an elevator one evening in Beirut, Chinmaya turned to me abruptly and asked seriously, 'What are you doing here?'

I tried to explain that Beirut had everything anyone could desire from the east or the west.

He put his arm around me and warmly said, 'Therefore it will also have the worst of the east and the west.' He sounded perturbed and as we were getting into the car, he looked at me intently and said firmly, 'You have no business being here.'

Only a few months after this encounter civil war erupted and I was forced to leave. Beirut and its 'Paris of the East' reputation contrasted starkly with Chinmaya's stoicism and total dedication to wisdom and inner transformation. He taught me that when money pours in through the door, wisdom flies out of the window.

The avalanche of western material development and progress was inevitably sweeping across the Middle East. The Muslim and Arab world, where the roots of religion were planted in too shallow ground, could not withstand the onslaught. The signs were on the horizon and it showed in all political, social, and economic events. The Arabs had fallen in love with wealth, comfort and petro-power without having truly earned it. This new dependency was like a drug, supplied by the western consumer of the fossil fuel – a case of instant 'west-intoxication'.

The civil war and the destruction of Lebanon was, as other events had been, an advance warning of the general disintegrating fabric of Muslim and Arab societies in the Middle East. Lebanon had been a clearing house between east and the west, whose dramatic collapse exposed a much wider and deeper rift – like an echo of 1492 and the fall of Granada in Spain with subsequent centuries of disconnection and mutual suspicion between the European Andalusian community and their neighbours.

> **Say: 'Oh people of the Book, come to a word that is just**
> **between us and you, that we worship none but Allah,**
> **and that we associate no partners with Him, and that**
> **none of us shall take others as lords besides Allah.**
> — Qur'an (3: 64)

A curious event occurred just a few weeks before the full-blown civil war broke out in Beirut in 1975. This was a delightful incident, which shows how with innocence, faith and trust, the best will always happen.

Foad Sami, a distant cousin whom I had not seen for many years, had come to Beirut for a brief holiday to escape the intensely hot summer in Iraq.

Foad was a simple, honest man, who worked in a government department in Baghdad. He phoned me one evening to ask for urgent help. I had to alert the concierge that I was expecting a visitor, as the main entrance to the apartment block was locked due to Beirut's street violence. He arrived promptly at half past eight in a disturbed state. This was at the time when sniping and kidnapping were rife in the country.

Foad had never before travelled outside Iraq. It was his life's ambition to visit Damascus and Lebanon. He had always longed to be photographed with his wife and children in some of the resorts, amongst Lebanon's beautiful cedar trees and ancient ruins and shrines. After a week's stay in Damascus he had come to Beirut in a taxi which had delivered him to a local hotel in the old quarter of Beirut, near the well known Martyrs' Square.

When Foad had settled in his hotel room, he discovered that his camera was missing. At the time, no one was permitted to bring a camera out of Iraq unless it was declared and recorded in the traveller's passport. Anyone returning without it would be sure to face severe penalties, possibly including imprisonment.

Foad was very nervous and concerned, and so was I, albeit for different reasons. He had put on a lot of weight and I feared he might have a heart attack if he did not calm down. He had already gone to the police station the day before and lodged a complaint of theft.

'They didn't seem at all interested,' he exclaimed indignantly.

'But can't you see the situation in the whole country is disintegrating?' I asked. 'Just this morning the editor of a prominent newspaper has been kidnapped. There's chaos all around. The police have enough on their plates without running after petty criminals who steal cameras.'

Foad kept interrupting me with, 'Mal al-hallal ma yathee' (that which is earned honestly will never get lost). I can still hear the sonorous tones of his deep voice invoking this mantra repeatedly. At times, it felt as though we could not communicate with each other on a normal, practical level.

Suddenly, Foad hit upon a solution and asked if I could introduce him to a lawyer. I wondered to myself whether the legal fees would be more than the cost of a camera, but due to Foad's concern of the Iraqi customs officials, I called my lawyer and put the two in direct contact.

After a few days, Foad phoned me to say that he was not happy in Lebanon and that he wanted to go back to Iraq, armed with a police report in the hope that this would ease his way through customs. He again reiterated on the phone several times, '*Mal al-hallal ma yathee.*' I truly marvelled at his faith and stopped myself from expressing doubt and scepticism.

'I wish you a safe return,' I said.

Three weeks after this event, the situation in Beirut really heated up. Miraculously, however, a letter arrived from Iraq in Foad's beautiful handwriting. Foad first expressed gratitude to God Almighty followed by large calligraphic lettering in Arabic: *Mal al-hallal ma yathee*. He then proceeded to recount the story of his return journey.

After a bit of questioning, the customs people let him go through out of sympathy for his two children, who were by now sick. As they entered their home, on the sideboard by the entrance was his camera awaiting his return.

The neighbours who had been looking after his house in his absence came over and explained that a Lebanese businessman had arrived the week before to deliver the camera. Apparently, the Lebanese man's wife was watching from their apartment and had seen the taxi driver put the camera on the roof of the car whilst off-loading Foad's baggage. She was shocked when she saw the taxi driver retrieve the camera from the taxi's roof and drive away with it.

She felt badly about this mistreatment of a foreign visitor to Lebanon, so she noted down the taxi number plate and insisted that her husband pursue the case. The husband was doing well with business transactions in Iraq and the wife pleaded to him to perform this gesture of goodwill and generosity, which might even bring blessings in his business dealings in Iraq. She was obviously a religious person and was outraged by the robbery.

And on Allah you should rely if you are believers.

— Qur'an (5: 23)

*'There was One, there was no one, other than God
there is no one.'*

'In a village along the Euphrates River, there was a pious peasant
who lived in true contentment with whatever came to him. He saw
only goodness in every situation that presented itself. There was no
fatalism in his attitude, just a simple man's realization of the miracle
of existence and the perfection of the Creator and His ways.

One day his donkey died, and the people came to express their
sorrow at his loss. He would have nothing of it and saying, 'Praise
be to God', went to bury it without distress. The next day his
cockerel and chickens got a disease and again he said, 'Praise be to
God, the All-Generous and All-Wise.' The following day his dogs
ran away, yet he remained unwavering in his praise and trust that
'God, the All-Generous' only bestows generosity, although we may
not understand the greater picture. Some of his neighbours thought
that perhaps the series of disasters had deranged the man.

A week later a group of robbers came upon the village at night.
As the village was widely spread, the only way the raiders could
discern where the houses were was by the braying of a donkey, the
crowing of a cockerel or the barking of a dog. By dawn, every
house had been burgled and ransacked except our pious peasant's.
Allah had saved him through the losses of his animals. (End of
story).

When relating this tale, Umm Hussein would hasten to add the
meaning behind: It is not that you welcome every disaster without
discrimination, but if something has happened, and you then see the
goodness in it, you will emerge wiser.

'And Allah knows best.'

• • •

I loved my time in Beirut. It was an exciting and hypnotic city of
contrasts and contradictions. However, it was clear that we were

living on the edge of a political volcano that might erupt at any time, although I was unaware of the scale of political turmoil that was to ensue.

The new horizons that appeared for me in Beirut ranged from the grossest worldly exposures to the most subtle spiritual openings and insights. The shameful extravagance and wastefulness of rich individuals, especially the ostentatious Arab weddings and receptions, contrasted harshly with the dreadful hunger and destitution of the poor and needy all around. The old world where traditional values and cultures – in isolated and self-governed communities – were being mercilessly uprooted by the new global culture of material pursuits and corporate power.

The cruel war in Lebanon forced me to make a hasty departure during a lull before the approaching storm. The next period of my life echoed the restlessness and confusion of my search for true belonging. For nearly two decades after leaving Beirut, I was to travel east and west looking for safe havens and people whose agenda in life was balanced between this world and their real purpose and direction in existence: to know and serve their Creator and not be enslaved by their unevolved lower selves.

Time has come to bid farewell to the mulberry tree,
To the faithful ancient olive bark;
For the time has come to embark
On the journey to meet destiny.

— Sufi Abu Ahmad

9

Cross Currents

Islam began as a stranger and will return as it was at the beginning.

— Prophet Muhammad

From the shockwaves of Lebanon until some twenty years later, my life went through a disturbing yet fruitful period of discoveries. The greatest gift was the ability to travel extensively, not as a tourist escaping the drudgery of bland middle-class life, but as a modern nomad searching for meaning and understanding amidst the confusing and conflicting currents of east and west.

This long period of wandering and restlessness was steadied by faith in God and an inner conviction that it would eventually lead to inner restfulness. There was certainty about the ultimate outcome of the journey, but apprehension about the unexpected twists and turns that my journey would force me to undergo.

Every now and then I found myself descending into misty, dark canyons and then suddenly facing endless desert plains without previous experience or prescribed guidelines, like the kites seen from the rooftops of Karbala, I was blown by the winds of destiny, fluttering up, down and sideways, the only control being a flimsy string – the breath in my lungs.

This state led me towards inner reliance and trust in the Glorious Creator and His purpose. Life begins with trusting the mother, then the family, then a widening circle of others, until the time comes for the discovery that the origin of all trust lies within the soul – a reflection of the Divine trust.

> *All I have seen teaches me to trust the Creator for all that I have not seen.*
>
> — Emerson

As Lebanon was exploding, I set up base in room 407 of the Sharjah Carlton in the United Arab Emirates, the first western-style hotel to be built on what was then a sparsely populated coastline. The almost empty beach stretched for about one hundred kilometres towards Abu Dhabi. Abu Dhabi had been a small desert camp with a square mud fort where the ruler, Shakhbout, lived.

It was rumoured that Shakhbout was upset to discover the paper money the British were giving him for his oil was being eaten by rats in his cellar and thus he insisted on being paid in gold bullion. He was most cautious and hesitant in spending his accumulating fortunes. This was an unacceptable state of affairs and thus Shaykh Zayed, his 'progressive' younger brother, eventually replaced him.

Abu Dhabi's neighbouring emirate, Dubai, was a trading settlement along a creek with a hundred-odd mud houses on either side. The ruler's small income came from duties on the cargo from the wooden dhows plying the creek to the Persian and Indian coasts. This included legitimate trade as well as gold smuggling. There were a few hundred metres of tarred road and the centrepiece was the town's only roundabout, a clock tower, whose hands were more often stationary than moving. Other than that, there was little else in Dubai, not even a traffic light. Dubai was not yet a commercial hub with a huge income to spend on western goods and ostentatious living.

> *Every people is subjected to a trial and the trial of my people will be through wealth.*
>
> — Prophet Muhammad

My family settled in an apartment in London, whilst I commuted between UK and the Gulf. In Sharjah, I moved into a small house with Narayan, my Indian Brahmin servant, who had served Chinmaya in the Himalayas and was on loan to me. He was a pure, perceptive soul. I never needed to ask him for anything, he would pre-empt my needs. I would arrive back in the Gulf from a trip abroad, without warning, yet he would have anticipated my return and would greet me well prepared.

●   ●   ●

The material development in the Middle Eastern countries was such that you could almost see the cracks and breaks in the socio-economic, political and cultural fabric of the communities.

The winds of change had blown into a storm that swallowed everything in its wake. In search of refuge or answers, some simple-minded folk became attracted to reactionary, unworkable and conservative or fundamentalist movements. The failure to maintain and develop self-governing societies connected to the rest of the world over centuries had left a legacy of desperation. A sincere, honest and pious people took to the hollow recourse of simply blaming imperial powers and 'infidels' for all their problems. Nostalgic, unrealistic ideas and instant solutions prevailed in the hope of restoring a past way of life that had suddenly vanished.

A wealthy man in Kuwait once lamented to me that for generations they had lived on very little, but had all the time to enjoy the desert, the sea and leisurely daily life. Now, they had all the wealth they needed and more, but no time to enjoy anything.

Unaccustomed to the comforts now available, consumption turned to excessive waste and luxury. Indulgence was starkly manifested in the huge quantities of food that was imported and resulted in gross overeating. This caused new illnesses, both physical and psychological. The innocent and impressionable Arabs took an instant liking to rich diets, refrigerators and microwave ovens. Digestive disorders and obesity became common ailments. The traditional import of Somali and Sudanese livestock was replaced by Australian intensively – farmed animal products.

> *Truly, the thing I fear most for my community is illusionary desire and excessive expectation, for desire bars one from the truth and expectation makes one love the world.*

— Prophet Muhammad

One local Arab friend managed to resist the onslaught of a foreign diet. He was exceptionally healthy and strong. We sometimes went night fishing offshore, under the light of the oil fields flares, near an island in the warm Gulf waters. He told me the secret of his well-being was due to his mother accepting only the food that came to her house from its source, on the back of a donkey. Any food that was frozen or had been imported was banned in her home. My father had been similar in insisting that all our food had to be freshly brought in daily with no left overs from the previous day.

When the Prophet Muhammad was asked why he did not store food in his house, he answered, 'If you were to trust in Allah with the trust that is due to Him, He would surely provide for you as He provides for the birds.

Alcohol, forbidden in Islam, became easily available in the Middle East, initially because of the influx of foreign workers and then to satisfy the growing tourist industry. Once I needed to rent a few houses in Riyadh for some European doctors and was surprised to find the prices of the seemingly similar villas varied considerably. Nobody could give me a satisfactory answer as to why this was so until the Lebanese housing agent took me into his confidence by showing me a kitchen cupboard with a well-concealed small electric distillation unit for alcohol production.

He produced a small booklet from behind the camouflaged

wall unit entitled '*The Blue Flame*', which explained, with clear instructions, how to produce a wide variety of alcoholic drinks, such as gin and rum. Aramco had anonymously produced the distillation instructions after several of their employees went blind from poisonous brews they had produced in desperation.

Only a non-Muslim could qualify for a liquor licence (to purchase alcoholic drinks from stores) in the petrodollar Arab lands. This was an ineffectual attempt to fence off western influences. How could the ruling families of these countries lead their populace in Islamic virtues, when they themselves did not always honour them? Their attempts to resist or slow down the onslaught of 'infidel ways' and the concomitant erosion of local customs and values, was and remains ineffectual, clumsy and more often than not counter-productive.

To this day the censors blot out with markers, the semi-clad breasts of foreign actresses pictured in western magazines, while some in the wealthy classes secretly indulge in licentious behaviour, drugs and alcohol. Congregational prayers, following the tradition of the Prophet, are meant to be reasonably brief in order to allow people to resume their daily business quickly. If, however, there is an official present, especially from the Ministry of Religious Affairs, the prayers take on all the pomp and ceremony – and length of time – necessary to impress him, leaving the worshippers hanging on for much longer than they bargained for.

A good example of the façade that is maintained in supposedly Muslim Arab countries can be seen in Dubai's wind towers. These ornate, tall structures had customarily been used to cool houses in the desert heat by channelling in the sea breeze. With the installation of central air conditioning facilities, the towers were made redundant. Nevertheless, there they remain, featuring solely as architectural embellishments, void of any utility, symbols of a past that has no connection with a strange and uncertain future.

'The wine's forbidden', says these honest folk,
But for themselves the law they will revoke;
The snivelling Sheikh says he's without a garb
When in the tap-house he had pawned his cloak.

— Al Ma'arri

In every aspect of life, opposites constantly meet and complement each other. It is experiencing this continual swing between two poles that makes us seek balance and equilibrium. The more I became upset and concerned with cultural erosion, the more I gained insight regarding the Prophetic path and the perfection of the Creator. My outer questions were often matched by inner answers that brought about deeper, subtler understanding and contentment. As Imam Ali has said, 'The answer is already within you.'

In my answers I read warnings at every level that we are not fulfilling the primal purpose of existence – to witness God's perfection and to strive towards realising His truth in every situation. It is a question of yielding to the One and His ways whilst doing your utmost in this world with modesty, courage, wisdom and justice.

As my outer success and financial ease increased, I began to lose interest in obtaining greater material gains. My goal became focussed entirely upon my personal search for meaning and the purpose of life, just as Chinmaya had predicted when I first met him.

It was Chinmaya who sent me along to the next stage in my life when, one day in 1977 in India, he put his arms around me. 'The time has come for you to leave me and return to your people. All you have learnt from me is already present in Islam's heritage. You must look for it, discover it, and live it fully. You must also rise above the institutionalised and structured 'official Islam' propagated by the mullahs and clergy and instead seek enlightenment with the Sufis', he said.

*To be a Sufi means to abide continuously in God and
to live at peace with men; whoever abides in God and
deals rightly with men, treating them with unfailing
kindness, is a Sufi.*

— Al Ghazzali

This felt like yet another abandonment, yet another ejection from the familiar. Rarely had I felt so vulnerable, bereft or directionless. A whirlwind of utter helplessness engulfed my entire being, for Chinmaya had been my guide and the only human being I trusted totally, certainly far more than I had ever trusted myself. It is often the case that an enlightened teacher will do something that seems harsh to those close to him.

Chinmaya had reminded me on several occasions that I did not have to become a renunciate, a Sanskrit scholar, or convert to a new religion, in order to discover the ever-present Truth. The time had now come to move on, but there was anguish in my heart at the separation from my spiritual teacher.

I cannot recall any blow as hard as this separation, but somehow could still see the glimmer of perfection in it. My inner voice said that it was necessary and wise as part of the weaning process, but the self was in agony.

'Who and what can I trust in this world? The solution must lie within me', I would often remind myself now that Chinmaya was no longer there. He had always told me that his soul was a reflection of mine, and in reality, there is only a state of pure consciousness.

Before parting, he gave me a piece of paper with two instructions written on it: First, take the first real opening that presents itself to you. Second, do not concern yourself with things that do not concern you.

*The teaching is the real teacher and the teacher is only
    a vehicle.
If you follow the teaching, you will always have the*

teacher with you.

— Swami Satchidananda

A day after my return to England from this watershed trip to India, I walked into a bookshop located on the ground floor of my apartment-block in London. An invisible guiding hand took me to a far corner of the bookshop, where the esoteric section was stacked. I went straight to a book entitled *'The Way of Muhammad'* and opened it on the page describing the Prophetic conduct: his nobility, integrity, forbearance and other admirable qualities. These attributes reminded me of Chinmaya and inspired me to seek the author of this book, who was a western Sufi teacher.

My dear friend Hosam Raouf who, like me, had come on a scholarship to Britain before returning to work for the IPC until the growing influence of the Ba'ath party made it impossible for him to remain in Iraq, had read a book called, *'The Book of Strangers'* at about the same time I came across *'The Way of Muhammad.'* We discussed our respective books not knowing then that the author was the same man, because different names were used in the different books.

Enquiries were soon made about how to reach the author, Shaykh Abdalqadir As-Sufi. I found that he was born and brought up in Scotland. His family name was Ian Dallas. He had become a writer and was associated with the world of music and films. He had been guided and illumined along the Prophetic path of Islam through a Moroccan Sufi 'Order'[1]. He was now a Sufi Shaykh of the Shadhili Darqawi tariqa and led a community of Muslim converts in Norwich.

As the book was published from California, it took a couple of weeks before I could trace the author's whereabouts. Eventually, after a month or so, one of his devotees came looking for me. A

---

1 The different Sufi orders are known as *'tariqas'* or ways.

young Englishman arrived at the apartment, dressed like a North African travelling trader with a green turban and prayer beads around his neck. Courteously he invited me to visit the Shaykh, who was at the time in London, recovering from a near fatal car accident.

The next day I went to meet him in a flat where he was a guest of one of his followers. He was resting his wiry frame on the floor at the end of a large living room, quite obviously in considerable pain. I could see he was a man of light and I was powerfully drawn to this dignified, forthright Scotsman.

'You are a Sufi Shaykh and an alchemist', he said, as I sat down next to him on the floor. 'Now I know I was kept alive to meet you', he muttered, with his face alight. I was startled and a bit alarmed by what he said. Was he a psychic or one of those aura readers? When I visited him again with my wife, she agreed with me that this was indeed a genuine man of light and truth. For the first time since my wrenching separation from Chinmaya, I felt I might have found my new teacher. I also knew he would be pivotal in my return to Islam although up to this point I had never even considered a spiritual or religious future.

> **The one who goes in search of knowledge is accompanied by angels until he returns.**
>
> — Imam Ali

The relationship between Shaykh Abdalqadir and his devoted Sufi community in Norwich was based on sincerity, trust and commitment to seeking enlightenment. It evoked in me memories of my childhood in Karbala and the reverence and respect people had for my father.The Karbala scene was gentle and sweet, the fruit of centuries of customs and habits continually reinforced and deepened by the passage of time. In Norwich, there was fervour, anticipation and excitement, often punctuated by jagged and jarring events. The sincerity and commitment of the '*murids*' (devotees) in Norwich was reflected in their imitating the Sufis of Morocco in dress, *Maghribi*[2] dialect and other domestic customs, such as the regular serving of sweet mint tea during the ceremonies of invocation (*dhikr*). It was like a small, Moroccan, English-speaking, extended family incongruously living in a dilapidated Elizabethan mansion. Flowing *djellabas*[3] and incense burning evoked the feeling of a zawiya or centre in Fez, yet outside lay foggy, drizzly Britain.

> *Your vision will become clear only when you look into your heart...Who looks outside, dreams. Who looks inside, awakens.*

— Carl Jung

A couple of weeks after our first meeting, I invited Shaykh Abdalqadir to visit the Emirates and stay as my guest in Sharjah to recuperate from his car accident. He arrived at Dubai airport in pain, but in good spirits. We had wonderful discussions; he seemed to understand fully my past pursuits and present needs. In the balmy air near the sea, his health began to improve.

My companionship with Shaykh Abdalqadir led to a deeper understanding of him and his work. He had a desire to move to the United States and establish a base in Tucson, Arizona, so I helped him to achieve this objective. An attractive large house was purchased, which he called the '*Ribat*'[4]. I went there with him.

In Tucson, I rented a small apartment in town, but spent most of my time in the company of the Shaykh and his community. For several months, he was fully engaged in talks, *dhikr* and writing. I was regarded by most of his companions as a

---

2 North West Africa is referred to as the *Maghrib* in Arabic, which means west. *Maghribi* means from the West and is the Arabic dialect commonly spoken there.
3 Robe commonly worn in various Middle Eastern countries.
4 The North African Shadhili/Darqawi Sufis used this name for their compounds which served as sanctuaries and teaching centres. The name literally means fortress. In Morocco, it is the name of the capital.

'special' insider/outsider – a visitor who had access to the Shaykh. Chinmaya had instructed me not to concern myself with what did not concern me and this teaching has saved me from blunders on countless occasions.

I also did not concern myself with the *murids*' personal or community dramas. Some of the followers lacked courtesy and sensitivity towards others and regarded me mostly as a wealthy donor. They had left their own cultural and religious background and had the difficult task of rooting themselves on the Sufi path without an umbilical cord attached to a living Muslim or Sufi nation. To live in the west as Muslims without belonging to a Muslim or Eastern nation made the need for an identity more desperate than most of them could cope with.

'What else am I to do but rescue them from the rubbish heaps of western society?' Shaykh Abdalqadir asked me.

The Shaykh told me one day that he could only help people who were truly fleeing mainstream, materialistic, western life. 'Counterculture' was a label often used by outsiders when describing the group in Norwich. What was, however, most impressive was the clear boundaries, direction and loyalty of the *murids*. They lived their religion wholeheartedly with obvious commitment and zeal; a challenging example to many born Muslims, who took their religion only at its face value.

Do people imagine that they will be left (at ease)
because they say, 'we believe', and they will not be tested
with affliction.

— Qur'an (29: 2)

10

Clear Currents

There will come a time upon people that those who wish to live their faith will flee from place to place and from one hill to another, like a jackal that seeks safety (from harm).

— Prophet Muhammad

When I felt the time had come to leave Tucson, Shaykh Abdalqadir asked me to stay a little longer so he could put me in seclusion or 'khalwa', which also means, literally, emptying out. He felt not only that I was ready, but 'over-ripe' for it. During this period, I was not to see or talk to anyone. My days and nights would be spent chanting the name 'Allah'. This I did in my small Tucson apartment.

My earlier preconceived notion of a far off secluded spot was soon shattered. I had always imagined myself tucked away on some mountaintop (but within easy enough reach of food and other amenities!), with birdsong and nature surrounding me, as I went deeper and deeper into meditative bliss. The reality was rather different.

The apartment was on the third floor of a block of flats located by a highway and the thunderous sound of passing juggernauts day and night. The unseasonal rain, which hammered onto the highway outside and on my windows, continued for my entire khalwa and added to the cacophony of the traffic. For someone with sensitive hearing this was quite a struggle, but surprisingly, I was soon able to ignore the noise.

I was in *khalwa* for three or four days; during that time I meditated and was given simple food. As my senses were denied stimulation, they became more heightened. I would weep every time the man brought me food. The carrots were radiant with light and colour. The peas were merging into what appeared to be a liquid state. It was beautiful.

I had vivid dreams and visions of great beings and prophets, especially the Prophet Muhammad. At one point, I saw myself lifted by him as a mother lifts her baby and carried for some distance across a barren desert, after which I was embraced and walked on by myself. There were many other visions, both disturbing and serene.

The idea of *khalwa* involves complete severance from the world. Periods of seclusion and isolation are necessary for spiritual health and development. They are prescribed and practised by all paths of enlightenment. The world of rationality is causal and its mysteries can only be unravelled through the exercise of a healthy intellect and what appreciation lies beyond. The spiritual world relates to the heavenly, inner, unseen realities in subtle ways that can only be tapped into by exclusion, silence and through transcendental states[1]. Giving up outer awareness and going beyond the world of causality is the only way to reach this subtle world, whose patterns are already in the soul and heart, but locked away for most people. The 'emptying' that takes place during *khalwa* reveals the cosmology of one's inner.

Nothing benefits the heart more than a spiritual seclusion whereby it enters the domain of true reflection.
— Ibn Ata' Allah Iskandari

---

1 It was during one of his frequent periods of seclusion and meditation in a cave outside Mecca that the Angel Gabriel came to the Prophet Muhammad and the first verses of the Qur'an were related.

The make-up of human beings is a combination of two worlds or domains. There is the identifiably physical person, with body, mind and intellect, and there is the emotional and spiritual side – which is more difficult to describe or define. The outer, physical and discernible 'ego' or '*nafs*' – 'lower self' – is the lens through which we relate to and experience this world but this differs from person to person.

The subtler component is the '*ruh*' – 'the soul'. This is essentially the same in each person and is the essence, root and source of life within us – it allows humans to relate one to another. The soul contains all the patterns in existence and the boundless truth, which reflects the eternal divinity within humanity. Only in this context can it be said, 'God created man in his own image.'

> **God resembles nothing and nothing resembles God. Anything that one can imagine about Him is a misrepresentation.**[2]
>
> — Prophet Muhammad

The soul has no possibility but to reflect the truth and to energise the emerging developing ego. The ego has no real independence for it is dependent on the soul for its existence. This is why spiritual exercises, prayers or religious services and devotions are uplifting and desirable. The soul is the only true and durable source of well-being, contentment, and thus happiness. The self or ego is subject to confusing changes. The soul is constant.

We can explain all motivations and desires in life by reference to the soul. Take, for example, generosity, patience, forgiveness and all other virtues. These qualities dwell in the soul, which reflect Divine attributes, and the self tries to mimic or experience these

---

2 There is a Hindu saying in which God is defined as, 'that which we cannot perceive, but by which we perceive, that which we cannot understand, but by which we understand.'

virtues. When you act generously and with tolerance, this is a reflection of the absolute Generosity and Tolerance of God. The person echoes the perfect patterns of the soul without reaching total satisfaction; we are forever worshipping at the altar of these perfections.

The soul is ever content and humans can only have moments of contentment – the absolute contentment of the soul is only reflected in relative terms in this world of change. The self seeks power, whereas in truth, the soul is the source of power – power as a reflector of God, the All-Powerful. The self seeks knowledge and the soul is the source of knowledge as it reflects God, the All-Knowing. The self yearns for all the Divine qualities within the soul and acts in the world to reproduce these states.

That is what was meant when Prophet Muhammad said, 'He who knows himself knows his Lord.' The trouble arises when the self or ego attributes the Divine qualities to itself, whilst in truth it is only a passing shadow without any substance except as a means of realising the light within.

> ***Your ultimate enemy is your (lower) self.***
> — Prophet Muhammad

All outer searches and quests are symptoms and reflections of the perpetual inner call of the soul. Seclusion and periods of withdrawal give one the opportunity to hear the call more clearly. When you hear the original Caller, silence and timelessness, all movements and change cease to exist. The transitory reality is absorbed by the timeless and boundless 'Truth' beyond this world. You come to recognise that, from the beginning to the end, all authority belongs to the One True Author.

You come to know that you do not exist, as you believed before. You die (to the transitory world) before you die (physically and irrevocably). You witness consciousness as a shadow of the Eternal, All-encompassing Divine Oneness. You transcend worldly consciousness to pure consciousness.

Your so-called death in this world is the recognition of the 'ongoingness' of the soul. When the self yields or dies, inner contentment is accessed and realised. This is the enactment of returning to the One through the soul or spirit within. This is enlightenment.

> *Someone once asked him, 'When will the Kingdom of God come?' He answered, 'The Kingdom of God doesn't come if you watch for it. It isn't in heaven. It doesn't come only after you die. No one can point to it and say, 'It is here' or 'it is there.' For the kingdom of God is within you.*
>
> — Jesus (Matthew 22: 17–21)

> *Seek truth – you will find it in your self. Therefore, know yourself.*
>
> — Prophet Muhammad

After a few days – the *khalwa* period usually lasts up to forty days[3] – inner awakening for the mature or ready seeker may occur in special and unexpected ways. After I emerged from seclusion, I wrote a letter to Chinmaya to thank him for his love and patience with me. 'Only now the obvious has become obvious', I wrote, with tears of joy streaming from my sleepless eyes.

> *True knowledge enables a man to realise that he is the soul with a body. Now, in his ignorance he thinks that he is a body with a soul.*
>
> — Swami Chinmayananda

---

3 Khalwa is sometimes referred to as '*chillah*', a Persian word, which means forty. This is derived from a Qur'anic story of the Prophet Moses, who left his people for forty days to go into seclusion.

It took about six months after khalwa for me to readjust to the outside world for I was feeling exceptionally vulnerable and found normal human activities, such as driving a car or being driven, unfamiliar and even frightening. The immediate effect of *khalwa* was to see the fallacy and uselessness of everything that one had previously considered important and significant. Whatever people considered as being responsible action or generous service was seen now as merely ignorant, short-term selfishness and self-deception.

I could see how every aspect of the lower self was demeaning or distracting, while at the same time there existed in the heart a most sublime essence and light, reflecting the primal truth of God's eternal light. My constant companion was the knowledge that everything in life has a reality, but none of it is durable compared to eternal Truth.

The Giver is One, and all of creation are receivers, it is not a question of finding God so much as realising that He is already within you and is the instigator of your needs and search. God is already there and has been there and everywhere, before time and in time. God is within you and around you, before you and after you.

In the Qur'an, God tells us that he is closer to us than the jugular vein. It is just that we do not always recognise this. There is a famous Christian story in which a man is looking back on his life as represented by footsteps in the sand. For most of the way, there are two pairs of footsteps in the sand and God tells the man that he was with him every step of the way. But the man notices that on the low points or difficult times in his life, there is only one pair of footprints and so he asks God why He left him in the times of difficulty. To this, God responds that those were His footprints for He was carrying the man.

In the Islamic tradition, there could never be another pair of footprints besides those of God. To presume this is to presume there is an 'other' and this is to be mistaken – for there is none but God.

*You are not veiled from Allah by the existence of
something that exists with Him since there is nothing
which exists with Him. You are veiled from Him by the
illusion that something exists with Him.*

— Shaykh Abdal Qadir al Gilani

The first thing Shaykh Abdalqadir asked me after khalwa was to teach Qu'ran to a group of ladies in his Ribat at Tucson. The Divinely revealed Book seemed now illumined, accessible and transformative. This was the first time I spoke and thought spontaneously, without effort or self-concern. From my childhood I had never felt the need for the label of a profession or occupation, but this new state took over. When people asked me a question which moved my heart, the answer came to my lips in spite of me! I had no option but to share what is not mine and submit to what comes through me.

Shaykh Abdalqadir gave me the '*idhn*' or permission to practice as a Sufi shaykh of the Shadhili order. Subsequently, two other Sufi shaykhs have given me the *idhn* of the Chishti and Rifa'i orders (incidentally, shaykh is a title I have never been very happy with, especially because of its connotations in more recent years and its spurious use). Because of my reluctance to teach, Shaykh Abdalqadir would, in jest, refer to me as 'the reluctant shaykh.'

I found myself in this new position without any desire for it. It was what God had allotted for me, and though I may have preferred to run away from it, it was my appropriate destiny. This feeling was re-enforced by my mother, aunt, brothers and sisters, who gave me a number of the family items from Karbala. Included amongst these were the prayer mats of my father, grandfather and great-grandfather, Shaykh Ahmad, Shaykh Muhammad Hussein and Shaykh Zainul Abideen. A couple of years before he died, my brother, Danish, had given me one of our father's rings, which he had from his youth. And, touchingly, the year before he died, my eldest brother, Sadrudeen, sent me Shaykh Ahmad's Qur'an (traditionally given to the eldest child) with a note saying that I was the heir to it and he had just been looking after it for me.

One day, Mashti told us a story about God's will and destiny.

'There was One, there was no one, other than Allah there is no one.'

'There was a young prince whom the soothsayers predicted would preside over a great new kingdom. When the prince grew up, he became an ascetic, fasting all the time and avoiding worldly desires, interests or attachments. A time came that he could no longer stand the excesses of his father's kingdom, so he left for the mountains with just one sarong.

He climbed up beyond the mountain villages and beyond the tree line to where there was a great plateau with a stream and a few shrubs, which produced the berries for his subsistence. There he found a cave and set up his frugal residence, content in meditation and fasting.

After a few weeks, the people of the surrounding villages heard about the presence of the prince who had forfeited his throne to lead a life of asceticism. A few of them decided to make regular visits to be in the company of such a sincere and godly man. They would continuously ask him if they could do or get anything for him. He always refused their tempting kindnesses.

As the visitors increased in number and regularity, he realized that it would be embarrassing if anyone were to see him while he was washing his one sarong in the river, so he accepted the offer of another cotton sarong. The new sarong soon arrived and the people continued to come – being more worldly and attached, they were challenged by this man, so free and detached. One does not want to be incumbent with the things of this world.

For a time, the prince was very content with his two sarongs, but then after a while, he began to notice that soon after he washed a sarong and left it on a bush to dry, field mice were tugging at it, damaging it and continuously moving it to another location. He thought it would be a good idea to have a cat.

This request was transmitted to the men from the villages and a cat was brought up the next day. The mouse problem was soon resolved, but the cat became very unhappy as the mouse population diminished. The prince, reflecting on the condition of the cat, concluded there to be no harm if there were a cow that could be milked for the cat. The cow arrived but our prince found that it too required maintenance. He was cautious not to let worldly activities engulf him or distract him from his joyful meditative state and so consented to the cow being looked after by a poor old man from the village.

Time passed with the prince, the cat and the cow living in harmony on top of the mountain, but the poor old man was growing unhappy. The mountain air, fresh milk and yogurt had quite rejuvenated him and he longed for company. The old man approached the compassionate and understanding sage prince and asked for permission for another person, preferably an elderly lady, to join him. The prince could not deprive this old man of such a basic request.

As the elderly lady arrived, she made her own demands. One thing led to another and within a year there was a small village. Within three years, there was a kingdom, presided over by a wise ascetic king. The moral is you cannot control what finally comes to you as part of destiny. This is influenced by the wishes of others as well. The prince gracefully submitted to what was written and remained in blissful contentment.

And Allah knows best.'

• • •

At the time of the *khalwa*, I realised that the outer rituals of Islam cannot be separated from their inner meanings and the inner meanings would not gel unless encased in the outer rituals. I gained particularly from prayer or *salat*. Some people find meditation frustrating because they have been unable to reap the benefits of it quickly – it is not for everyone. *Salat*, however, is useful for everyone and rewards people according to the level they can manage.

At the very least, leaving aside the spiritual benefits, for the duration of the *salat* you can stop an argument, stop being angry and stop other stresses. *Salat* takes you away physically from distractions. You stand facing the Ka'aba and praise and thank your Source. Then you bow, seeking entry into the inner sanctum. Then, you 'disappear' in the prostration, your 'you-ness' hidden in submission. If you are able to 'plug in' properly, especially with the prostration, it gives you increasing access to an inner dimension. I found that the very core of the salat for me was the prostration, *sajda*, which is the ability to disappear from all sensory stimuli. It takes you into a subliminal state or a state of sensory deprivation and therefore into a state of spiritual rejuvenation.

I do not like proselytising, but when people came to me for guidance, I could only guide them to what I had discovered. I would say to them if you can do your *salat* properly, put your head down and disappear, then the inner, higher dimension of you will appear.

The only way I could talk to westerners interested in Islam was by expanding on the inner meanings of Islamic worship. As time went by, I found that Muslims needed this knowledge just as much if not more. They needed to know about the transformative part of the rituals they performed.

Trying to fulfil this need became an ongoing quest and source of great benefit for me as I researched, both in existent Islamic literature as well as through experiencing these rituals, the inner meanings of ablution, prostration, fasting, and hajj. There had already been a good deal of literature produced on the subject, but usually not presented in a way the modern Muslim or sincere seeker can assimilate.

• • •

Soon after leaving Shaykh Abdalqadir, I felt I needed to contribute something to the people and the land where I was, in this case the US where I had spent such a beneficial and enjoyable time. Perhaps there a haven for seekers could be created – a working and functional Muslim community. This would be something I could provide, even in my capacity as a 'reluctant shaykh'.

Whilst I was searching for a place to set up the centre, I came across on a map, a tiny town called Medina in the hill country of Texas. '*Medina*' in Arabic means 'city' and is the name of the city where the Prophet Muhammad established the first Islamic community. I took this sign as a good omen and travelled to tiny Medina and the nearby large town of San Antonio. In San Antonio, I stayed at an attractive hotel built around a Spanish style courtyard. When I called room service, the man who answered the phone spoke with a Persian accent. Recognising this, I told him I had not eaten a decent meal for several days and would very much like a rice dish. Hussein soon arrived at my room carrying a pot of food that his mother had cooked for his supper.

Within half an hour, he was enthusiastically encouraging me to set up the centre there. Later on that evening, he brought along a few members of the small Persian community of San Antonio. After a few days, I felt at home there and Allah made it easy and pleasant for me to think seriously of a teaching base in the area.

I first bought a property perched on a hill to the north of the city. To the existing house, several buildings were added, including a small wooden cabin for myself. This secluded room without any furniture was my home for three years. Soon a group of Sufi men and women gathered around for teachings and worship. As the numbers increased, farmland, half an hour away on the route from San Antonio to Austin, was bought. On this 140-acre land, a spacious community centre was built with sufficient accommodation for over a hundred people.

I planned that 'Bayt ad-Deen', as it would be called, was to be a place where people could come and stay for a few weeks or months to learn and feel they were in a dynamic community. At the time, I had no full-fledged programme of learning apart from the Qur'an and the basic practices of Islam. I did not have a modern curriculum, but was able to create the 'hardware' and arena for it. As the 'Institute for Quranic Studies' developed, Razi Bilgrami, a retired Pakistani Brigadier General came out of retirement to administer it. He was a man of great integrity who devoted himself to the work

Even at the time, I had a sense that I would not be wholly successful at establishing anything that was sustainable there. The whole edifice was far too dependent on my input alone. That is not how a community should be. So I designed a large teardrop shaped grassy patch at the entrance to symbolise the fact that I could only shed a tear on this land and depart.

The reward in this for me was that the people who came were sincere and serious seekers, fairly representative of the American public, who were healthy, positive, generous, but also cut off from the rest of the world. It was through the people who came that much opened up for me. Indeed, people arrived from different parts of the world and from diverse professional backgrounds to attend talks or to live on the land. Cultures as diverse as Indians from the Sub-Continent, Persians and Arabs to Native American Indians, White Americans, South Americans, Slavs, Britons and many others. A number of these people were new converts to Islam.

We were in that teacher/learner mode on a daily basis and the setting was beautiful, quite idyllic. Not too gentle a landscape, rocky but with beautiful lakes and waterfalls and a delightful climate. The whole setting was very suitable for diving into the Qur'an. Therefore, for me, it was truly a period of going into the inner meanings of the Qur'an on a daily basis.

We dwelt upon Arabic terminology in the Qur'an at great length and with great depth. We examined the sources and the roots of key words, for the root of the word often reveals far more than the word itself. This allows greater access to the nuances and vistas contained within the single word. The Prophet Muhammad has described the Qur'an as having many levels.

I noted that serious seekers who wanted to learn the Qur'an found Qur'anic Arabic very easy. It took people within six months to a year to read and understand it better than many Arabs. The Arabs tend to take it for granted that they understand a particular word to have a certain meaning, whereas the word has deeper layers and flashes and sparks resonating within it, above and beyond its specific usage.

The Qur'an is always difficult to translate. However, it must be made accessible and therefore translation is essential, but it makes sense to leave some of the terms with multiple meanings as they are. One example is *Iman*, which means 'to have trust and faith with knowledge', rather than just 'belief'. There are probably some 300–400 such terms that must be preserved. Otherwise, the language will be denuded of its subtleties.

Whilst at Bayt ad-Deen, I often arranged for some of the more serious seekers to travel the world, as the Americans lacked this international exposure. I arranged for several groups to travel to India, Sri Lanka, Pakistan, and the Middle East for Hajj. On one occasion, 19 people were sent for Hajj.

When they returned, I thought it would be good to hear their impressions of their trip. Each one of them said that had they not embraced Islam in the US, they would have rejected it after seeing the conduct of Muslims. People who have come to deen, expecting the right conduct and quality of good character from those born into the deen, are disappointed!

For me, Bayt ad-Deen represented real spiritual growing up, the discovery of the foundation of Haqq (Truth) and Nur (Light). It was my Meccan period, in a way. It was to do with inspiration, revelation, the light of creation, the perfection of it, delighting in it, and the beauty of the Qur'an.

Generally speaking, we lived in Texas in relative peace without outside interference despite the conspicuous nature of the centre. We did have a difficult neighbour who brought several legal suits against us, including accusation of stealing stones from his property. Finally, his long suffering wife divorced him and came over to show us photographs of her husband shooting his automatic rifle towards our buildings. She eventually embraced Islam and married a Tunisian.

On two occasions, FBI helicopters came to investigate the place, but they soon realised we were harmless and that they were wasting their time. This was two decades before every Muslim became suspicious, but after the Iranian Revolution, western governments became more generally suspicious.

Say (O Muslims), 'We believe in God and in what has been revealed to us, and what was revealed to Abraham and Ishmael and Isaac and Jacob and the tribes and what Moses and Jesus were given and what all the prophets were given from their Lord, We make no differentiation between any of them. And to Him we have surrendered.

— Qur'an (2: 136)

The 'Islamic Revolution' in Iran erupted in 1979, when Ayatollah Khomeini, riding on an incredible wave of popular support, swept the Shah and his American backed regime aside. This shocked the Americans to a point of hysteria matched only by the hysteria of the anti-American demonstrations in Iran.

The Shah had aligned himself totally with the US and Israel and when the Arab countries withheld their oil to certain Western countries, which had aided Israel in the 1973 Arab–Israeli War, Iran stepped in to bridge the gap. After 1973, Iran became the most important buyer in the world of American arms. The secret police, SAVAK, brutally suppressed even the slightest evidence of dissent to the Shah's autocratic rule and kept him and his political elite out of touch with the popular sentiment.

One commentator describes how, 'The celebrations of the 2500th year of the Iranian monarchy, staged in Persepolis in October 1971, were the epitome of all that separated the Shah and the small elite surrounding him from the rest of the Iranian people. The ceremonies were financed and conducted on a grand scale, but ordinary people were only used as mere props. A huge tent city was set up to house foreign heads of state at the foot of the plateau on which the ruins of Persepolis stand. It was designed in France, manufactured with the most costly materials and filled with the most luxurious furnishings, all imported. The Shah's guests ate French food and drank French wines. The high point of the proceedings was a ceremony at the tomb of Cyrus the Great, the founder of the Persian empire, where the Shah reassured his predecessor that he could sleep in peace 'for we are awake'!'[4]

It did not seem to matter to the Shah that he was the son of a subaltern with no connection whatsoever to the past glories of Iran, nor did he mind (or was it an advantage?) that Persepolis was inaccessible to the general population. Like others had done before him throughout the Middle East, he dissociated himself from his country's Islamic history, despite his people's deep religious beliefs, and harked back to romantic notions of what had gone before.

> *Vain the ambition of kings*
> *Who seek by trophies and dead things,*
> *To leave a living name behind,*
> *And to weave but nets to catch the wind.*

— John Webster

Ayatollah Khomeini returned from exile in France to Tehran as the undisputed leader of the Revolution. The foreign powers had little

---

4 Baqer Moin, *Khomeini: Life of the Ayatollah*, p. 163–164.

understanding as to what was really going on in Iran. They had minimal comprehension of the country they had been manipulating for so long.

They set out to try and determine whether the Ayatollah was on their side, and once it was realized he would not toe the American line, he was vilified in the Western media, particularly after the US embassy hostage crisis in the early 1980s[5] . At the time, the spectre of the 'American' Mossadegh coup, though alive and remembered in Iran, was seldom mentioned in America. It has been recognized by a number of commentators[6] that the inflamed anti-US sentiments in Iran were a direct result of the US role in re-instating the Shah and supporting his rule. The Mossadegh coup had been orchestrated from the US Embassy in Teheran in 1954. It is also easy to see against this backdrop and with the Shah seeking refuge in the U.S., why the American embassy should have been a target for the angry masses.

> ***Finality is not the language of politics.***
> — Benjamin Disraeli

The first time I had heard of Khomeini was when he was in exile in Iraq. My impression was that he was a sincere and seasoned theologian with deep Sufi spiritual qualities and wisdom. Saddam's government offered him asylum in the hope that they could use him as a pawn against the Shah. Later on, pressure was put on him to leave Iraq and he chose Kuwait, which had already granted him a visa. At the border, the Kuwaitis were not sure what to do as the Shah's court was reeling in turmoil from the unrest born of Khomeini's popular, anti-Shah discourses, smuggled across the border in audiotapes.

---

5 When students stormed the US embassy in Tehran and held 52 members of the staff hostage for 400 days.
6 The most recent is Stephen Kinzer in his book, *All The Shah's Men*.

Khomeini and his son, Ahmad, were kept waiting for hours at the Iraq–Kuwaiti border post, with nowhere to sit or rest. Ahmad started to curse the unpleasant Kuwaiti authorities, but Khomeini reprimanded him. He told him to look at the meaning and message behind the event. 'Goodness is within whatever has happened', was his constant refrain. He told Ahmad to contemplate the plight of millions of people all over the world who were homeless or displaced. Khomeini was eventually given a visa for France. Soon after arriving at a house in a Paris suburb, he asked his attendants to take flowers to the neighbours, as it was Christmas time. He commented that it was courteous to treat people according to their customs.

Treat people according to their understanding and what they know for people are enemies of what they are not familiar with.

— Prophetic teaching

Shortly after the Revolution, I was invited to visit Iran along with nearly seventy Iraqi dissidents and opposition leaders from around the world. Seyyid Mehdi al Hakim was a close friend of mine and had come to teach at the centre in San Antonio on several occasions. He was one of the most prominent people in the Iraqi opposition movement and was adamant that I should go, insisting that I accompany him on the same flight. A few years later, he was assassinated in Sudan by one of Saddam's hit-men.

The Iran–Iraq War was at its peak and bombs were raining on Tehran when we arrived. As I entered my hotel room, a relative of mine who had helped me to renew my Iraqi passport (not an easy matter) was on the phone from London. He complained that the Iraqi Ambassador, upon whom he had prevailed for my passport renewal, had angrily called him and assured him I was amongst those meeting in Tehran. He had even been given the number of my hotel room. The Iraqi regime clearly had their informers, even in a Tehran hotel.

With this ended any future hope I had of renewing my Iraqi passport. I was only one of the millions of Iraqis who were constantly concerned about their vulnerability regarding their nationality. No wonder one Iraqi friend of mine had become perhaps the world's greatest collector of passports – eleven in all.

Fortunately, the Saddam regime did not concern itself too much more with me – although there was the occasional encounter, as my mother, who had left Iraq and was living with me in San Antonio, experienced on her flight from Egypt to America. She met and was greatly assisted by, a charming and most helpful Iraqi, who was particularly curious about the activities in San Antonio. He transpired to be one of Saddam's more active hit-men. My mother could not believe it when she found out. He had been exceedingly helpful to her, helping her through the VIP lounge and customs. You get what you expect in this life just as one often experiences the worst of one's fears. Allah says that He is as good as you expect of him. My mother always expected the best and so she got it – even from the hands of an assassin!

God says; 'I fulfil the faith of whoever puts his trust in me,
— Prophet Muhammad

The highlight of this trip to Iran was meeting Ayatollah Khomeini in his small compound north of Tehran. We all gathered in a hall adjacent to his modest room. No sooner had we done so than Iraqi jet fighters started bombing nearby and the buildings shook and rattled. It was mid-winter and the chilly concrete floor of the hall was covered only by thin *kelims*[7]. Press and TV presence was much in evidence and I tried to sit away from the cameras, but somehow ended up being seated right in the front. When Khomeini came in, he sat only a couple metres in front of me. Thus, to my

---

7 A type of Persian carpet, which is simply woven with no pile.

embarrassment, I appeared as one of the prominent faces on the news the next day.

Khomeini sat serenely and quietly. The Iraqi dissidents and exiles spoke with passion, defiance and unrealistic hopes, whilst I sat quietly praying for some Divine message or insight. Immediately, my eyes fell upon a word woven in the carpet that separated Khomeini and myself. In fact Khomeini's feet were just above this word: '*irfan*' – 'gnosis' or 'enlightenment'. The metre long sentence in the rug was '*Khanaqah Jamiran Irfani*' – The Jamiran centre for gnosis.

The next day, the Iranian newspapers announced that the meeting of the Iraqi opposition leaders had been a great success, claiming that Khomeini had given them his support. In fact, the Ayatollah did not utter a single word throughout the long gathering. Many things have been incorrectly attributed to Khomeini while other things, sometimes intentionally understated by him, are scarcely known; for example, the influence of Sufism[8] on Khomeini that is clearly evident in his poetry.

> *Oh, I desire a cup of wine from the Beloved's own*
> *hands.*
> *In whom can I confide this secret?*
> *Where am I to take my grief?*
> *I have yearned a lifetime to see the Beloved's face;*
> *I am a frenzied moth circling a flame,*
> *A wild rue seed pod roasting in the fire.*
> *See my stained cloak and this prayer-rug of hypocrisy;*
> *Can I, one day, tear them to shreds at the tavern door?* [9]
>
> — Ayatollah Khomeini

---

8 The study of *Irfan* is essentially akin to Sufism, but is considered 'more acceptable' in the orthodox Shi'a world on account of people's ignorance as to what Sufism entails and the taint of people who claim to be Sufis, but who do not abide by the *Shariah*.

There were both interesting and undesirable people around Khomeini. Dr. Naqshabandy was of Kurdish origin and belonged to a large Sufi group, known as the Naqshabandia[10]. His brother was a popular Naqshabandi Shaykh with over a million followers. He was a cultured and dedicated Muslim with sincere love and trust for the Ayatollah, who had wanted him to take a position in the government. A group of fanatical Shi'a clerics, however, warned him that if he did not leave the country, they would kill him. When he protested that he was in Iran on account of Khomeini's wishes, they said they would also kill the Ayatollah. Eventually he left, disappointed and concerned about the ignorance of the power hungry mullahs.

People in Muslim countries often mistakenly, assume that by virtue of their religious status, the mullahs or Ayatollahs must necessarily be very wise and pious. This is often – but not always – the case. On a later trip to Iran, I met one of the most prominent and powerful Ayatollahs in the Khomeini government. He cornered me and discussed at length issues about which he seemed to know very little, but irrespective of that, forcefully expressed his opinions. His resoluteness made me question myself on these issues. When I managed to escape, I turned to a friend who was present and asked him what he thought of this man. 'He is an ocean of knowledge', responded my friend. At this stage I doubted my sanity, but my friend continued, 'He is an ocean of knowledge…but only 2 feet

9 This poem was published after Khomeini's death. The reference to 'wine' and the 'tavern', that any reader of Hafez or Omar Khayyam would be familiar with, are clearly metaphorical (it would be absurd to claim that Khomeini was not in or did not want to be in Shariah!), but those unfamiliar with such a manner of expressing overwhelming love for the Creator could be misled. Hence, Khomeini's reluctance to publish.

10 The Naqshabandia is the only known Sufi order, which traces the genealogy of its lineage of transmission of knowledge back to Abu Bakr, the first Caliph of Islam. All the other Sufi orders trace their origins back to Imam Ali. The Naqshabandi *tariqa* is particularly strong amongst the Kurds and the former Soviet Republics.

deep!' Certainly, it is a mistake to assume that the size of a man's turban is proportional to the size of his knowledge[11].

Nothing is so good for an ignorant man as silence; and if he were sensible of this, he would not be ignorant.

— Saadi

Originally, of course, Islam did not have a clergy. The reasons for its development were in some cases political, but also because of the lack of education of the public and the limited availability of religious books. A major Shi'a reference book that contains many thousands of traditions as related by the Imams and collected some 400 years ago is called, *'Bihar al Anwar'* – 'The Seas of Lights'. Seyyid Mehdi told me that his father, the most important Shi'a cleric of his time, didn't even have all the 17 volumes that the book typically used to come in (either hand written or printed with 'old style' techniques)[12]. Seyyid Mehdi recalled how his father would send him to a local merchant to collect one of hefty volumes (each weighing several kilograms).

I complained to Seyyid Mehdi about the hypocrisy, arrogance and ignorance of some of the mullahs and religious leaders around Khomeini. He listened to me patiently and then said, 'What do you propose? Should the Imam exile his people and import others from another country? These are his followers and his job is to reform them.' Enlightened men accept their destiny doing their best to serve others at all times, acting with total sincerity and submission to God's will with no expectation of personal rewards.

Khomeini had issued instructions to all religious clerics and scholars (wearing a turban) to declare annually everything in their

---

11 In my childhood turbans were a common headgear. Within 50 years turbans became almost exclusive to religious scholars in the varying ranks. The Arabic word for turban is, *'ammamah'*, the root of which means common or public. Ironically, today it is used to distinguish official religious status.

12 The collection has more recently been published in Lebanon in 110 volumes.

possession, in order to safeguard against a religious position becoming a means of self-enrichment. He was the first to declare all that he possessed. The list was one page long and included personal clothing and books, even those that he had borrowed. He kept his possessions in a wooden chest in his room. Khomeini had freed himself from worldly needs and desires and lived in readiness to leave this life for the boundless hereafter. He was never seen to be anxious, despondent or excited by events and news, whether good or bad. His inner balance and constancy always dominated over outer changes and uncertainties. He witnessed the truth of perfection of '*al khair fi ma waqa'a*' – 'goodness is in what has occurred'.

> *If things do not turn out as we wish, we should wish for*
> *them as they turn out.*
>
> — Aristotle

Although the Islamic Revolution temporarily delayed the erosion of the traditional way of life in Iran, it produced immense expectations from millions of Muslims in every land. It brought to the surface many of the deep sicknesses of the society, which had been neglected for centuries. The advent of Khomeini and the Revolution signified the perennial human need for a balanced and just life on this earth based on constant accountability and reference to the absolute Lord, who had created man in order to be worshipped and obeyed. Muslims everywhere and the Muslims of Iran particularly were given another chance to awaken to the true Prophetic path.

A year after the death of Khomeini, I was invited to Iran to attend the anniversary of the Revolution. It was a cold winter night with a blizzard blowing over Tehran airport as we landed. When I got into the taxi to take me to the hotel, I realised I had made a mistake in coming. The country's political, religious and social life had changed. The spiritual light seemed to have departed. The airport loudspeakers were blaring out revolutionary songs and marches. I knew I had no business there. The days of spontaneous heart-felt actions and sacrifice had now become days of existential hardship, difficulties in reconciliations and defiance of the outside world, which had bought Iran onto its knees.

At 5 am, on the same morning of my arrival, I headed back to the airport. I bought a ticket for the first flight out of Tehran, which happened to be for Karachi, and proceeded to customs. A grim looking airport official shook his head as he inspected my passport, shocked to see I had entered the country only a few hours earlier. 'Why are you leaving?' he asked. I told him I had come as a guest of the government, but I did not want to stay and listen to exaggerated praise and polemics from politicians of the revolution. He smiled at me knowingly and requested, 'Please sir, can I talk to you alone for a minute?' I asked for what reason and he said that he just needed to talk to someone like myself. He closed the barrier and told the queue of passengers to go to the next kiosk behind him.

He took me aside to a quiet corner and said, 'I believe you are a good man and I want to ask you if you think I am acting within the religion or am a sinner. I believe in God, in the Prophet and in being honest and correct, but I cannot survive on the salary the government pays me as an airport inspector. I live in the south of Tehran with a wife and three children and half of my salary goes on transport alone. Thus, I am obliged to take a small personal tax from the passengers, just enough for my family needs. Do you think this is allowed in our religion?' I said that I was not a theologian and could not give him a *'fatwa'* (a religious edict or authorized opinion). He suddenly started to weep loudly, the tears darkening his grey beard. He begged me, 'Please, put yourself in my position, what would you do?' I tried desperately to avoid this emotional involvement, but he was insistent. Eventually, I had to admit that I would probably do the same, if I had no other option. This drama was delaying me for my plane, but he rushed me through a special channel. As I boarded, he thanked me profusely. In many countries, corruption is the consequence of a lack of responsibility of the governments. Government employees are left with little alternative but to compromise their natural dignity and in the process become accustomed to thievery, misconduct and corruption.

> *You are free from that which you despair of attaining*
> *and a slave to that which you covert.*
> — Ibn Ata' Allah Iskandari

The centre in San Antonio, Texas, was visited regularly by several Sufi Shaykhs and men of light. Shaykh Jamali, a Yugoslavian teacher of the Rifa'i Sufi order was one. The Rifa'is had a centre in upstate New York, where the resident master was Shaykh Asaf Durakovic, a Bosnian Sufi Shaykh, medical professor, scientist, poet and a dear friend.

Shaykh Asaf's ancestors were large landowners in Bosnia, who ruled firmly and autocratically over the population. With the advent of communism they were pushed aside and he had to escape from the family estate to Belgrade, where he studied medicine. Then he immigrated to America where he first studied veterinary medicine, then general medicine and eventually nuclear medicine, earning a professorship as well as a senior position in the U.S. Army Medical Corps. He speaks over six languages, beside the Divine language of inner silence and joy.

On an early visit to Shaykh Asaf's centre in upstate New York, there were several other Sufi teachers present from Eastern Europe. During the gathering, Shaykh Jamali performed the Rifa'i's 'Miracle of the Sword'. After a period of invocation and Sufi chanting, he called out several times *'Allahu Akbar'* (God is greater) and then inserted a metre long sword through his abdomen, right in front of me and of my companions. Shaykh Jamali then pulled the sword out smoothly and with ease, without evidence of pain or blood. At the end of the proceedings he hugged us warmly before we left. Razi Bilgrami, who was with me, had expressed some scepticism about this practise before the event. When we got home, a trace of blood was found on Razi's shirt, as a reminder that the event was materially true, although seemed logically inexplicable. Sometime later, through Shaykh Asaf and Shaykh Jamali, I was invited to join the Rifa'i order. I accepted this honour with delight

> *The likeness of brothers is the likeness of two hands*
> *washing each other.*
>
> — Prophet Muhammad

In America, I met Shaykh Muzaffer Al Jerrahi many times. He often related stories of *Ashuras* he had spent in the Dervish tent in Karbala, which had attracted me so much when I was a young boy. His sonorous singing continues to resonate in my heart and ears. Shaykh Muzaffer Khalwati Al-Jerrahi was the Shaykh of a popular Sufi line in Turkey, which continued to flourish in spite of the official ban on Sufis. Each year his group of singers would come to America for '*dhikr*' recitations and invocations that were held in mosques, churches, cathedrals and other halls, attracting large crowds.

Dhikr (or *Zikr* in India and Turkey) is group or singular invocation of a Divine name or quality of Allah. The purpose of the act is to focus the mind and heart on the quality invoked. Through *dhikr*, especially if it is held in the presence of an enlightened teacher, the zone of higher consciousness, from the sound and meaning of what is being recited, becomes more accessible. Through the voice and appropriate thought, one may find it easier to transcend both physical and mental consciousness to a higher realm.

> *God says, 'I am with him and near him, when he*
> *remembers me.'*
>
> — Prophet Muhammad

From my first meeting with Shaykh Muzaffar in New York, I recognised his high station, loved his company and travelled in ecstasy many times along the sound waves of his booming voice. He would joke with me that cigarette smoking was his only vice, as he knew of my aversion to smoking. He would excuse his habit on the grounds that he at least saved on matches by only lighting one match in the morning – from this one, all successive cigarettes were lit.

He had my father's habit of throwing cigarettes across the room at his *murids* (devotees) and visitors. Every few minutes, a cigarette would come flying from his hand towards its human targets. The act was a sign of love and informality between the thrower and recipient. Shaykh Muzaffer exuded tremendous charisma and spiritual effulgence. He owned a small bookshop in the Istanbul bazaar, but during the last fifteen years of his life, he had travelled extensively outside Turkey. His trips to the west would last a few months of every year and his western followers, who numbered many hundreds, were in constant contact with him and would regularly listen to him on tape, or read his books.

During one visit to Shaykh Muzaffer, I asked permission to sing some of the Jerrahi *diwans* (odes). He graciously called a couple of his *murids* and asked them to give me all the tapes that were available. He then declared that I had complete permission to sing and perform *dhikr* according to the Jerrahi tradition. Several of those present were surprised at the Shaykh's open generosity to one whom they viewed as an outsider.

> **Dogs bark at everything they don't know.**
> — Heraclitus

Shaykh Muzaffer's gatherings were attended by a stream of newcomers and esoteric types, including non-Muslims. During one of his early trips to America, there were several couples in the audience holding hands and occasionally embracing each other. This caused several Muslims present at those gatherings to criticise the Shaykh for allowing such 'western' discourteous behaviour in his company. I trusted that Shaykh Muzaffer's patience, compassion, and tolerance would eventually bring about the appropriate conduct at the right time. On his last visit to America, before his death, he announced to a large gathering just before sunset that all those who had been with him during his several visits over the years should by now know how to perform the evening prayers. He then invited those who were able to pray and wished to do so to stay, while those who did not should leave. Several hundreds performed the Muslim prayers that evening. A few months later, his body was carried to its final resting place in Istanbul, followed by thousands of his followers in defiance of the government ban on such mass gatherings. His *murids* still hold circles of *dhikr* in America, Turkey and elsewhere.

> *Pass the rest by follow and love, O heart;*
> *Reality's folk obey love, for their part;*
> *Love is more ancient than all that is known to exist:*
> *They sought Love's beginning, but found it had no start.*
> — Shaykh Muzaffer Al Jerrahi

In the mid-80s, I felt it was time to move on and so I left America without any regrets, and have never looked back. There were other callings, particularly those involving my own understanding and reconciliation with my past and the state of the Muslim people at large. I moved back to England with my whole family, which by this stage was enlarged by six more children, (and was to increase by another two – making up a total of six daughters and four sons). From my new Berkshire base in England, I continued my search and travels.

> *I am satiated and I oscillate between here and there;*
> *always on the move. And I press my impoverishment at the*
> *centre of richness and this is my secret, for my existence*
> *was prior to all manifestations.*
> — Shaykh Ahmad al-Alawi

11

People and Places

He saw the lightning in the east and he longed for the east, but if it had flashed in the west, he would have longed for the west. My desire is for the lightening and its gleam, not for places and the earth.

— Ibn Arabi

Over a period of about 15 years, through the 1980s and early 1990s, the physical component of my search was particularly concentrated. The travelling was partly driven by a desire to satisfy my need for belonging, generally sustained by a yearning to understand, but always directed towards the meaning and purpose behind events, actions and intentions. For this reason, there was an attraction to people with a greater inner knowledge, and places where such knowledge had or still pervaded. In places I have been and the people I have met, I was truly fortunate.

As well as alchemy, my father also practised astrology. On the inside of his Qur'an, he recorded astrological charts for each of his children. On my horoscope, he wrote that throughout my life, I would have good companions and friends. This has come to pass. My friends, associates and family enhanced my well-being and progress, at all levels, and made it easy for me to witness the perfection of life. Even events that appeared as undesirable were seen later on as contributing to my spiritual unfoldment. Humans are like mirrors, susceptible to every light which impacts upon the surface or self. We are affected by what we experience through the senses, windows and channels to the self. If the signals enhance the higher in us, then the self is closer to the soul; otherwise we become more egocentric and drift further away from the zone of inner joy, which is ever-present in our heart.

> *A man said, 'Oh God, make me independent of Your creation.' The Prophet told him, 'Never say such words, but rather say, "Oh God, make me independent of the worst of your creation", for the believer cannot do without his brothers.'*

Many of my travels during this time were in the Sub-Continent. Here, my initial motivation was to establish centres for teaching and living. My first step was to try and set up a model village near Ahmadpur in the Pakistani Punjab. The Punjab[1] district (Punjab means five rivers) is similar to Iraq in climate and agricultural crops, as well as its old Islamic tradition and culture.

The land belonged to Dr. Khalid Iqbal, whom I had met a few years earlier in the USA. At that time, he was a post-doctoral researcher in biogenetics. I had encouraged him to return to the village of his birth in order to set up a model farm and other related agribusiness activities, based on profit sharing with the workers. We established a clinic, a cotton ginning mill and other related business facilities as well as houses, a mosque and a school. The clinic offered homeopathy, physiotherapy and basic education on hygiene and diet for the villagers. It developed a good reputation in the whole province, even becoming popular with some of the wealthier landowners.

It was there that I first met Seyyid Ikram Seekri, a Pakistani Sufi Shaykh of the Chishti order, a *hakim* (Muslim healer) who uses

---

1   The Punjab was divided between India and Pakistan during partition in 1947.

traditional herbal and mineral remedies. A descendant of many generations of Indian Chishti Sufis, he combines diet and herbalism with spiritual guidance and healing.

The Chishtis were amongst the original introducers of Sufism into India some nine centuries ago and were responsible for the conversion of many Hindus to Islam. Moinuddin Chishti is credited with being the founder of the movement, whose roots lie in the *Qadiri* and *Suhrawardi* orders from Baghdad. Singing and chanting were a popular and effective method used by Chishtis to open people's hearts. This was particularly useful in India where music was traditionally part of the spiritual practices. The present day 'qawali' singers of the Sub-Continent have their origin in the spiritual chants of the past Sufi Masters, which were part of their programme for enlightenment.

It was an unusual event that brought Seyyid Ikram to establish a *'khanaqah'*[2] or centre in the Punjab. Seyyid Ikram's chief pupil, who ran the clinic and the centre, was the reason Seyyid Ikram had come to the Punjab a few years before from his base in far away Hyderabad, Sind. The pupil's father had vowed to dedicate his son to the path of Islamic healing when the boy was born, but apparently he had forgotten his vow and became mainly concerned about his son's success in secular studies at the government school.

One day, as the boy was on his way to school to take an exam, he was gripped by severe stomach cramps. He was next to a small bridge and whilst he was immobilized in agonising pain, a ghostly looking man suddenly appeared on the bridge before him. He told the sick boy that only a man called Seyyid Ikram from Hyderabad could cure him and that this man would also be the boy's teacher and guide. He informed the pupil that his father had made a vow and should be reminded of it.

---

2 Sufi Centres are often called '*khanaqah*' in Iran, India and Pakistan. In North Africa, such centres are called '*ribat*' (fortress) or '*zawiya*' (corner). In Turkey and Central Asia, they are also called '*tekkiah*' (where you rest your back) or '*dergah*'.

This strange man had already appeared a few times before in the village declaring that he was a dead Sufi who had been buried some five hundred years ago in Damascus and, once his task was over, he would disappear. The concerned father traced Seyyid Ikram; the son was cured and became the Seyyid's pupil.

My relationship with Seyyid Ikram grew deeper as he took an active part in my work in Pakistan. We shared many wonderful experiences together, including a memorable visit to Moinuddin Chishti's Shrine in Ajmer, India.

We sat together in a corner under cover with the intention to meditate and access the spirit and light of the saint. Soon we were disturbed by the noisy appearance of a semi-naked Hindu fakir, circling the Shrine with incomprehensible gesticulations. I was unable to concentrate and Seyyid Ikram noticed my agitation. I then had to ask him what this fakir's mantra meant.

'He is asking Moinuddin Chishti for a hundred rupees', Seyyid Ikram explained.

'Who will give him that?' I muttered disparagingly.

'Oh! There are all kinds of fools in this world!' said, Seyyid Ikram with a gleam in his eye.

Some fifteen minutes passed and I still couldn't concentrate with this fakir's noisy circumambulations. My mind began to reason that it was worth my while giving him what he was asking for and be rid of the disturbance. The trip had already cost many thousands of rupees and my visit to this Shrine was its highlight. It would be foolish now not to buy peace for a mere hundred rupees.

After having paid the fakir what he was asking for, I returned quietly back to my meditation. Next to me Seyyid Ikram smiled from under his head-shawl and told me, 'Did I not tell you there are all kinds of fools who will oblige such a destitute'?

Such is the '*barakah*' (blessing) of the Shrine, that both the naked beggar and the well-endowed seeker were granted their wishes.

A man of knowledge is like a good date palm which
you watch and wait for something good to fall down.

— Imam Ali

There has always been some controversy about visiting of shrines amongst Muslims. Some Muslims object to such practices, equating it to idol worship and thus condemning it. However, in its symbolism there can be meaning. The love of visiting shrines comes from devotion and respect for those who have travelled successfully before us along this testing worldly path. A person who was illumined and lived according to divine justice in a world of constant change and apparent injustice is worth remembering. Visiting the tomb of a saint is an attempt to enhance the higher in us. A pilgrimage to holy places will benefit us more if we reflect upon the life values of the enlightened being and tune our soul with his to resonate at a similar frequency.

Generally, people's conduct improves whilst visiting a shrine or place of worship. They behave more compassionately and become more tolerant, accommodating and giving. In poor Muslim lands, even with thieves around, you find the shrines are safe as far as rugs, carpets and fittings are concerned. Hardly anyone steals or removes anything that belongs to the shrine even though many amateur and professional thieves visit them and even take refuge in them. In fact, criminals often bring gifts and offerings along with them.

One of my favourite shrines is another famous Chishti shrine in the village of Pakpattan, in the Punjab. Baba Farid, who died there in 1265 CE, was famous for his ascetic life and long periods of seclusion and meditation. His shrine is often full of qawali singers and intoxicated dervishes. On my first visit to his tomb, I felt an immense love engulfing me. On subsequent visits, I felt welcome and at home in the presence of Baba Farid's spirit and light. During the first visit, the shrine-keeper gave me an inscribed green cloth that covered Baba Farid's grave. I keep this grave cover close at hand for use at my own burial.

Don't give me a knife, give me a needle. The knife is for cutting and the needle is for sewing together.

— Baba Farid

It is only possible to visit the Shrine of Baba Ali[3], just off the coast of Bombay, through a causeway at low tide. Beggars on both sides flank the causeway. I had carried a bag of small coins on me to distribute along the long walkway that led to the shrine. As I was leaving the Shrine with its high thick wall protecting it from the sea, my eyes caught the silhouette of a solitary fakir who was sitting on part of the wall. He had long matted hair and beautiful clear eyes. I felt I should give this special man some money but all my coins had already been distributed. So I pressed upon him a 100-rupee note. He held the note between his fingers and let it fly in the evening breeze over the wall. Then he lifted his index finger to the sky muttering '*Omm, hoo, omm, hoo*' (God).

All sense of worldly awareness disappeared, dissolved into pure stillness and light. The wandering sage continued in a deep trance. His ecstasy was contagious as our faces met and our eyes and minds drifted into horizons beyond discernment. My clumsy token gift to him opened up the sublime channel through which this man was travelling and drawing nourishment. These few moments were stretched to timelessness. I am transported to this state every time I recall the visit.

This event and its transcendental effect remain a handy switch in my mind's 'exchange station', whenever its button is pressed. I relayed this incident to some Bombay friends, who were not surprised. They were aware of similar encounters at Baba Ali's tomb and they believed that his soul manifests sometimes to greet his visitors.

• • •

---

3 Baba Ali was a Sufi saint, held in great esteem by many Muslims and Hindus, with many miracles attributed to him.

The famous Sufi Barkat Ali was always alive to the moment, free of past baggage or future fears, living in the now, but beyond bounds. Ever free as a soul, he was ever-enslaved to the real call. I always looked forward and enjoyed my visits to Sufi Barkat Ali, near Faisalabad, in the middle of the Pakistani Punjab. When I first met him he was in his mid-seventies. My visits to him continued at least every other year for fifteen years, until his departure from this world.

Sufi Barkat Ali's centre was called '*Dar al-Ihsan*' (the abode of selfless action). It was an intriguing and most unusual set up a few kilometres outside the town. In this centre, several charitable, educational and religious activities took place simultaneously. There was even a free eye clinic, where daily treatment and frequent operations for serious eye problems took place. Doctors from different parts of the country would perform these operations for the poor villagers as an act of charity.

Dar al-Ihsan housed several hundred children, mostly orphans, who were taught basic reading, writing and Qur'an. There was a large square courtyard in which all the children would sit and chant, whilst in one corner Sufi Barkat Ali would be typing away on an ancient English typewriter. He even wrote to heads of state and other leading politicians inviting them to embrace Islam. There were rarely any replies.

Sufi Barkat Ali had one set of clothes made from locally woven rough cotton, which he wore for a whole year until it was threadbare and full of inkblots. All his old clothes were left folded up in a corner as a mark of the years gone by.

The cooking and feeding of several hundred people who invariably assembled every day at Dar al-Ihsan was quite an affair. At the end of each day, however, no food or perishables would be left in the centre. Everything would be given out to neighbouring peasants and no gifts or charities would be received after sunset. Barkat Ali trusted that worldly provisions would seek the needy, who serve their Lord and obey His commands. He was secure in the presence of the Ever-Generous Sustainer.

Promise me two things and I promise you
enlightenment; no anxiety about your provisions and
no fear of creation.

— Abul Hassan ash-Shadhili

The central building was a high walled mud fort that housed a hospital and museum for Qur'an manuscripts. The several large halls contained thousands of handwritten as well as printed Qur'ans stacked from floor to ceiling. Some of these Qur'ans were so tiny you could hardly read them even with a magnifying glass. One huge book had pages each two meters long.

Hundreds of people would scout for dilapidated, torn and neglected Qur'ans all over the country and from abroad to bring them for Sufi Barkat Ali for repair and proper placement on a shelf. Boxes of broken pages would arrive at the workshop, where a dozen dedicated workers would sift through the materials, reconstruct and rewrite missing pages, then bind the reconstituted Qur'ans before they were placed on shelves in the halls.

In the centre of one of these halls, there were piles of rose petals in different stages of preparation. Sufi Barkat Ali used them as remedies for diverse ailments. There were rose petals of every colour and size, in plates and baskets, scattered all around; only he knew what each was for.

During one of my visits, he gifted me four old hand-written Qur'ans as a special acknowledgement. I was told by one of his devotees that this was the first time such Qur'ans had ever left the centre. Qur'ans came by the dozen, but never left!

On another visit, he gave me eight printed Qur'ans for different centres connected with my work. His students and older followers were always intrigued by my special relationship with Barkat Ali. He had taken a vow of silence, yet whenever we were together he spoke in English and laughed all through our brief delightful conversations.

Sufi Barkat Ali often joked with me about his early life, especially when he was forcibly recruited into the Indian Army only to be released after a few months of service. His British Commanding officer was unhappy about his lack of worldly concerns and after detailed cross-examination, he reported that this man was not suitable for army duty due to 'God intoxication'. Sufi Barkat Ali would grin joyfully, showing the gap left by his missing front tooth. 'God Intoxication, to be mad about God, is the only true sanity!' he would say.

One time, an excited assistant reported to him that the then Prime Minister of Pakistan was visiting Faisalabad and wanted to pay his respects to Sufi Barkat. However, he showed no interest in meeting the politician and prayed for it not to happen.

> *Do not keep the company of anyone whose state does not inspire you, and whose speech does not guide you to God.*
>
> — Ibn Ata' Allah Iskandari

Towards the end of his life, there was some dispute about the trusteeship or management of *Dar al-Ihsan*. This event upset him so much that he decided to leave the place that had taken him decades to build and develop. He simply walked several kilometres away until he reached a river. There he stopped and set up a small new camp. Soon, several devotees and followers arrived and within a few months, a new centre sprung up in this place. Whilst construction was taking place, Barkat Ali would walk around the orchards by the small river, with his five-meter long rosary beads trailing behind him, carried by one or two assistants. Every now and then, he would recline upon his *charpoy*, (a simple wooden bed) for a brief rest.

One day, without prior warning, I decided to visit his new place. Somehow he knew, and had informed his followers to expect me. Just before my arrival, he had even walked up the road to the bridge, near the main entrance to welcome me. When I arrived, he was beaming with his infectious smile, his arms stretched open for a warm embrace. Our hearts overflowed with delight whenever we were together.

Cheerful welcome and a happy face reflect love and closeness to God, and a frowning face and a cold welcome produces distance and ignorance of God.

— Prophet Muhammad

During this visit, I felt embarrassed by the way he honoured me and told his followers that I was his heir. A few Swedish seekers, both male and female, were with me. He turned to them.

'I have in me both the male and female in perfect proportion. I am also the Shaykh for cows', he said.

One of the Swedes asked what he meant by referring to himself as the 'shaykh of cows'. He replied that he is always asked by the peasants who come to him for remedies for a sick cow, for advice on the healthy delivery of a calf, or for increased milk production. Then he added with a mischievous smile, 'You must follow your own Shaykh (pointing to me) for real teaching.'

On another day, Barkat Ali had declared in front of a large crowd of his followers that I am the teacher of the future and I must help to teach the ladies.

'But why the ladies?' I exclaimed!

'Because the men are too distracted and diverted with business and money, the future lies with women who seek knowledge and their offspring who will carry on the work. In our time, most men are misled and will mislead', he replied.

Guide us on the Straight Path. The path of those you have blessed, not of those with anger on them, or the misguided.

— Qur'an (1: 6–7)

I had always thought how fortunate Barkat Ali was in being settled and established in one place, whilst I was constantly roaming the world with no real base or a country to return to or belong to. I told him how I longed to stay with him in this remote rural setting. He then stood up as though on a stage and announced authoritatively, whilst waving his stretched arms: 'You have to go to north, south, east, and to west, you have to travel and teach.' Barkat Ali had obviously already read the course that lay ahead of me and thus, was confirming it by indicating all the directions of the compass.

> ***To will what God wills is the only science that gives us rest.***
>
> — Longfellow

In Pakistan, I had a friend who specialized in locating interesting Sufis, dead or alive. He could almost smell out any sage or dervish with mystical or spiritual inclinations; I labelled him the Sufi hunter. Samandari Baba was one of his recent finds. He had been visiting him for a while, before taking me along one day to meet him, near the shores of the Arabian Sea.

Samandari Baba (the title means father of the sea) lived amongst sand dunes and hills, east of Karachi, near the beach. This was some twenty kilometres away from a new town development and housing scheme that belonged to the Army Trust. He had built a beautiful little mosque, which was always kept locked to remain pure and sacred until the advent of Imam Mahdi[4], the awaited Saviour.

When he had begun building the mosque, an army officer arrived

---

4 Numerous prophetic traditions from wide sources relate that the prophet had said there would come a time when the world is filled with darkness and then one of his progeny will come to this earth to bring justice. On numerous occasions, Muslim leaders and scholars have predicted that this time has arrived. Thus, in the history of the Muslims, you find dozens of people claiming to be the Mahdi, some of who made a big impact upon the people such as the Mahdi of Sudan. Note, that to claim to be 'a Mahdi' (guided one) is very different from claiming to be 'the Mahdi'.

with an eviction order as the land belonged to the army. Samandari Baba was given one day's notice to leave the area. Early the next morning, this officer was taken ill with inexplicable, severe abdominal pain. After a few days in the intensive care unit, the officer's superstitious wife became desperate for any relief for her husband. After hearing about the incident with Samandari Baba, she came rushing to him asking forgiveness and the removal of her husband's pains, which she thought were the consequence of a curse from the Sufi hermit.

Baba asked for a lorry load of cement and another lorry of bricks, as an expiation cost. The next day, after these gifts were presented, the officer was back on his feet. In time, he became one of Baba's closest devotees and his 'official' protector. Eventually, he was promoted to colonel, but still came for a visit almost every evening.

Samandari Baba lived in a small wooden crate, about two metres by one metre wide, perched upon cement blocks, some ten metres away from the mosque. He would sit on a couple of wooden benches in front of his box, whilst one of his attendants would bring us the customary strong black tea, thickened with condensed milk. Several cats jumped on and off his lap, whilst Baba pointed towards Karachi, cursing its inhabitants, its industrial money and military masters. He predicted the doom of the corrupt, abusive government, the army and the unjust businessmen and industrialists.

One starry night, Baba tried to explain how the light and energy of the unseen descends into creation and activates events. He warned that if Muslims do not awaken to the Divine purpose, they would be doomed by their ignorance; which is compounded by the assumption and illusion of living on the proper path of salvation. On one occasion, Baba took me inside the ever-locked mosque and the two of us prayed on the gleaming tiles. It was like diving into a timeless celestial ocean of light.

On a subsequent visit to Karachi, I was informed that whilst Baba was on a visit away from his seashore base, he had departed from this world. Following some inspiration, Baba had travelled to the rocky dry hills north of Karachi to help in digging a water well for the poor peasants living there. After a week or so, he had unexpectedly left this world to the join the abode of constant joy.

> *No self knows in which land it dies.*
>   — Qur'an (31: 34)

As part of my desire to understand the Muslim culture in India, I visited several of the princely states that maintained a feel of the by-gone days. Notable amongst these was Mahmudabad, in Lucknow – a state with particularly strong connections to Karbala and my family. The father of the last Raja of Mahmudabad had been a good friend of my father, and the last Raja had come to Iraq to get married. In recognition of the family connection, my father agreed to perform the marriage ceremony, though it was very rare for him to agree to do this at that stage in his life.

The last Raja had supported the Partition of India and Pakistan and so he left India, first for Iraq (where he stayed in Karbala and Najaf), and then to England where he died and where he opened the mosque in Regents Park, the first mosque in London.

My host in Mahmudabad was Mahraj Kumar, the brother of the last Raja. In its heyday Lucknow was a vibrant centre of Islamic scholarship and culture, but as I went through it, it was very much rundown with very little of the old traditions. Similarly, the once beautiful and dignified '*qila*', or ancestral fort of the Raja's, was crumbling all around. In the once manicured gardens, the grass had died, and the flowerbeds were choked with weeds.

All around the garden were replicas of the famous Shi'a tombs (Imam Ali, Imam Hussein, Hazrat Abbas), and inside each of these tombs was dust from the originals. William Dalrymple visited Mahmudabad more than a decade after me, and wrote about the visit in his book '*The Age of Kali*'. His host was Suleiman, the son of the last Raja, but besides that his description fits almost exactly my own experiences – right down to lunch being served at 5 o'clock!

Dalrymple tells about the fort, 'all flaking yellow plasterwork and benign baroque neglect', of how in the once magnificent library 'cobwebs hung like sheets from the walls (with)... the chintz literally peeling off the armchairs.' He goes on to describe the floors with no carpets and holes in the ceiling with 'bushes sprouting from the fort's roof [5].

After lunch the Mahraj took me into one of the wings and showed me a large *ferman* – a formal decree by a Sultan or chief religious figure. The *ferman* was in a large frame and decorated with beautiful calligraphy that stated the duties of Muslim rulers. The *ferman* was from my great-grandfather, Shaykh Zainul Abideen, and it ended by appointing the Raja (at that time) as his representative in that area, with the duties of establishing charitable institutes and collecting alms.

• • •

Sri Lanka was a delightful country to visit. Attempts had been made to undertake a range of activities there, relating to human development. The natural beauty and simplicity of life around the southern coast and in the eastern and northeastern parts were most appealing, with its mixed population of Tamil, Muslims and Singhalese.

Apart from a planned centre near Colombo, there were other projects in which my close friend Hosam and others had initiated and sponsored. Orphanages and children's hostels were a favourite venue for service. On one occasion, two days after the Eid celebrations, I was taken to visit a boys' orphanage and a school in a suburb of Colombo where we had already been helping with scholarships. There we met a few dozen boys who seemed to be well cared for and lived in a lush rural setting, full of exotic flowers and chirping birds. We then wanted to visit a girls' orphanage.

5 See William Dalrymple, 'Tha Age of Kali', p. 40–48.

Saheed, our host and the Sri Lankan agent for our work, who was from an old and established 'Moor' family, had just the right girls' orphanage in mind. The Muslims in Sri Lanka are called 'Moors' due to the history (mixed with legend) of their early arrival in the land. It is said a ship of North African Muslims was on its way to China, but needed repairs. It landed in what is now the city of Galle to the south of the Island.

The king of that time encouraged these Moors, who were a well-behaved community of traders, to stay in his kingdom. These early North African Muslims (or Moors) were the ancestors of the present Muslim population of the country. Their names are adapted to local pronunciation. Saheed, our friend's name, derives from the Arabic name '*Shaheed*', which means 'witness' or 'martyr'.

Their customs and habits are like the North African Shadhili Sufis in many respects. At the time of my visits, the Muslim population of the country was some eight percent. Muslims were mostly businessmen with a good reputation in the country.

The country that honours you is indeed your country
—Imam Ali

The girls' orphanage was a half hour drive into a poor suburb of Colombo. In front of the modest house were piles of sand, rubble and wood planks. We soon discovered that a roof had recently collapsed and that repairs were slowly taking place. At the door, we could hear the soft melodious voices of girls chanting '*la ilaha il'allah*'. The '*dhikr*' was serene and hypnotic, so we waited outside listening with enchantment and anticipation, whilst Saheed quietly went inside the house to announce our arrival.

After a while the *dhikr* quietly came to an end and a short stocky lady with a radiant, but wrinkled face emerged at the door. She had a light complexion with bluish brown eyes, yet with eastern-looking features, and was wearing a thin white cotton scarf over her white hair and around her face. Mrs. Junaid, for that was the matron's name, stood calmly at the entrance to greet us and to explain the reason for the piles of building rubble.

I apologised for disturbing their *dhikr*, but she waved her hand dismissively and said that our arrival was what the orphans were waiting for. She went on to tell us that for two days, since the Eid, the children were without sufficient food, though it is customary that for the festive occasion the children be well fed, given new clothes and possibly books and stationery. This year, however, her school had received nothing. So she had decided that all the girls would sit in vigil and ask God's help around the clock, taking it in shifts until mercy came to them.

As this was the condition that they imposed upon themselves, the girls did not interrupt their chanting with the first signs of our arrival. They only stopped when our presence was announced by Mrs. Junaid, who was convinced that Allah had answered the two days of supplications.

I was delighted with the strength of her conviction and faith, but was concerned that we had come with insufficient funds. Quietly, I fumbled in my pockets and discovered some currency, which together with what my companions had between them presented an adequate sum. It turned out that what we had between us was enough for the seventy or eighty girls to eat well and have some new clothes and sandals. Whilst we were emptying our pockets, Mrs. Junaid stood facing us with a confident smile at Allah's promised generosity. Her face expressed her deep conviction and trust in the One Glorious Provider.

On a second visit to Mrs. Junaid I asked her if she could find us another lady like herself who could dedicate her life to our work in Sri Lanka. After a long contemplative silence, she lifted her face and looked at us with an apologetic sadness that expressed her inability to do this.

Mrs. Junaid's personal qualities, saint like purity and commitment to service without expecting worldly rewards was the secret of her spiritual wholesomeness. You could see that all grief and calamities would evaporate at her smile. She lived her faith and trust in God fully and her soul's light overflowed from her.

A few years later, I heard that Mrs. Junaid had become too frail to run the orphanage and had left for the village of her birth, near Kandy, in the central mountains with its cooler climate. I shall never forget her piercing yet shy eyes and their constant expectation of Divine mercy.

> *...but Allah was their protector, and in Allah should*
> *the Faithful (ever) put their trust.'*
>   — Qur'an (3: 122)

I first met Bashir Uthman whilst still based in the Gulf following which he visited me a number of times in the US and England. I also visited him in Medina, where he lived for more than twenty years. He was another remarkable person whom I came to love and respect dearly. He came from a prominent family of leaders in a well-known tribe in Eritrea. He was modest, generous and an illumined being, who exuded spiritual presence and power.

Early in his life he had managed his family's wealth in land, cattle and properties in different parts of what is now Somalia and Eritrea. Naturally, he was drawn into the national revolts and struggles against the Italian and British colonizers. Through a newspaper he owned, he advocated independence and care for their Islamic heritage. As he was not a typical politician he was unable to deal with party politics, so he withdrew to Medina in search of the answers to life's eternal questions.

He was now the senior companion of a well-known Somali Sufi master called Shaykh Al Bukhari, who lived modestly in the outskirts of Medina. The Shaykh had a large following of devotees from the areas around the Horn of Africa, who visited Medina frequently.

Bashir was a healer endowed with the knowledge and science of making Islamic talismans and protective amulets. He selected the appropriate talisman according to the supplicant's need. He once told me that in the past he had chosen the appropriate verses from the Qur'an when preparing the talismans, but now he only used *Surat-ul-Fatiha'* ('the Opening' – the first chapter of the Qur'an). However, while he would be writing the talisman he would think of the person and his or her needs, thereby potentiating the inscription appropriately. In this way, one Qur'anic verse was used for varying messages and outcomes.

> *Will they not ponder on the Qur'an? If it had been from other than Allah they would have found therein much incongruity.*
>
> — Qur'an (4: 82)

Bashir Uthman was skilled at the art of interpreting dreams. Once I had a shattering dream of a car accident in which I was blown to bits. The dream seemed so real that I woke up in a state of shock and remained much disturbed. He explained to me that the extent of my travels was such that an accident like this could well have happened. Instead, the accident was transferred from the physical world to the dream world. For Bashir Uthman, the two worlds of the seen and unseen were complementary and interactive.

He also practiced as an herbalist and prepared his own remedies. On one occasion, some people had contacted him from the United States requesting medicine for a lady with severe chronic internal pains. He prepared a special medicine that took days to make. When he arrived in the States, he was unable to locate these people. Nevertheless, Bashir Uthman was confident his potion would find someone who would benefit from it. The last place he visited during his trip was our centre in Texas and sure enough, there was a lady who needed Bashir's exact remedy and experienced a dramatically positive response from it.

There were also numerous occasions with Bashir Uthman when miracles and strange events occurred. Most people around were surprised with these happenings, except him. On one occasion, I travelled with Hosam to Medina to visit the Prophet's Shrine and to meet Shaykh Al Bukhari.

We arrived several days later than planned and booked into a new hotel without informing Bashir of our revised schedule. In the late afternoon, soon after arriving at the small hotel and just as I was about to look for Bashir's address in my bag, I heard loud voices from the lobby. My room was on the first floor overlooking the atrium where the reception was and at the reception desk, I saw Bashir Uthman. He was insisting that I was there, although he had not been informed which hotel we had booked at and the man at the reception desk had told him that nobody by the name he had given them was staying there. I had been registered according to the name on my passport, which was different to what he knew.

I greeted Bashir from the first floor banister and hurriedly joined him in the lobby, to be whisked off to the Prophet's mosque before the *Maghrib* prayer. The crowd was a solid mass of humanity, but Bashir assured me that there would be a place for me beside the Shaykh, right next to the Prophet's tomb.

The clear signs of Allah's acceptance of my visit overwhelmed me. After manoeuvring amongst the crowd, I landed next to Shaykh Al Bukhari with ample space to pray next to the blessed tomb. After the prayer, I asked Shaykh Bukhari if he had any special instructions for me.

'You see all of that endeavour to know the truth?' he asked calmly, as he pointed at the bookshelf next to him with the pile of Qur'ans and books of supplications. I nodded. He then looked at me with eyes that were seeing beyond and said, 'Know that '*La ilaha illa'llah*' (There is no God but Allah) is higher than everything else. It is the first and last of all knowledges, as Noah's ark of safety and arrival is but a drop in the ocean of *La ilaha illa'llah*'.

He is the First and the Last, and the Outward and the Inward; and He is the Knower of all things.

— Qur'an (57: 3)

One day Bashir Uthman gave me a special Qur'anic recitation to read after each morning and evening prayer whilst holding my head with my right palm. He told me that if I adhered to this litany, I would never have any severe illness during my life. He also authorized me to give it to others at my discretion. He assured me that due to this supplication he had not been ill except for the occasional cold or flu.

Before Bashir went to bed every night the last thing he would do was to perform his ablutions and put on his shroud, in readiness for departure from this world. He remembered death at all times and kept his slender, agile body impeccably clean, observing a strict diet and regular fasting. He used to say, 'It is only the wise man who tries to discover what Allah wants of him, rather than what he wants of Allah.' This was his way to harmony and contentment.

Bashir's eldest son, Abdul Qader, was educated in the U.S. and had a good connection with me. One day, I received a letter from him saying that his father had been taken to hospital in Medina and had just returned to his home still unwell. After fifteen days, he passed away peacefully.

A momentary doubt came into my mind regarding the effectiveness of the Qur'anic vigil to ward off illness, which I had been performing diligently for a few years by now. Why was Bashir sick for two weeks? That night it became clear to me that the two weeks illness was a preparation for the sake of his family, before his death.

After Bashir Uthman had passed away, Abdul Qader came to see me in England and narrated an amazing event which he wished to share with me. The night before Bashir passed away, two important, Arab looking guests had come to the house with an official government car. They intimated that Bashir might pass away that night and that they would come the next morning to arrange for his burial. The family thought that the men were influential officials who were connected with Bashir's work as a healer and Sufi teacher, for he had many friends and followers not known to the family.

Bashir Uthman passed away that night and he was buried the next day, as arranged by these two men, in the most prestigious cemetery, *Jennat al Baqi* in Medina. This is the oldest Muslim cemetery in which many of the prominent men and women from Islamic history are buried, including numerous members of the Prophet's family. It is rare nowadays that anybody gets buried there for it is almost impossible to get official permission. Soon after the burial, these two men simply disappeared and Bashir's son could not trace them, as much as he tried.

• • •

The purpose of my first trip to Morocco was to meet the people of Allah, dead and alive. Soon after arriving in Tangier, I went to the *zawiya* and tomb of Shaykh al Harraq of Tetuan, whose love of Allah has reverberated for generations. His songs, to this day, open the hearts of seekers at many Sufi gatherings all over North Africa.

A companion and I walked early morning through the attractive crafts souq in Tetuan as it stirred. The zawiya was next to one of the old gates of the city, adjacent to an extensive graveyard. In the courtyard of the gate, piles of charcoal and bunches of green fodder for goats were being offloaded for sale, as had been done for centuries.

A clean-shaven attendant greeted us outside the zawiya and we were encouraged to go up the steps. We climbed two levels of steep steps up to the entrance. There an old man met us, showed us in and waited while we prayed and greeted Shaykh Harraq's tomb. Then we exchanged more greetings with him and discovered that he was the *Muqaddam* (senior Sufi) of the *zawiya*. He made a supplication for us, and then showed us around the numerous rooms of the centre with their colourful stained glass windows and alcoves. He invited us to come back in the evening at the time of the sunset prayers to attend the usual weekly gathering with the traditional singers.

Just beyond the gates of Tetuan, there was a blind man sitting in a palm orchard, repeating the Qur'anic verses in his haunting melodious voice, '*O my people who have wronged yourself, do not ever despair of the mercy of Allah.*' This verse reverberated amongst the palm trees, as though it had emerged from the eternal garden. I heard the voice from quite far away and was drawn to it like a magnet. The blind man was sitting next to a mud wall, totally absorbed in his recitation. He seemed most distant from the material world and its confusions. I stood still for a while next to the Qur'anic reciter contemplating his intoxicating state, whilst recalling it within my own heart. Allah's mercy showers upon us from where we do not expect.

Our next stop was to visit Moulay Abd As-Salam Ibn al Mashish (died 1228), the spiritual master of Shaykh Abul Hasan ash-Shadhili, who was considered the *qutb* (spiritual axis) of his time. Ibn Mashish was a Berber and had lived as a recluse in the Rif Mountains, not far from Tetuan. His Shrine in the Jebal Alam is a well-known place of pilgrimage.

The most famous legacy of his writings is the '*Salat Al-Mashishiyyah*' – a prayer and spiritual portrait of the Prophet and thus depicts '*al-insan al-kamil*', 'the perfect man'. Ibn al Mashish was martyred by a local gangster who saw him as a threat to his unlawful ways.

> '*O First, O Last, O Outward, O Inward, hear my petition, even as You heard the petition of Your servant Zachariah; succour me through You unto You, support me through You unto You, unite me with You, and come in between me and other-than You; Allah, Allah, Allah!*'
> — Abd as-Salam Ibn Mashish (taken from his Salat Al-Mashishiyyah)

It is commonly said that a visit to Ibn Mashish's shine is always fraught with obstacles, for he tests the sincerity of the visitor by the difficulties on the way. The distance we were travelling was comparatively short on a well-travelled road. The early morning rain gave way to intermittent bursts of sunshine, and we drove in high spirits through the beautiful mountain valleys on the road to Chauen.

We then turned off from the main road and began to follow the narrow road that leads up into the mountains. It was paved to start with, but before long, asphalt gave way to a dirt track – still the going was easy, though a little bumpy. As we went up, the clouds came down; the moisture in the air increased and the road's surface became muddy and slippery.

We passed a village where peasants gathered for the market day. People were buying animals to sacrifice for the Eid festival, still a few days away.

A man with a black beard and wearing a thin white shirt drenched by the cold rain tried to stop us for a lift, but we continued on the muddy path upwards. The higher we went, the worse the road surface became until finally we could go no further. We were well and truly stuck. There was no way we could continue, although we were only a few miles from the Shrine. There was nothing for it but to turn back and try an alternative route.

This entailed a one hundred mile detour around the other side of the mountain and even then, we had no guarantee of the road being passable. We decided to risk it anyway. So we slithered back through the thick clouds and mist down the mountain. After a short while, we passed the man with the nylon shirt and black beard again, who waved us down. We stopped this time, opened the window and through the cold moist air he asked for a cigarette. 'Certainly not', I replied impatiently, 'We do not smoke,' and with that we began to slide back down the mountain towards Tetuan.

After praying *dhuhr salat* at midday and having snacked on some dates and nuts, we braved a second attempt. Once more as we reached the cloud level the dampness in the air turned the road's surface into a layer of liquid clay. It reminded me of driving on oil spills in Kirkuk, where you have no control over the car. Somehow we kept going, sliding this way and that across the road, sometimes forwards, sometimes sideways and sometimes backwards. Mercifully, there was no traffic whatsoever.

The clouds were so thick that visibility was down to a couple of yards. Suddenly, the road turned into a stream of water and I thought we were not going to make it. Just as we were ready to give up, the car somehow swam through the water and emerged on terra firma. A muddy, but stone road was under the wheels again.

Then, through the swirling mist, we reached a junction, which joined the first road and where the familiar black bearded face was waving at us. He must have been waiting all these hours, because according to where we had left him before, several hours ago, he should have arrived at the Shrine long ago. This time we did not hesitate to open the car door and motioned him to get in. He slid in, his clothes dripping mud and his wet white shirt stuck to his thin chest. He seemed oblivious to the cold. 'What's your name?' I asked. 'Abd as-Salam' came the reply! It suddenly occurred to me that he was a guide sent to take us to Moulay Abd as-Salam's Shrine, and we had twice ignored him. Had we not done so, the trip might have been easier, but Allah knows what is best. We crept cautiously through the dense cloud again and eventually reached our destination. As we stepped out of the car and walked on to the cork floor that surrounds the great tree, which is the site of the Moulay Abd as-Salam's grave, the *adhan* for *asr* was being called. It had taken us over eight hours to complete a journey which should have taken an hour or two at the most.

Just before Abd as-Salam left us, I gave him some money as a gift, at which point he said he would advise us to carry some cigarettes in the car. As we left him, several beggars came to him to share the token charity, still in his hand.

The next day we set off for the southeastern deserts of Tafilalet to visit a living Sufi Shaykh called Sidi Bukhorshid. During a hot afternoon, as we traversed a rough road over a hundred miles long, we suddenly noticed steam emerging from the engine - the radiator was leaking water. There was little traffic on the desert road, but we managed to stop a car to ask for help to get to the nearest garage or town.

The driver looked at the water leak and asked if we had any cigarettes on us. A strange recurring request it seems in these parts. As we looked puzzled, the driver walked to his car and came back with a packet of local cigarettes. He pulled out several cigarettes, crushed them between his fingers and dropped them in a small can of water. He then poured the tobacco concoction into the car's radiator carefully, whilst advising us that you could not travel in these parts without cigarettes for they were an instant cure to seal holes, as the tobacco leaves expand in hot water. We fell silent remembering Abd – as Salam's request.

> *Do not look down at anything in creation for in it may*
> *lie your salvation.*
>   — Sufi Abu Ahmad

There is something about cemeteries that leaves an indelible mark on our psyche. As we approached the city of Rashidiyya in the desert of Tafilalet one particular graveyard attracted us and one specific grave propelled us towards it. We sat down in silence and were soon enveloped in ecstatic peace. We learnt later that the 'wali' who was buried there was known by all the tribes for his uncompromising piety and devotion to Allah. They informed us that even before the age of puberty he had scarcely spoken nor heard a sentence, unless it had to do with Truth or God. He shunned all company and would walk out of any conversation, unless it was about Allah.

His Shrine was a blaze of light in the darkness of the other tombs surrounding it. A few kilometres behind the shrine, was the Sufi Sanctuary of Sidi Bukhorshid. It was a desert caravanserai, built out of local mud with many cavernous passages, private and public quarters. A hundred or so people made up this blessed community, living a simple life in an isolated desert oasis. One could feel the dynamic harmony between them and the desert.

Soon after the exchange of greetings was over, the call to prayer assembled us all in one of the courtyards. Afterwards we had lunch, which was followed by seemingly endless glasses of sweet mint tea. We were then gifted with baskets of provisions for our return trip.

I did try to explain to Sidi Bukhorshid that we did not need all these kilos of sugar, loose and in cone form, nor were we likely to go through the sacks of dates and other provisions. He would hear none of this and continued to behave as though we were setting out to cross thousands of miles of desert on foot or on camelback.

At the gate of the caravanserai, Sidi Bukhorshid stood in humble dignity, praying for our safe journey and assuring us that there will always be havens of light and islands of refuge on this earth for the sincere seeker. The gentleness and the love of the community was matched by the starkness and the harshness of the desert landscape outside. We learnt sometime later that Sidi Bukhorshid was sending some of his disciples a few hundred miles further to the south, away from the encroaching civilisation. It is said that when society's morals weaken, men of light flee.

> *O my slaves, you who have faith. My earth is wide, so worship Me alone.*
>
> — Qur'an (29: 56)

Bahalil is a small old settlement, nestled in the foothills of the Northern Atlas Mountains. The hillside is lined with poplar trees. Streams of water cascade down to the village square into a large rectangular water tank, surrounded by platforms and taps for clothes washing. When we arrived, several groups of young women were busy thrashing clothes and chatting away. A few donkeys and carts were moving, carrying firewood, hay or other produce. A herd of sheep could be seen on the nearby hill and three or four young shepherd boys accompanying them. There were several goats wandering around chewing on anything they found edible. The winding narrow streets were paved with stones and lined up with simple single story houses with flat mud roofs. It was a typical, small, North African town living in the present day with minor changes from its past – an ancient setting, as yet undiscovered by tourists and modern traffic.

The purpose of the visit was to meet the illumined sage, Sidi Saleh. His popular name was the '*Wali of Bahalil*' (Saint of Bahalil). It is known that Sidi Saleh had served at least forty enlightened masters of varying stations during his lifetime by that stage. Blind and probably in his eighties, he was homebound and in constant invocation when I saw him. His home was a modest two-room house with one simple water tap on the roof, from which all the water needs of the household was drawn. He sat cross-legged on his Moroccan banquette in a long sitting room that had one window slightly open to the alleyway.

Although the *Wali* was blind, his other senses more than compensated for the loss of physical sight. He was in good health and fully alert. He constantly recited rhythmically, '*All praise belongs to Allah and all gratitude to Him*' (*al hamdulillah wa'sh-shukrulillah*) over and over again with an expression of contentment on his face. Whilst sitting with him I felt an inexplicable familiarity, as though I had known him before.

Since the *Wali* had been fasting continually for the past twenty or thirty years, I preferred not to eat or drink in his presence. Upon his insistence, I chewed on a few dry dates and local raisins. The Prophet had encouraged hosts to always offer some food or drink to guests, saying otherwise it was like visiting a grave.

Fasting is a shield that protects you from the ills of this world.

— Prophet Muhammad

The *Wali* had one daughter who was living with him and looking after him. As I was thinking about giving a gift of money to this hard working young girl with a child strapped behind her back, the *Wali* told me not to give any money to any one other than him. I was so startled that I didn't ask the reason.

I thought how true it is that a man of knowledge is often unrecognised by his people. I had come a distance of a few thousand kilometres to spend a couple of hours in the presence of the *Wali*, yet most of the villagers around only regarded him as a blind, pious, old man. The highlight of our meeting was communion in silence.

Before parting, he prayed that I should go out to the world and witness it with his insight, and relate to it with his wisdom and knowledge. He confirmed our deep connection some years later, when my wife and two of my daughters visited him. They were told that I am his eyes and they are his daughters. He had also surprised a group of British Muslims who had enquired as to who is worthy to receive *sadaqah* (charity or poor due) for distribution, to which he answered he and Shaykh Fadhlalla were eligible.

One day, a few years later, one of my daughters wept, telling us that her Shaykh had died. Days later, we learnt that the *Wali* had passed away on that day.

> *And the Garden is brought close for the pious, no longer far. This is what you were promised – for those oft-returning in penitent and, and those who preserve their covenant with Allah. Who fears the Beneficent in the unseen and comes with a patient heart. Enter in peace. This is the Day of Immortality.*
>
> — Qur'an (50: 31–34)

On one trip to Tangier, I asked my host Qassimi if we could go to visit the shrine of his ancestor Shaykh Ibn Ajiba. The road out of Tangier was being hurriedly patched up in preparation for the

King's visit. Qassimi described this welcome activity as the one good outcome when the King once in a while visits a city. He said that the only way that the corrupt administration does something for the public is out of fear of the autocratic King who can punish or reward as he wishes.

The old international checkpoint out of Tangier, a relic of the past when it was an independent international zone, had been deserted since the country's independence. Qassimi described how in the old days, miles long queues of cars would wait for clearance in and out of the international zone of Tangiers.

The Americans, French, Spanish, British and Italians had all claimed their stake in this 'interpol' enclave. The local population would flock there for legitimate employment, as well as shady deals.

We left the main road for a narrow and winding dusty trail full of potholes. Thistle grew over two meters high on each side of the road. An occasional wind swept fig tree shaded shepherd boys and girls. Hardy North African cacti grew in clusters everywhere.

Qassimi had originally planned to take a four-wheel drive to negotiate the last few miles up to the rugged hills, but like most Moroccan planning, it had been changed without real reason or explanation. So, the Renault 5 was put to the test and my faith in French technology began to weaken as the thermometer on the dashboard showed red. The car, however, held out through a steady climb, between young pines and old cork forests with the road a shallow stream of water. Egg shaped boulders of all sizes caused the tires constantly to slip and bump. Apart from one donkey loaded with firewood, we did not see any sign of human habitation, until we arrived at the village.

The shrine of Shaykh ibn Ajiba stood on top of a knoll facing a steep and long valley, which dropped hundreds of feet below. It reminded me of the tomb of Abd as-Salam Ibn al Mashish. At the door as we were coming out, an old *majdhub* (a holy tramp) woman begged for alms with quivering hands.

An attempt to take her photograph made her dart swiftly behind the door to avoid being seen. She muttered her objection. Two small boys laughed, looking curiously and mischievously at us. By now, the midday sun was fierce and the dozen or so houses in the village fell into silence, as the villagers took their siesta.

Next, we visited the nearby shrine of the son of Shaykh ibn Ajiba. A modest jewel of a tomb perched on an adjacent hill at the edge of a vertical drop into the valley below. Several other small shrines littered the area below the mountain, which Ibn Ajiba had named 'the Saviour'. It certainly had saved him from the tyranny of the village population, who every now and again attacked him and looted his house in the early years when he came to live there.

Ibn Ajiba's family origin is from an Andalusian mountain village, called the Ain al Ruman, (the source of the pomegranates). Eight generations later he ended up on the opposite side of the Mediterranean Sea, following the orders of his Darqawi Shaykh. He was instructed to stay amongst the unruly Berber villagers to guide these people to the Prophetic path and, at the same time, write a comprehensive commentary on the Qur'an.

> *Sufism is the most honoured of all sciences for it contains the foundations of ethics and morality and the path to be followed towards the lights of truth.*
>
> — Ibn Ajiba

Ibn Ajiba's commentary of the Qur'an had several levels of explanations. It is monumental in size and content. Before undertaking such an enormous task, he had asked his Shaykh to pray for long life. The Shaykh promised that he would be given sufficient lifetime to finish the work and ordered Ibn Ajiba to hurry up with it. It is reported that the last chapter of the commentary was finished at sunset and Ibn Ajiba passed away with the sunrise on the following day at the age of 63, the same age as the

Prophet Muhammad.

Upon the urgent recommendation of Bashir Uthman, I had commissioned Qassimi to research the original manuscript of this Qur'anic commentary with a view to publish it. Several years later, an excellent edition, printed in Lebanon, came out in eight volumes.

The journey back to town was quicker, but more dangerous than the trip there. We slid downhill with a fierce wind at almost gale force, blowing bits of earth, rocks, dry leaves and branches and a host of insects at us. Along the rivulets, the villagers were cutting down old trees for firewood and construction work, denuding the countryside as they had been doing for generations. Poverty and conservation are always as loggerheads.

We drove towards the ocean to the nearest point across from the Iberian Peninsula, where the early Arab invaders had crossed to make reconnaissance raids before the final conquest. A few white shrines shimmered in the villages that dotted the road. One Muslim saint with healing powers for the mad and the mentally disturbed was the reason that, during the Spanish occupation, a large mental hospital was built where he had lived. It had since been neglected and was now in ruins.

We visited Qassimi's uncle, a most noble and dignified patriarch, who was a renowned scholar and Islamic judge. He was in his nineties and the oldest member of the family. The orchard and compound of this old Shaykh was thirty kilometres west of Tangier on a beautiful hill that rolls all the way down to the Atlantic.

At the entrance to the property, there was a newly constructed mosque, with several courtyards where school children were grouped in different corners to be taught religion. Walking along the steep path down towards the sea, there were half a dozen houses for the extended family. Ancient fig trees, plums, vines, pomegranates and olives all competed for the rich soil and brilliant sun.

In his private library, the Shaykh produced several Sufi manuscripts which he had hoped to publish whilst he acknowledged sadly that people nowadays are not interested in religion. He filled a white cotton sack with fresh figs, mulberries and pomegranates for us before we left.

. . .

Once whilst still based in the Gulf with Hosam Raouf, Shaykh Abdal Qadir phoned to recommend that we visit Damascus to spend a few days in the company of Shaykh Fayturi, who was one of his Shaykhs. He lived in Libya, but was then visiting Damascus.

The airport in Damascus was filled with throngs of people waiting for arriving passengers. It took us two hours to clear passport control, but as we emerged, a tall, handsome man confidently approached us. He was one of Shaykh Fayturi's attendants and he drove us immediately to meet the Shaykh, who was an old and ailing man in his eighties.

Several times over the next few days, we had the delight of being with a man of his light and wisdom. At our last meeting, Shaykh Fayturi told us he would be soon leaving this world because his time had come. He passed away shortly after his return to Libya. Shaykh Fayturi was one of the spiritual heirs of Shaykh Ahmed al Alawi and was an example of how outer sobriety can cover inner intoxication. You could see in him a meeting point between beauty and majesty, his outer boundaries leading to inner vastness.

> *O seeker of truth, leave your desires behind if you want*
> *deeper divine secrets,*
> *And then take onto the Path and maintain the*
> *companionship...*
> *Until all shadows vanish and the original love engulf you.*
> — Shaykh Faytouri

. . .

I have been for Umrah[6] three times and for Hajj once. As much as these visits are outwardly inconvenient, they are always a delight inwardly. The perceptive seeker is rewarded with a heightened sense of awareness and sensitivity to the meanings behind intentions, actions and thought.

I knew the Hajj to be the most difficult of the five 'pillars' of Islam. When two million people are in one spot at the same time attempting the same ritual, it makes you learn to give up much of your normal concerns.

The first part is the standing on the plains of Arafat, realising that you are nowhere, calling for that which can't be seen or touched. Whether you are a king or a pauper, Arafat is all to do with seeking knowledge of where you came from, where you are going, the desperate search for guidance and light while navigating life.

Having realised that there is only the One Creator who sustains creation and guides it, in the second part of the Hajj you accept the truth that you do not own anything and you do not control anything. Then you follow in the footstep of Abraham when he questioned his ability to sacrifice his beloved son, Ismail. As with all human beings, the inner voice says, 'you need to free yourself from all attachments,' whilst to the reasoning voice, it doesn't make sense.

This confusion, or debate, ends with the manifestation of the ram. Once you are free from attachments, you have already made the sacrifice. Once you inwardly submit, then the outer is symbolic.

It is indeed due to unending miracles that one is saved all the time from the consequences of one's mistakes. The seen and the unseen often mingle noticeably during Hajj. Most pilgrims encounter situations that shake them out of their exclusive identification with the rational world of cause and effect. Hajj leaves an impact on everyone; the depth of the impact is according to the person's ability and readiness to realise subtler consciousnesses.

---

6 When you perform all the requirements for the hajj but it is not during the designated month of Hajj, this is known as 'Umrah'.

For many, it is a ritual of inconvenience or status. However, in every case, to walk in the footsteps of the great patriarch Prophet Abraham who was willing to sacrifice his dearest possession, his beloved son, is a great liberation.

• • •

My scholarly or spiritual teachers have helped show me the meaning and purpose of life. They gave me wise counsel and loving companionship which helped me to refocus my orientation. However, there have also been numerous small incidents and encounters with ordinary people that taught me as much.

From these hidden teachers, who were often amongst the poorest of people or peasants from rural areas, I have learnt much about my inner state. Whether it was from the generosity of the waiter in one small hotel in Northern India who, realizing I was not fond of restaurant food, brought me food that his wife had cooked from home, or the dignity of the old Sudanese peanut seller, outside the tomb of the Prophet in Medina, these events have stayed with me throughout my life.

One afternoon, I had come out of the Prophet's shrine and on my way back to the hotel felt quite hungry. There in front of me was squatting a large old Sudanese woman on the marble floor adjacent to the shrine entrance. She had a basket of freshly roasted peanuts and different sizes of paper cones as packaging material.

I asked her for the middle-sized cone. I did not have any change in my pocket so I gave her a note. She took out the largest cone, filled it to the rim and handed it over to me. I asked her to give me only half of that amount and keep the change. She said, 'No, you have to take it as it is.' I explained that I wouldn't eat the entire amount. To my utter surprise she abruptly emptied the content of the cone back into the basket and returned the paper cone back on its stand and returned my money.

I protested that I did not want to offend her, but I would not be able to consume all of the nuts she gave me. This is why I only asked for half the amount and the rest was my gift to her. She ignored me whilst I still waited for reconciliation. Finally, she turned to me and said, 'For a certain amount of money, I have to give you a certain amount of goods. What you do with it is your business. I am not responsible whether you are going to eat it or leave it.'

I apologized, gave her the money and took back the full large cone. On the way back to the hotel, I enjoyed feeding the noisy happy pigeons that surrounded me near a pavement. The lady street vendor was not anxious to increase her sales or gain extra money. Her integrity was a result of simple trust in Allah, the Provider.

Whoever engages in travel will arrive.

— Ibn Arabi

12

Making Sense

My heart has become capable of every form: it is a
pasture for gazelles and a convent for Christian monks
and a temple for idols and the Pilgrims' Ka'ba and the
tablets of Torah and the book of the Qur'an. I follow the
religion of Love: whatever way Love's Camels take, that
is my religion and my faith.

— Ibn Arabi

Making sense of life, its direction and purpose, didn't come to me in an easy or dramatic way. Every time I turned away from worldly nonsense and what I knew to be false or temporary, I gained more insights and 'sense'. Ever since I left Karbala on scholarship to study in England I felt like a straw blowing on the winds of an unknown destiny. Eight times in my life I have completely re-located to a different country. As I grew more aware and mature, the need and desire for a place and people to belong to and identify with increased.

Most of my travels as a grown-up were in some way motivated by this drive. My feeling of being 'out of place' was highlighted by the fact that I had never voted for anything or anyone in my life. Indeed, I have scarcely ever been qualified to vote.

The Iraq and Karbala of my youth had vanished forever. I had outgrown my childhood attachments and had gone beyond nostalgia for Karbala or Iraq. I also came to know that in the new globalised world there are an increasing number of people who suffer from cultural alienation, physical displacement, the stresses and depressions of being uprooted and a lack of belonging. Even in the environs of one's own culture, there exists a strong tendency to search for roots, which is just a reflection of the primal human need for safety, stability and security. This drive is called the soul.

Everywhere there are individuals, families, groups of people and indeed nations who are looking for an identity and direction. This need is strongest when individuals, people or nations are vulnerable or insecure. Hence the appeal for new ideological and nationalistic movements throughout the so-called 'developing world' in – America, Europe, Africa, the Middle East or Asia.

The search for outer personality or identity is a reflection of the perpetual need and search for the inner reality or truth or the inner light within the heart. Outer search and longing for freedom – freedom from basic needs, freedom from oppression, freedom from injustices, and freedom from fears and anxieties – are all echoes of the freedom of the soul within the heart.

The self is never free and the soul is forever free. The outer world only appears with boundaries and limitations that are time/space based, whereas the inner world is boundless. Confusion and conflicts arise due to the lack of understanding of this basic situation.

Our perpetual search for roots and security is because the soul within us is beyond the limitations of time and space and is forever secure in the certainty of its eternal and perfect origin. The person – whose existence is only made possible by the soul – strives to emulate or challenge this 'master' directly or indirectly at all times. The usual human interest in ancestral roots is an echo of the souls' heavenly roots beyond bounds.

We human beings essentially seek what is already etched within the soul.

My life's experience simply confirms this perpetual quest to the point that constantly witnesses this balance and the relationship between meaning and form, seen and unseen.

> *I am in this world like a traveller who takes shade*
> *under a tree, only to resume his journey.*
> — Prophet Muhammad

At all times, we are attempting to be fulfilled through an attribute or quality of God. From this point of view, all human endeavours are directed at trying to reach a Divine attribute within ourselves and to be absorbed in that particular consciousness.

The eternal good is ever present in one's heart and soul, reflecting God's mercy and bounty. By reference to that constant goodness within me, I will be able to experience all relative and transient good and bad with equanimity and steadfastness.

The so-called bad is only the shadow of the good. The bounds and limits are only the shadow of the boundless and limitless. If you deny limitation, you will be denied the limitless. If you deny your uncertainty, you will be denied the light of constant inner certainty. If you deny your ignorance, you will be denied knowledge. The seeker who recognises these laws will then embrace boundaries, limitations, responsibility, sincerity and commitment. These disciplines will enhance his inner awareness, giving access to the constant light of the soul within the heart. Outer sobriety is a door to inner joyfulness.

Because the soul is free and infinite, the self wants freedom and boundlessness. It is the wise seeker who realises that the self or ego needs restrictions and boundaries for its grooming. Apparent freedom actually betrays ignorance. You think you are free to eat as much or whatever you want, but if you care for good health, then you will only eat the correct quantity and quality. Thus, you are not free.

Appropriate or virtuous action is very specific, like the centre of a sphere. The optimal amount that one should eat is specific. If a child asks for chocolate, generosity is not to give him or her the whole box. You should give that which is appropriate at that moment. The virtue is to balance between excess and meanness, and this can best be done through constant awareness.

It is through the discipline of habitual reflection, meditation and prayer that we can reach that zone of pure awareness. As the Qur'an says (13: 28), '*Truly in remembrance of God do hearts find rest.*' This is why Muslims go on pilgrimage, fast and pray. The five daily prayers are prescribed so that we punctuate the days with constant awareness and taking reference with the Absolute. Everything that is prescribed in Islam is for human benefit and spiritual awakening for these two aspects cannot be separated.

God does not need to be worshipped; we need to love, know, adore and worship the Ever-Perfect, Ever-Present, Ever-Generous and thus attain a tranquil and contented heart. When this state is realised, then the outer obligations, limitations and obedience, which at first seemed inconvenient and constricting, will become a pleasure and the door to the state of inner joy.

• • •

In the same way I witness the cosmology of the self, containing the worldly, rational and causal, and the spiritual zone of the soul, so I look at groups of people and nations. Individuals make up society and a tribe or nation only represents the sum total of its individuals. Therefore, if you look at the root of discord, whether it is between individuals, or nations, you realise the cause arises from outer dispersion and confusion with opposites.

Harmony is based upon gatheredness and union in essence and Oneness before the manifestation of duality, individuality and differences. When this paradigm is borne in mind, you can then 'make sense' of historical and current events. If we don't see the One before the two, then we are confused and unable to act appropriately along the path of harmony and truth of the One.

In history, we find empires which have been successful and

lasted longer have had a 'greater purpose' and unifying factor than simple power politics, economics and finance – though this may have been inadvertent. The British Empire was built on a rallying point of service to the King and country. It was when Commerce completely relegated the other two of Livingstone's three Cs (those of Civilization and Christianity) that the glue dissolved.

> *The truth is ever constant and absolute and all*
> *experiences and realities are different reflections of*
> *truth. The more real and durable, the closer to truth.*
> — Sufi Abu Ahmad

Making sense relates to the realisation and understanding of the innate paradox within humans and nations. You walk in this world on the two legs of rationality and spirituality; you recognise the seen and unseen, earthy and heavenly, inner and outer. Making sense is based on understanding and accepting all five outer senses and the five inner senses[1], so that to realise pure consciousness lies beyond the relative awareness of the senses. We are in this world but not of it, so we need to interact with this world while recognising its temporal nature through insight and enlightenment.

The dominant world cultures are increasingly concerned with material acquisition, increase, efficiency and rationality. The generous Creator gives the children of Adam what they seek and the consequences become destiny.

In the East we had not built upon reason and we have collectively failed to awaken spiritually, although there were always wise men, religious scholars and rare enlightened beings around. Muslim leadership had become worldly with only spiritual pretence. The Muslims' drift from Islam Original started from the time of the Prophet's death and accelerated during the past five centuries, leading to the misery of the present predicament with its violent

---

1 5 inner senses are acknowledged and listed in traditional Islamic teachings.

eruptions and criminal madness, attaching the name of Islam to bombs and rockets.

For centuries the majority of Muslim rulers were autocratic with little accountability to anyone. We had not developed rules, standards or procedures for constitutional representation or defined boundaries on our rulers. Original Islam was free of clerics, professional intermediaries, but the dynastic rulers of Muslims cultivated a class of 'court priests,' who obeyed the rulers and exercised power over the ignorant masses whilst the despots covered up their decadence and vices behind palace walls.

Collectively, we Muslims have been and are feeling the full effect of deviating from the path of enlightenment and the consequence of isolation from the western world, which we ignored and conveniently labelled as 'infidels'. Take the story of the sick Moroccan peasant who, after exhausting local remedies, ends up in a French clinic. As he opens his eyes after treatment, he sees the face of the blonde colonial doctor appear above him. He spits up in contempt towards the doctor's face (an infidel and an enemy of Islam) only for his vertical projectile to fall back on to his own face. Such is the tragedy of most Muslims, who are attacking their image in the mirror.

It is natural for victims to blame others, for desperate people with no homes to expect miracles, magical fixes and triumphant heroes. Only deep reflection, responsibility and self-criticism, as we look for the root cause of the malaise without being overwhelmed by the symptoms, can save us from wasting time and energy on desperate and futile struggles, most of which are generally counter-productive.

Access to truth which will bring lasting success comes about as a result of living Islam along the Prophetic footsteps.

An especially important paradigm for Muslims to take note of is the Prophetic phases of the Mecca/Medina interplay. The Qur'an first descended upon the Prophet in Mecca where most of the verses were to do with absolute truth (*haqiqah*). The verses are overwhelmingly to do with the purpose of creation and the issue of existence and the role of human beings and their duties in the world, the animals and the plants, how everything in nature emanates from and returns to Allah. It is to do with emancipation and awakening to the higher.

In Medina, the teaching was mostly to do with personal conduct and the rules and duties (*shariah*) necessary for the growth of a harmonious society. The world Muslims face today is more akin to that of the early years in Mecca, when they were surrounded by non-believers, than the ideal of the Medina community. Muslims look back nostalgically on a time when Islamic culture dominated with justified superiority, and forget the negligence and decadence of succeeding centuries. This hubris and nostalgia is blinding and distorting in present day terms.

We have failed to follow the way of Muhammad and build upon our heritage now we are resentful and in denial as we are dominated by the secular culture of the West.

If Muslims conduct themselves as though they are with the Prophet in the first few years of Mecca, qualities of humility, courage, steadfastness, modesty, wisdom and justice will emerge as dominant characteristics of conduct. These characteristics are recognized and desired globally. The Muslims must return to Islam by accepting all the practices of reasoning and be as in Meccan Islam, tolerant, patient and willing to accommodate others.

We have now to accept the empowerment of the masses through variations of Western democracy. You can't just love western manufactured goods and egalitarian laws without accepting their practices. The more simplistic minded clerics with their peasant mentality will only retard spiritual development and popular acceptance of the religion of Islam. We must accept reason and logic, and then the Prophetic values and higher virtues will become evident. People cannot be forced and subjugated by religious police. Once there is an illumined society, then through choice people will live Islam and not simply repeat rituals in the shadow of ignorance and superstition.

There is no compulsion in religion.

— Qur'an (2: 256)

On my last trip to Saudi Arabia, whilst I was at the airport in Jeddah, a porter made off with my briefcase. The Saudi authorities caught him and returned my briefcase. They wanted to punish him (which would have amounted to cutting off his hand), but under *shariah* they could not do so without my participation. They got my hotel information, I asked my Saudi friend to change the hotel I was supposed to stay in, to avoid being tracked down to testify in the case. My Saudi friend commented, 'Here, if you steal billions, you are a Saudi Prince, you'll have a street or airport named after you, but if you steal a few Riyals, you'll have your hands cut off.'

Many of the *shariah* injunctions are applied without taking into consideration the full circumstances and context. Cutting of the hand is only meant for professional thieves and repeated offenders. It cannot be applied in situations where the person is desperate and where there is no welfare situation. Another example of *shariah* misrepresentation is with adultery and stoning, brought to the fore recently by the *shariah* courts in northern Nigeria.

For an adulterer or adulteress to be found guilty, there must be four witnesses who actually saw the copulation – a difficult requirement to say the least! What is more, there must not be extenuating circumstances. There was an example of a woman who was accused of adultery and was taken to Imam Ali. Imam Ali discovered that there was a well in the desert and the owner had been charging for people to use it. This woman had no money and the only way she could get water was by agreeing to sleep with him. The woman was let off and the man punished.

Shariah is a luxury that works fully only in a proper functioning community along the 'Medina model.' The Prophet Muhammad even discouraged too much questioning which could lead to theological hair-splitting. People should do their best to follow the injunctions – inevitably the more particular and specific the questions that were asked, the more rigid the specific injunctions would be.

> *The path of Islam is ease and whoever finds himself burdened with it cannot continue. Thus do not be extreme, but aim for perfection and you will be rewarded.*
>
> — Prophet Muhammad

The same misapplication and taking out of context as exists with *shariah* also exists with the 'sunna' of the Prophet. They have tried to fix *hadith* and the *sunna* or the way of the Prophet, and as such sometimes applied them out of context. To support and justify an action, some scholars often refer to sayings of the Prophet without questioning as to whom he said it to, in what context and why. Only after taking into consideration the whole context can we claim to follow the Prophetic Path[2]. Structural and formal religiosity often misses out on the light and meaning behind the form. That is why millions of people profess love of God, but uncertainty about formal religion.

It is impossible to reform Islam. The religion is perfect, for all times and all places. It is the Muslims who must undergo a reformation and deeper knowledge and application of the Path. Allah in His wisdom and generosity has put us under the hammer and has subjected us to difficulties and constriction so that we realize our transgressions and return to His Ever-forgiving presence.

---

2 It is important to mention that even some things that are purported as having been said by the Prophet are questionable. For example, in the works of the major '*hadith*' collectors, thousands of *hadiths* are related through a man called Abu Huraira, who was not regarded with great respect by the close companions of the Prophet including Abu Bakr and Omar. In fact the Prophet's wife Aisha forbad him to narrate *hadith*.

We each associate ourselves with one group or another, highlighting the minor differences that exist between Muslims. If the division is not between Sunni and Shi'a, then people will make it between one school of law (*madhhab*) or another, or between one nationality and another. Even amongst the Sufis there are those who try to distinguish one grouping from another.

On one of my visits to Islamabad I was invited to the house of a government official, where the guest of honour was a Naqshabandi Shaykh with a reputation for miracles and foretelling the future.

When the Shaykh was informed that I was a Shadhili Shaykh, he reflected for a while seriously and then announced that a few nights ago he had been visiting the Prophet Muhammad, who had several Shaykhs from different Sufi orders with him, but Shaykh Abu'l Hassan ash-Shadhili was absent. There was a silence and many faces turned towards me for explanation. I could only smile and then said solemnly that this was not surprising as Shaykh Shadhili had already been with the blessed Prophet and is now with Allah!

> ***Allah will not change peoples' situation unless they change themselves.***
>
> — Qur'an (13: 11)

Having reconciled myself with roots that stretched further and deeper than home and nationality, it was fitting that after 40 years of wandering, I should eventually find for myself a physical location which I could call home, albeit as a foreigner. I remember once Shaykh Abdal Qadir had asked Hosam and myself to visit Shaykh Ahmad Abdul Aziz, who was the head of the Abu Dhabi Shariah court, and to ask him where in the Islamic world could new Muslim converts from Britain go where would they be respected, treated as equals and allowed to trade freely.

When we visited him for the first time he did not answer, but told us to come back the following week. When we returned to his 'majlis', he asked the people who were there to leave. Once they were gone, he began to cry. He said that there was no such place, and then he related a verse by Imam Ali, 'And when I open my eyes, I see many, but I don't see any (worthy).'

A number of years later, I had asked a descendent of Shaykh Abdul Qadir al Gilani,[3] Seyyid Ala-ud-Din, who had escaped the tyranny of Saddam and was living in Karachi, 'Where should my earthly abode be?' His immediate answer was, 'Furthest from the Middle East, in a country where the Muslim minority has no chance of taking over power.'

> *Die, then, to creatures, by God's leave, and to your passions, by His command, and you will then be worthy to be the dwelling place of the knowledge of God.*
>
> — Abdul Qadir al Gilani

I had by now come to believe and understand that what affects me of the outer world is a true reflection of my inner state. I had to leave Europe for it had no resonance in my heart. From 1993, I had clear indications that I should move towards Africa. I had tried to relocate my family and myself to Pakistan, where I had bought land in the outskirts of Karachi and the developments were near completion when I was warned strongly by my trusted friend, Razi Bilgrami, against moving there. Part of my family had already gone ahead and lived there for a year, but almost at the last minute I had to cancel all previous plans.

Africa, especially South and East Africa, had always attracted me and as South Africa began emerging from the grip of decades of apartheid, I decided to explore the country in the early 1990s, travelling with three companions.

---

3 Abdul Qadir al Gilani (1077–1166) was a great Sufi master who is considered the founder of the *Qadiriyyah* order. He lived in Baghdad but had been born in the province of Gilan or Jilan (which is adjacent to Mazanderan) in Persia.

In Cape Town I received a clear sign in favour of my moving to South Africa as the next step in my life. One day, I was invited for an evening meal at the home of an old business associate, who had retired to Constantia in Cape Town. He picked me up from the hotel, but as we neared his home, he thought I may enjoy visiting one of the well known Sufi shrines before dinner. This place was within walking distance from his house, so he suggested dropping me there. I could then walk back leisurely to his place.

The shrine stood in a small pine forest with an air of peace and grace about it. As I gently pushed open the creaking door, I made the intention to receive some sign regarding my search for an abode. Upon entering the dark windowless shrine, I sat in a corner and proceeded to meditate upon the soul of the departed Sufi sage. When my eyes adjusted to the darkness of the interior, I could see three figures sitting motionless and in silence near me.

After a period of stillness, I felt the stirring of the person near me, and when I opened my eyes I saw an old man removing the shawl that was covering his head. He moved gently towards me and said in a soft clear voice, 'If you move to South Africa, you will have the best of times and you will be most honoured by the people here.' Then he withdrew back under his shawl.

After a while I got up and left, lingering outside in the hope of meeting this man again. The door creaked open, the old man, a younger man in jeans and a young lady in *hijab* came out. The old man introduced his son who was a doctor, and his daughter who had been ill for a long time. She was revived once a week whenever they visited the shrine. The man told me that what he spoke inside the shrine was not from him. He simply conveyed the message from the soul of the Sufi.

In the wake of the elections in 1995, I relocated to South Africa as thousands were leaving. In the Sub-tropical Lowveld, on a small Macadamia nut farm called 'Highwood Orchard', I found a shady spot under the African Sun.

The lonely soul, all souls,
Yearning for rest, like the rest,
Longing for the Promised Land,
Where passions can rest,
And the heart is stilled,
And at its best;

— Sufi Abu Ahmad

My mother joined me at Highwood along with the rest of my family. She settled well into her new surroundings, but became increasingly frail and it was clear that she did not have much longer in this world. Two months before her death she needed a wheel chair, then was bedridden for a few weeks, but with no pain or complaint. We tried to diagnose what was wrong, but with no success.

She passed away gracefully and peacefully with most of the family around her. In the last few days of her life, she stopped taking any food or drink. On the last day we called the local GP, who had grown fond of my mother, to see if anything could be done. After setting up the drip connection for an intravenous injection, the doctor turned to me and said she did not think it would do much good.

I held my mother's right hand and saw her drift peacefully towards the hereafter. After a few minutes, a deep sigh of relief came from her, ending this world's journey. As I held her soft, cold hands, my mind drifted to the days of childhood when I would run towards her for a hug whenever she came back home from a visit to the bazaar or Imam Hussein's shrine. Her disappointed cousin who wished to marry her and had exiled himself in grief and anger flashed across my mind.

Her beautiful face, which I had kissed thousands of times, was now lifeless and distant although only a few inches away from me. The kind words of the doctor who was standing behind me, returned me to the solemnity of the occasion and the grief of the surrounding family members.

My eldest daughter, Muna, who had nursed my mother in the last week of her life, was visibly affected, yet calm and content with the inevitable. My youngest sister, Fodhla, was in deep grief. She had been very much dependent on her mother's emotional support during her exile in England since her husband's premature death.

Even the cats had congregated at the door, as though they felt something strange had taken place. About ten furry creatures had abandoned their usual personal differences and had collectively crowded the doormat.

My mother passed away on Saturday evening, the 20th September 1997. She was washed the same night in her living room and buried midday on Sunday at our South African community farm cemetery 'Umdeni', near Belfast.

Her death somehow signalled a turning point in the lives of our family and the close friends who loved her. The day of her burial was a majestic reminder of the transience of life on earth. My friend, Shaykh Asaf, who was visiting South Africa at that time, sent a message that he wanted to attend the funeral. When he arrived at the cemetery, late morning, the group of mourners prayed on the coffin and then carried it towards the prepared grave. I climbed down into the six-foot deep grave with my brother Fazel and my dear friend Hosam Raouf to receive my mother's body and to rest her on her right hand side facing Mecca.

I often reflect upon my great fortune to have had the company of my mother for so many years of my life. Her departure seemed only temporary as her memory and light always shines through my heart. Whenever I remember my mother, an inner warmth of contentment and joyful acceptance engulfs me. She always expected the best and was scarcely ever sad or upset other than for a flash of a moment. Her faith in God's perfect decrees and unconditional love for creation was the foundation of her life's journey.

> **Certainly, the friends of Allah have no fear, nor do they have sadness.**
>
> — Qur'an (50: 62)

Most human beings believe in another phase of life after this worldly experience. The Muslim concept of the afterlife beyond time and space relates to the soul's experience of what the self has gathered in this world of vices or virtues. The soul is permanent, whilst the body is temporary. Death brings about the separation between the physical part of a person and the incorporeal part.

During her last weeks, my mother's weakness often reminded me of how true Plato's saying is that the body is the prison of the soul and death brings about the release. He believed the soul descended from the Divine realm and that birth, not death, is the cause of sleep and forgetfulness. When the soul comes into the body, its high state of awareness is reduced and it forgets its pre-corporeal state of perfections and bliss. Plato added that after death the soul faces Divine judgment with regard to every good or bad action that it has done in its life.

The Tibetan Book of the Dead describes various levels through which the soul passes after death. It enters into an inter-space accompanied by a 'shining body' which is of more perfect consciousness. Then one's entire life is reflected upon to see it with no misinterpretation.

The Bhagavad-Gita presents the soul as immortal in nature and that death is conquered by identification with the All-Knowing All-Loving God. Thus, the real self or soul is never born nor dies; the wise man is not slain when his body is cut. The enlightened one is described as being in perfect equilibrium in both pleasure and pain, passing through the ever-changing conditions of life undaunted. The wise man does not mourn death, for he knows the soul is indestructible.

> *Death is not extinguishing the light; it is putting out the lamp because dawn has come.*
>
> — Rabindranath Tagore

As I look out over my beautiful farm, the trees and the mountains shimmering under the South African sun, my mind goes back to Karbala and the roof of my father's house. It goes back over my travels, my time in England, in America, in the Gulf, and in the Sub-Continent. It is as if I am a canoeist on the river of life who has descended rapids and cataracts, and is now sitting silently on a calm lake with colourful vistas and magical horizons.

The tumultuous past experiences and the calmness of the lake are unified and reconciled within me, in the same way as earth and heavens are ever connected. My heart overflows with inexplicable gratitude to have experienced contrasting perfections, all of which are unified.

The healthy wayfarer in this world sees all things and events as messages for meanings, patterns and divine laws, interacting and relating subtle energies with physical and material entities. The enlightened traveller sees the perfect light behind and within countless changes, shadows and forms. The Truth is that there is One Absolute Truth, whose generosity is as Ever-Present as a soul in the heart of a seeker.

> *Your remedy is within you – but you do not sense it.*
> *Your sickness is from you – but you do not perceive it.*
> *You presume that you are a small entity –*
> *Whereas within you is concealed the vast world*
> *You are indeed that magnificent book –*
> *By whose alphabet the hidden becomes evident.*
> *Therefore, you have no needs beyond yourself*
> *Your essence and secrets are in you – if you can reflect.*
>
> — Imam Ali

And Allah knows best…

O

is a symbol of the world,
of oneness and unity. O Books
explores the many paths of wholeness
and spiritual understanding which
different traditions have developed down
the ages. It aims to bring this knowledge
in accessible form, to a general readership,
providing practical spirituality to today's seekers.

For the full list of over 200 titles covering:

- CHILDREN'S PRAYER, NOVELTY AND GIFT BOOKS
- CHILDREN'S CHRISTIAN AND SPIRITUALITY
- CHRISTMAS AND EASTER
- RELIGION/PHILOSOPHY
- SCHOOL TITLES
- ANGELS/CHANNELLING
- HEALING/MEDITATION
- SELF-HELP/RELATIONSHIPS
- ASTROLOGY/NUMEROLOGY
- SPIRITUAL ENQUIRY
- CHRISTIANITY, EVANGELICAL
  AND LIBERAL/RADICAL
- CURRENT AFFAIRS
- HISTORY/BIOGRAPHY
- INSPIRATIONAL/DEVOTIONAL
- WORLD RELIGIONS/INTERFAITH
- BIOGRAPHY AND FICTION
- BIBLE AND REFERENCE
- SCIENCE/PSYCHOLOGY

Please visit our website,
www.O-books.net

Some recent O Books

The Wisdom of Marcus Aurelius

ALAN JACOBS

The Meditations of Marcus Aurelius have been described as the best book of practical philosophy ever written. The message is simple but powerful; we have a short time on earth, we don't know what is going to happen, and it doesn't matter. It is the best defence available against the problems and stresses of our time. Most translations are literal and arid, but here Alan Jacobs, a distinguished poet, uses contemporary free verse and added metaphors to convey the essential emotional meaning of the text.

ALAN JACOBS *is Chair of the Ramana Maharshi Foundation UK. He is author of Poetry for the Spirit, The Bhagavad Gita (O Books), The Principal Upanishads (O Books).*

1-903816-74-2
£9.99 $14.95

Is There An Afterlife?

DAVID FONTANA

The question whether or not we survive physical death has occupied the minds of men and women since the dawn of recorded history. The spiritual traditions of both West and East have taught that death is not the end, but modern science generally dismisses such teachings.

The fruit of a lifetime's research and experience by a world expert in the field, Is There An Afterlife? presents the most complete survey to date of the evidence, both historical and contemporary, for survival of physical death. It looks at the question of what survives-personality, memory, emotions and body image-in particular exploring the question of consciousness as primary to and not dependent on matter in the light of recent brain research and quantum physics. It discusses the possible nature of the afterlife, the common threads in Western and Eastern traditions, the common features of "many levels," group souls and reincarnation.

As well a providing the broadest overview of the question, giving due weight to the claims both of science and religion, Is There An Afterlife?

brings it into personal perspective. It asks how we should live in this life as if death is not the end, and suggests how we should change our behaviour accordingly.

DAVID FONTANA *is a Fellow of the British Psychological Society (BPS), Founder Chair of the BPS Transpersonal Psychology Section, Past President and current Vice President of the Society for Psychical Research, and Chair of the SPR Survival Research Committee. He is Distinguished Visiting Fellow at Cardiff University, and Professor of Transpersonal Psychology at Liverpool John Moores University. His many books on spiritual themes have been translated into 25 languages.*

1 903816 90 4
£11.99/$16.95

Good As New

A radical re-telling of the Christian Scriptures

JOHN HENSON

This radical new translation conveys the early Christian scriptures in the idiom of today. It is "inclusive," following the principles which Jesus adopted in relation to his culture. It is women, gay and sinner friendly. It follows principles of cultural and contextual translation. It also returns to the selection of books that modern scholarship now agrees were held in most esteem by the early Church.
A presentation of extraordinary power.

ROWAN WILLIAMS, *Archbishop of Canterbury*

I can't rate this version of the Christian scriptures highly enough. It is amazingly fresh, imaginative, engaging and bold.

ADRIAN THATCHER, *Professor of Applied Theology, College of St Mark and St John, Plymouth*

I found this a literally shocking read. It made me think, it made me laugh, it made me cry, it made me angry and it made me joyful. It made me feel like an early Christian hearing these texts for the first time.

ELIZABETH STUART, *Professor of Christian Theology, King Alfred's College, Winchester*

It spoke to me with a powerful relevancy that challenged me to re-think all the things that I have been taught.

TONY CAMPOLO, *Professor Emeritus of Sociology, Eastern University*

With an extraordinary vigour and immediacy, Good As New constantly challenges, surprises and delights you. Over and over again you feel like you're reading about Jesus for the first time. Ship of Fools John Henson, a retired evangelical Baptist minister, has co-ordinated this translation over the last 12 years on behalf of ONE for Christian Exploration, a network of radical Christians and over twenty organisations in the UK.

1-903816-74-2
£19.99 $29.95 hb
1-90504711-8
£11.99 $19.95 pb

The Wise Fool's Guide to Leadership

PETER HAWKINS

Nasrudin is the archetypal wise fool, who lived in the Middle East over 600 years ago, though his stories have travelled the world and been updated in very generation. Peter Hawkins has given a modern spin to 84 of these stories by turning Nasrudin into a management consultant. Simple truths are told in a straightforward and highly entertaining way. They shock us into seeing situations and ideas with which we have become familiar from a different perspective. Each story slips into our house by its engaging good humour, but once inside it can start to rearrange the furniture and knock new windows through the walls of our mind-a process that can be releasing and refreshing, but at times disconcerting!

The book also provides an introduction to Nasrudin and his stories, and a chapter on "Telling Tales; the positive use of stories in organisations."

I commend this book to you-wiser even than The Hitch Hiker's Guide to the Galaxy, far, far funnier than In Search of Excellence, so much thinner than The Harvard Business Review Encyclopedia of Corporate Strategy, and astoundingly cheaper than Catch 22!

PROFESSOR MIKE PEDLER

D<small>R</small> P<small>ETER</small> H<small>AWKINS</small> is co-founder and Chairman of Bath Consultancy Group, which operates internationally in helping all types of organisations manage change.

1 903816 96 3
£7.99/$11.95

The Secret Journey

Poems and prayers from around the world

S<small>USAN</small> S<small>KINNER</small>

A gift book for the young in heart and spirit

These prayers, verses and invocations are drawn from many faiths and many nations but they all reflect the same mystery: the mystery our passage from birth, through life, to death. We are born from the unknown. Our life, except perhaps to our friends and family, is a secret journey of joy and sorrow. Our death is shrouded in questions.

In the words of St Paul, "now we see through a glass darkly.." But we do see some things, if we respond to the spirit within. Most faiths, personal or communal, acknowledge the inspiration of the spiritual life founded on truth, love and compassion.

This anthology is a small reflection of the inspired and enlightening words that have been passed on down the centuries, throughout the world. They sing to the child within us all, to the spirit which always remains open and free and clear-sighted. In the words of Master Eckhart: "The eye with which I see God is the same eye with which God sees me."

Each reflection is stunningly illustrated in full colour, making this an ideal gift book for the young and anyone starting on the spiritual journey, or seeking images and verses for inspiration and meditation. A map and short introduction to the world religions, along with notes on sources, make it a useful addition to all libraries in homes and schools.

S<small>USAN</small> S<small>KINNER</small> is an artist who has made a life long study of world religions, working their themes into exquisite images. She lives near Hastings, England.

1 905047 08 8
£11.99/$16.95

The Ocean of Wisdom
Alan Jacobs

The most comprehensive anthology of spiritual wisdom available

The first major anthology of this size and scope since 1935, The Ocean of Wisdom collects over five thousand pearls in poetry and prose, from the earliest of recorded history to modern times. Divided into 54 sections, ranging from Action to Zen, it draws on all faiths and traditions, from Zoroaster to existentialism. It covers the different ages of man, the stages of life, and is an ideal reference work and long term companion, a source of inspiration for the journey of life.

Frequently adopting a light touch it also makes a distinction between the Higher Wisdom, which consists of pointers leading to the understanding of philosophical and metaphysical truth, and practical wisdom, which consists of intelligent skills applicable to all fields of ordinary everyday life. So Germaine Greer and Hilary Rodham Clinton have their place alongside Aristotle and Sartre.

The carefully chosen quotations make this book the perfect bedside dipper, and will refresh the spirit of all who are willing to bathe in the ocean of the world's wisdom.

Few individuals have as wide an acquaintance with the world's traditions and scriptures as Alan Jacobs. He is Chairperson of the Ramana Maharshi Foundation (UK), editor of Poetry of the Spirit, and has translated The Bhagavad Gita (O Books), The Principal Upanishads (O Books) and The Wisdom of Marcus Aurelius (O Books).

1 905047 07 X
£19.95/$29.95

Head Versus Heart-and our gut reactions
The 21st century enneagram

MICHAEL HAMPSON

Head versus Heart plots a map of humankind and of the spiritual journeys we take. Based on the enneagram, it is the most important new material on it in thirty years. The enneagram is generally presented as a system of three parts; a list of nine types of people, their arrangement in a circle in a specific order, and their interconnection by a distinctive pattern of internal arrows. Over a hundred books have been published on this material, endlessly describing it, but never explaining it. Most assume ancient Eastern sources as its authority, but none such exist. Into "the gap where the explanation should be" comes the present text.

Written by a highly experienced, wise and practical parish priest, it guides the reader gently and firmly through a whole programme of discovery and-in the proper sense-conversion. This particular reader was forced again and again to recognise the challenging sense of the analysis offered, and hopes that many more will find the same excitement and prompting to growth in these pages.
DR ROWAN WILLIAMS, *Archbishop of Canterbury*

Michael Hampson is an ordained priest of the Church of England, with degrees from Oxford University in Philosophy and Psychology.

1 903816 92 0
£11.99/$16.95